NIETZSCHE'S *THE*

Nietzsche's *The Gay Science* (1882/1887) is a deeply personal book yet also an important work of philosophy. Nietzsche conceives it as a philosophical autobiography, a record of his own self-transformation. In beautifully composed aphorisms, he communicates his central experience of overcoming pessimism and recovering the capacity to affirm joyfully the tragedy of life. On the basis of his experiments in living, Nietzsche articulates his most famous philosophical concepts and images: the death of God, the exercise of eternal recurrence, and the ideal of self-fashioning. This book explains the ancient and modern philosophical contexts that shape Nietzsche's central concern with the affirmation of life. It surveys Nietzsche's philosophy as a whole, explains the pivotal place of *The Gay Science* as the source of his ideal of tragic joy, and shows how he revives an ancient conception of philosophy as a way of life and the philosopher as physician.

MICHAEL URE is Senior Lecturer in the School of Social Sciences, Monash University. He has published widely on Nietzsche's philosophy, including his book *Nietzsche's Therapy* (2008).

NIETZSCHE'S *THE GAY SCIENCE*

An Introduction

MICHAEL URE

Monash University, Victoria

CAMBRIDGE
UNIVERSITY PRESS

CAMBRIDGE
UNIVERSITY PRESS

University Printing House, Cambridge CB2 8BS, United Kingdom

One Liberty Plaza, 20th Floor, New York, NY 10006, USA

477 Williamstown Road, Port Melbourne, VIC 3207, Australia

314–321, 3rd Floor, Plot 3, Splendor Forum, Jasola District Centre,
New Delhi – 110025, India

79 Anson Road, #06–04/06, Singapore 079906

Cambridge University Press is part of the University of Cambridge.

It furthers the University's mission by disseminating knowledge in the pursuit of
education, learning, and research at the highest international levels of excellence.

www.cambridge.org
Information on this title: www.cambridge.org/9780521760904
DOI: 10.1017/9781139019354

© Michael Ure 2019

First published 2019

Printed in the United Kingdom by TJ International Ltd, Padstow Cornwall

A catalogue record for this publication is available from the British Library.

ISBN 978-0-521-76090-4 Hardback
ISBN 978-0-521-14483-4 Paperback

Contents

Acknowledgements

Some material in Chapter 6 of this volume appeared in a different form in M. Dennis and S. Werkhoven (eds) *Ethics and Self-Cultivation: Historical and Contemporary Perspectives* (New York: Routledge, 2018), Chapter 5.

I would like to thank Hilary Gaskin of Cambridge University Press for her extraordinary patience and acuity. I am deeply indebted to Keith Ansell-Pearson, Aurelia Armstrong, Carita Bengs, Felix Bengs-Stattin, Cam Bontaites, Jeremy Cantor, Michelle Clay, Gillian Cohen, Peter Cryle, Richard Devetak, Alan Dorin, Andre Duarte, J. Peter Euben, Tom Gibson, Ian Hunter, Martin Jay, Robyn Kath, Manny Le Ray, Paul Loeb, Cat McGregor, Masha Makosh, the Mentone Athletics Club, Ruggero Milici, Ticky O'Connell, Francesca Rocca, F. Scott, Matthew Sharpe, George and Martha Mildred-Short, Colin Solomon, Christian Stang, Mikael Stattin, Neil Switz, Gudrun von Tevenar, Sander Werkhoven and my graduate students.

I am eternally grateful to my mentor and friend Michael Janover, whose joyful wisdom has sustained me over many years.

I give my heartfelt thanks to Anita Harris, Jules Harris-Ure, Louie Harris-Ure and our cats Jaffa and Quill.

Finally, I dedicate this book to my mother, Elizabeth Ure.

Abbreviations

A   *The Anti-Christ*, trans. R. J. Hollingdale (Harmondsworth: Penguin Books, 1985).

BGE   *Beyond Good and Evil: Prelude to a Philosophy of the Future,* ed. and trans. W. Kaufmann (New York: Vintage, 1996).

BT   *The Birth of Tragedy or Hellenism and Pessimism*, ed. and trans. W. Kaufmann (Toronto: Random House, 1967).

CW   *The Case of Wagner*, ed. and trans. W. Kaufmann (Toronto: Random House, 1967).

D   *Daybreak: Thoughts on The Prejudices of Morality*, trans. R. J. Hollingdale (Cambridge: Cambridge University Press, 1982).

EH   *Ecce Homo: How One Becomes What One Is*, trans. R. J. Hollingdale (Harmondsworth: Penguin Books, 1979). Sections abbreviated 'Wise', Clever', 'Books', 'Destiny'; abbreviations for titles discussed in 'Books' are indicated instead of 'Books' where relevant.

GM   *On the Genealogy of Morality*, ed. K. Ansell-Pearson and trans. C. Diethe (Cambridge: Cambridge University Press, 1997).

GS   *The Gay Science*, ed. B. Williams, trans. J. Nauckhoff, and poems by A. Del Caro (Cambridge: Cambridge University Press, 2001).

HH 1   *Human, All Too Human: A Book for Free Spirits*, vol. 1, trans. R. J. Hollingdale (Cambridge: Cambridge University Press, 1986).

HH 2	*Human, All Too Human: A Book for Free Spirits*, vol. 2, Part 1, trans. R. J. Hollingdale (Cambridge: Cambridge University Press, 1986).
HL	*On the Uses and Disadvantages of History for Life*, in *Untimely Meditations,* trans. R. J. Hollingdale (Cambridge: Cambridge University Press, 1983).
KSA	*Sämtliche Werke: Kritische Studienausgabe,* ed. G. Colli and M. Montinari (Berlin: Walter de Gruyter, 1967).
NCW	*Nietzsche contra Wagner*, in *The Portable Nietzsche*, trans. W. Kaufmann (Harmondsworth: Penguin Books, 1994).
PP	Parerga and Paralipomena, vol. 2, trans. E. F. J. Payne (Oxford: Oxford University Press, 2000).
PT	*Philosophy and Truth: Selections from Nietzsche's Notebooks of the Early 1870s*, trans. D. Breazeale (Atlantic Highlands, NJ: Humanities Press, 1979).
RWB	*Richard Wagner in Bayreuth*, in *Untimely Meditations*.
SE	*Schopenhauer as Educator,* in *Untimely Meditations*.
TI	*Twilight of the Idols or How to Philosophise with a Hammer*, in *The Portable Nietzsche*. Sections abbreviated 'Maxims', Socrates', 'Reason', 'World', 'Morality', 'Errors', 'Improvers', 'Germans', 'Skirmishes', 'Ancients', 'Hammer'.
WP	*The Will to Power*, trans. Walter Kaufmann and R. J. Hollingdale (New York: Random House, 1967).
WS	*The Wander and His Shadow*, in *Human, All Too Human*, vol. 2, Part 2.
Z	*Thus Spoke Zarathustra: A Book for Everyone and No One*, trans. R. J. Hollingdale (London: Penguin Books, 1988).

ABBREVIATIONS OF SCHOPENHAUER'S WORKS

BM	*The Basis of Morality*, trans. E. F. J. Payne (Indianapolis: Bobbs-Merrill, 1965).
WWR 1	*The World as Will and Representation*, vol. 1, trans. E. F. J. Payne (New York: Dover, 1966).
WWR 2	*The World as Will and Representation*, vol. 2, trans. E. F. J. Payne (New York: Dover, 1966).

Introduction

Nietzsche is widely recognised as one of the most influential philosophers of all time. He is also one of the most fascinating. One does not merely read Nietzsche, as Thomas Mann astutely observed, one experiences him (Mann 1959: 141). *The Gay Science*, first published in 1882, is one of his greatest experience books. It is so partly because in *GS* Nietzsche recounts what he elsewhere describes in a letter from this period as his "inner disturbances, revolutions, solitudes" (Middleton 1996: 187). By 'experiences', he stresses, he does not mean "crude 'events' impinging from without" (*D* 481); rather he signifies radical upheavals and transformations within his own life. *GS* is a deeply personal book, yet also an important work of philosophy. Indeed, Nietzsche claims that philosophy is only significant if it traverses the personal. In the 1887 Preface he doubts whether someone "who has not experienced something similar could, by means of prefaces, be brought closer to the *experiences* of this book" (*GS* P 1). If we are to understand this book we must not simply comprehend a theoretical perspective; we must also move nearer to certain kinds of experiences.

We can therefore mark out *GS* as a philosophical autobiography, a record of his own experiences. Nietzsche identifies these as experiences of self-transformation. *GS* expresses what he identifies in *Daybreak* (1881) as "the vicissitudes and convulsions that befall the most solitary and quietest life which possesses leisure and burns with the passion of thinking" (*D* 481). Great philosophers, he argues, require such experiences and their readers cannot comprehend their philosophies without themselves undergoing similar transformative experiences (*D* 481). Clearly, Nietzsche's book is a profoundly unconventional text by the standards of his German contemporaries and today's academic philosophers.

To understand *GS* therefore we first address a fundamental question: 'How does *Nietzsche* understand the discipline of philosophy?' We shall answer this question in the Introduction before turning to a detailed exegesis of *GS'* five books and a preface. In broad-brush strokes, I argue that Nietzsche follows the ancients in conceiving philosophy as a way of life that entails a set of philosophical practices, disciplines and techniques that enable philosophers to transform and cure themselves. The significance of *GS*, I claim, lies in its radical transfiguration of the ancient model of philosophy as a way of life and the insights into modern culture that Nietzsche believes he derives from applying this model. Nietzsche's 'meta-philosophical' view that philosophy is a way of life, a matter of wise *living*, not just theory construction, is controversial and unfashionable. Yet, as we shall see, only this account of his meta-philosophical view allows us to comprehend *GS'* meaning and significance.

Let us consider these claims in more detail. For all of his popularity among avant-garde painters, writers, musicians and left and right wing political leaders and activists,[1] to name just a few of his avid readers, in academic philosophy circles Nietzsche has been and remains an 'untimely' philosopher. Until fairly recently Nietzsche was rarely taught in mainstream academic philosophy. We have witnessed several waves in the rehabilitation of Nietzsche as a respectable philosopher. Partly due to the fact that his sister Elizabeth Förster-Nietzsche succeeded in making Nietzsche popular with the Nazi leadership he was often considered the 'godfather' of fascism in Germany and Western Europe. As early as 1937 there was a backlash against her conscription of Nietzsche to the Nazi cause in the form of the aptly titled 1937 special issue of the French surrealist journal *Acéphale, Réparation à Nietzsche*. Scholars have not stopped making reparations to Nietzsche ever since. In the opening essay of this journal, Georges Bataille claimed that "fascism and Nietzscheanism are mutually exclusive ... on one side life is tied down and stabilised in an endless servitude, one the other there is not

---

[1] Steven Ascheim (1992) records the extraordinary impact of Nietzsche's work on the German artistic avant-garde and political actors.

only a circulation of free air, but the wind of tempest; one on side the charm of human culture is broken in order to make room for vulgar force, on the other force and violence are tragically dedicated to its charm" (Bataille 1985: 185–186). In the post-war period Albert Camus, also suggested that "we shall never finish making reparation for the injustice done to [Nietzsche]" by fascists' uses and abuses of his philosophy, yet he also acknowledged that rebellion "placed in the crucible of Nietzschean philosophy ... ends in biological or historical Caesarism" (Camus 1981: 67, 71). Most famously in the English-speaking world, Walter Kaufmann attempted to save Nietzsche from Elizabeth's malign intervention by describing the theme of "the anti-political individual who seeks self-perfection far from the modern world" as "the leitmotif of Nietzsche's life and thought" (Kaufmann 1974a: 418).

More recently there has been a polarisation of Nietzsche interpretation. On the one side, in the 1970s and 1980s French and Italian philosophers sought to advance beyond Heidegger's interpretation of Nietzsche's philosophy as a defence of a metaphysical doctrine of the will to power. According to Heidegger, Nietzsche's metaphysical doctrine brought to completion the demand for the total technological organisation of the world that he (Heidegger) claimed was implicit in Western metaphysics.[2] Against the Heideggerian interpretation, these philosophers identified a 'new Nietzsche' whose philosophical style aimed to overthrow the metaphysical demand for the truth about being in the name of transforming philosophy into a playful, open-ended, undecidable form of rhetoric or 'nomadic' thought (see Derrida 1979; Deleuze 1983; Allison 1985; Vattimo 2006). On the other side, philosophers trained in the so-called analytic tradition reacted against the 'new' Nietzsche and sought to reclaim his philosophy as an intellectually credible 'naturalism' of one stripe or another (Clark 1990; Janaway 2007: 34–53; Leiter 2007; Janaway and Robertson 2012). For the most part, however, Nietzsche remains an outlier or oddity for academic philosophers. "In the twentieth century", as Werner Stegmaier explains, "Nietzsche

---

[2] For Heidegger's clearest elaboration of his interpretation of Nietzsche as the last metaphysician and the connections he draws between the history of Western metaphysics and technological domination see Heidegger (1977: 53–114 and 115–154).

became famous but remained infamous. No matter how popular his catchwords became, his thinking never acquired the status of a common philosophical ground like that of Aristotle, Descartes or Kant. Most of our academic colleagues outside of Nietzsche research still hesitate to accept his ideas, not to mention adopting them" (Stegmaier 2016: 384).

Yet at the same time, we cannot seriously doubt that Nietzsche's work, including *GS*, is in some sense philosophically important. In Bernard William's words, *"The Gay Science* is a remarkable book, both in itself and as offering a way into some of Nietzsche's most important ideas" (Williams 2001: vii). Written in a series of scintillating, beautifully wrought aphorisms, it contains some of his most famous and important themes and images: the death of God, the ideal of self-fashioning, with the closely connected, enigmatic doctrines of '*amor fati*' and the eternal recurrence and the vexing, unresolved problem of the value of truth. Why should we pursue truth and not untruth? Is the search for truth compatible with living a flourishing life? Does an unconditional will to truth undermine life? In *GS* Nietzsche also elaborates one of the most compelling and influential accounts of the modern crisis of values that he later called nihilism. His goal in *GS* is to measure the depth of this crisis and show the so-called free spirits among his readers how it might be overcome through a new art of living.

However, if, as Williams rightly maintains, *GS* is an important philosophical text, we must concede that it is so in a highly unusual way. As any reader of Nietzsche will attest, his style of philosophy does not fit neatly into the folds of academic convention. Among the central reasons for scholarly perplexity or hostility towards Nietzsche's philosophy is the fact that he seems to abhor systematic theory and style. Indeed, as Williams famously remarked, his texts seem "booby-trapped" against the extraction of philosophical theories (Williams 2006: 300).

This is especially true of the so-called free-spirit trilogy: *Human, All Too Human*, vol. 1 (1878), *Assorted Opinions and Maxims* (1879), *The Wanderer and His Shadow* (1880), which were subsequently published together as *Human, All Too Human*, vol. 2, *Daybreak* (1881) and *The Gay Science* (1882/1887). In these texts Nietzsche eschews conventional German philosophical styles and self-consciously adopts the 'aphoristic' style of the French moralists from Montaigne to La Rochefoucauld. In fact, he forges a style that recalls Greek and Roman philosophy's blend of philosophy and poetry, Montaigne's classically informed essays and La Rochefoucauld's art of the maxim. The free-spirit books are composed of continuously numbered sections with italicised titles[3] of varying length and styles, from one-sentence maxims to sustained meditations. Nietzsche organises these numbered sections into separate books, with titles announcing their themes in the case of *HH* 1, untitled in the case of *HH* 2 and *D*, and three untitled and two titled in the case of *GS*, which is also bookended with 'Jokes, Cunning and Revenge: Prelude in German Rhymes' and an 'Appendix: Songs of Prince Vogelfrei'.[4] The sections within each book are mostly arranged paratactically, that is to say, they are simply placed side by side without any indication of how (or if) they are related to or co-ordinated with one another. If there seems to be

---

[3] In *HH* Nietzsche occasionally published sections without italicised titles – e.g. *HH* I, 133–135, *HH* I, 136–144 and *HH* I, 630–637. These sections stand as an exception that proves the rule. Nietzsche mostly arranged the sections of the trilogy 'paratactically', or at least without any discernible co-ordination among the continuously numbered sections apart from assigning groups into separate books. In the case of *HH* 132–135 and *HH* 629–337, however, Nietzsche deliberately organised and marked these sections into a continuous run of argument. *HH* 132, for example, announces a theme in its title, '*On the Christian Need for Redemption*' and the following four untitled sections unmistakably develop a sustained argument that this need is based on a false psychology. Indeed, by beginning 135 with the word 'thus' Nietzsche explicitly indicates that it is the logical terminus of the argument he had developed across 132–134. The same principle of organisation applies to *HH* 1, 136–144 and *HH* 1, 630–637. In *D* and *GS*, however, there are no exceptions to Nietzsche paratactic arrangement of titled, continuously numbered sections grouped into separate books.

[4] Kathleen Higgins develops the most detailed treatment of Nietzsche's prelude of rhyming verse, arguing, among other things, that they are call for the rebirth of the chivalrous spirit of the troubadours as a model of living and their practice of courtly love or fin' amor; or more generally, that they express his goal of replacing "the moral perspective on life's significance with an aesthetic sensibility toward everyday matters". They also, she suggests, express his playful, childlike opposition to traditional morality akin to Goethe's singspiel after which Nietzsche named these verses (see Higgins 2000: 14–41; 16, 18, 21). On Nietzsche's poetry more generally see (Grundlehner 1986). James Luchte, the editor of the most recent English language translation of Nietzsche's poetry makes a strong claim for their philosophical significance: "Nietzsche's poetic expression is no mere supplement, nor an attempt to appeal to the baroque aspects of thought, which exceed logical, mathematical and scientific expression . . . It is through poetry – and music – that he not only descends into the depths of existence so as to gain a glimpse of truth in her own domain, but also to open up – and hold open – a creative space for his own convalescence as one who has tirelessly attempted to overcome the nihilism of the Platonic-Christian epoch" (Luchte 2010: 38–39). Robin Small expresses a conventional lament about Nietzsche's decision to conclude GS' final edition with songs, dismissing the final poem, for example, as a "blustery farrago" (Small 2017).

a logical chain of argument that connects some sections together Nietzsche leaves it unmarked and ambiguous. Nietzsche's 'paratactic' style frustrates and challenges readers seeking to identify a systematic philosophical perspective.

The many attempts to reconstruct Nietzsche's theoretical system not only face the challenge of his paratactic style, they must also confront the fact that within the numbered sections themselves he rarely develops anything corresponding to a systematic logical argument defending or rejecting a philosophical proposition. Nietzsche supplies very few syllogisms. Indeed, Nietzsche's numbered sections contain a bewildering array of different literary and philosophical genres, including maxims, confessions, parables, consolations, anecdotes, exhortations, notes of advice and dialogues (between anonymous As and Bs or the wanderer and his shadow). In arguably his most famous section 'The Madman' (125), for example, he does not offer a standard philosophical defence of atheism, but an extraordinary, hyperbolic dramatisation of the death of God. Nietzsche dramatises this event through a recycled version of an ancient Cynic *chreia* (or anecdote), which Diogenes Laertius reports in the *Lives of Famous Philosophers*, the text Nietzsche researched intensively as a young, aspiring classicist. Nietzsche reworks the *chreia* of Diogenes the Cynic who is reported to have "lit a lamp in broad daylight and said, as he went about, 'I am searching for a human being'" (*DL* 6.41; Desmond 2006: 233).

From the perspective of the then dominant tradition of academic philosophy, Nietzsche's free-spirit books are simply unrecognisable *as* philosophy. Anecdotes as a medium of philosophical insight and communication did not figure in works of nineteenth-century German philosophy. Nor do they appear in contemporary academic philosophy. It is a measure of Nietzsche's departure from philosophical convention that, in sharp contrast to Kantian and Hegelian scholarship, it still remains a live question in Nietzsche scholarship whether he intended to present any 'theory' at all (metaphysical, epistemological or ethical) or regardless of his intentions his books contain any such 'theory'.[5] As Richard Schacht writes of *HH*: "Even

---

[5] Nietzsche scholars find it difficult to agree upon his philosophical goal. For example, commentators are divided over whether he intended his account of the 'will to power' in

if [it] had been published by a professional philosopher ... it very probably would not have been regarded as a contribution to the philosophical literature by academic philosophers either in Nietzsche's own time or subsequently. Nor is it clear that it should be; for there is much in it that does not seem to have much to do with philosophical matters. Even the ideas on philosophical topics it addresses are seldom presented in recognizably philosophical ways" (Schacht 1986: xi). The same is true of *GS*. In the 1887 Preface Nietzsche does not describe it as advancing a metaphysical or scientific theory, but as a memoir of his own experiences of illness, convalescence and recovery that sheds light on the psychology of philosophy, or more particularly on "the relation between health and philosophy" (*GS* P 1).

How then are we to conceive Nietzsche's strange book of *"experiences"* (*GS* P 1), which challenges conventional academic expectations of philosophy? Clearly, we must acknowledge that he is an unconventional or 'untimely' philosopher: he does not write in the style of his contemporaries, or, it seems, share their scholarly aim of writing systematic theoretical treatises. Is *GS*, as many assume, a "delightful but disunified book" (Sinhababu 2014) that makes the task of writing a coherent account of its philosophy quixotic? Is *GS* a philosophically irrelevant autobiography?

In addressing these questions, we should note firstly that Nietzsche himself conceived the free-spirit trilogy itself as unified project. On the back cover of its original 1882 edition, he wrote that *GS* represents "the conclusion of a series of writings ... whose common goal is to erect *a new image and ideal of the free spirit*" (see Kaufmann 1974a: 28; Schaberg 1995: 86). Second, Nietzsche's untimely approach to philosophy was the flipside of his criticisms of professional philosophy. Indeed, he caustically dismissed what passed for 'philosophy' among his peers. In his judgement the work of German academic philosophers bore no connection to philosophy understood as 'love of wisdom'. Who among them, he exclaims, "would not be ashamed to call himself a 'wise man' or even merely 'one who is becoming

---

BGE 36 as a defence of a theoretical doctrine – e.g. a panpsychic metaphysics or cosmology of will to power – or as a *reductio ad absurdum* of all such doctrines (see Loeb 2015).

wise'!" (*PT* 47). Wisdom, in the ancient sense of living wisely, he lamented, is simply not on modern philosophers' agenda.

Nietzsche's judgement that modern philosophy is disconnected from or hostile to the ancient notion of philosophical wisdom bears further consideration. As Stephen Grimm observes, wisdom in this sense of knowing how to live well went "from being a central concern of ancient and medieval thinkers to a near afterthought" for much of the nineteenth and twentieth centuries (Grimm 2015: 140). Pierre Hadot contrasted the ancient model of philosophy as a way of life with the late modern assumption that all philosophers worthy of studying strive "to invent, each in an original way, a new construction, systematic and abstract, intended somehow or other to explain the universe, or at the least, if we are talking about contemporary philosophers, a new discourse about language" (Hadot 2002: 2). Yet "in [the ancient] view", he asserts, "philosophy did not consist in teaching an abstract theory – much less in the exegesis of texts – but rather in the art of living" (Hadot 1995: 83). "The philosophical act", as Hadot observes, "is not situated merely on the cognitive level, but on that of self and of being. It is a progress which causes us to *be* more fully, and makes us better" (Hadot 1995: 83).

In this book I argue that *GS* is a distinctive part of a unified philosophical project: viz. Nietzsche's effort to revive the ancient model of philosophy as a way of life, and the closely connected idea of the philosopher as physician. Nietzsche's untimeliness derives from his transfiguration of the ancient model of philosophical wisdom. Nietzsche challenges modern philosophy and philosophers to reassess the meaning and purpose of their discipline by appealing to and drawing on this ancient model. For Nietzsche philosophy *is* an art of living and the point of philosophising is to contribute to the flourishing of life. Philosophy's primary purpose, he suggests, is not 'merely' theoretical or academic, but curative. In the ancient view, as Hadot explains, philosophy "is a *conversion* . . . which turns our entire life upside down, changing the life of the person who goes through it" (Hadot 1995: 83). The ancient schools argue that conventional beliefs and values are not only false, but also that they create distress and illness. For this reason, they also adopt the view that if individuals are to flourish philosophers must perform a medical or therapeutic role: they must cure illnesses. "In the view of all philosophical schools",

Hadot asserts "mankind's principal cause of suffering, disorder, and unconsciousness were the passions ... Philosophy thus appears ... as a therapeutics of the passions ... Each school had its own therapeutic method, but all of them linked their therapeutics to a profound transformation of the individual's mode of seeing and being. The object of spiritual exercises is precisely to bring about this transformation" (Hadot 1995: 83).[6] The great Roman politician, lawyer, and orator Cicero succinctly expresses the medical analogy on which Hellenistic philosophies pivot:

> There is I assure you, a medical art for the soul. It is philosophy, whose aid need not be sought, as in bodily diseases, from outside ourselves. We must endeavour with all of our resources and all our strength to become capable of doctoring ourselves. (Cicero 1927: 3.6)

Nietzsche's conception of philosophy accords with the essentials of the ancient model: it conceives philosophy as art of living whose exercises convert or transform one's being and do so therapeutically so that by means of philosophy one realises a joyful life. Like the ancient philosophical therapists Nietzsche also believes we flourish by living according to nature. In *GS* his overarching project is to "*naturalise* humanity with a pure, newly discovered, newly redeemed nature" (*GS* 109). Nietzsche aims to rediscover and redeem nature for the sake of making humanity 'more' natural or more purely natural.

It is Nietzsche's debt to this ancient legacy that explains why, from the standpoint of professional academic philosophers, much of what and how he writes does not seem to belong to 'philosophy' as they conceive it. We might consider just one minor example of the many seemingly personal, non-philosophical diversions that pepper his books. *GS* 312 is located at the very heart of Book 4:

> *My dog.* I have named my pain and call it 'dog' – it's just as faithful, just as obtrusive and shameless, just as entertaining, just as clever as every other dog – I can scold it and take my bad moods out on it that way others do with their dogs, servants, and wives. (*GS* 312)

---

[6] I follow Hadot in conceiving Nietzsche as one of the few modern philosophers to revive the ancient idea of philosophy as a way of life. However, as we shall see, he radically challenges the ancient conception of the good life (see Ure 2009; Mitcheson 2017). Ultimately Nietzsche disagrees with Hadot's claim that "Epicureanism and Stoicism ... could nourish the spiritual life of men and women of our times" (Hadot, 1995: 280).

If we frame *GS* in terms of Nietzsche's own attempt to revive ancient philosophy as a way of life and the philosopher as a physician we can avoid treating such sections as inexplicable aberrations or irrelevant asides. In this section Nietzsche writes in the first person: it is his own pain for which he prescribes a cure. He also writes as physician to his own soul: he does not articulate a theory, but identifies a simple practice designed to alleviate his suffering. Following Hadot, we might say that Nietzsche describes a spiritual exercise the aim of which is to transform his life by attenuating his suffering. Nietzsche's amusing description of this psychological analgesic, which operates by comically deflating the significance of his pain, also alludes to the Cynic philosopher Diogenes the Dog, who conceived human flourishing as a completely self-sufficient and painless life. Diogenes realised this godlike self-sufficiency by living according to nature, which, so he assumed, required eliminating all unnecessary, conventional desires for 'external goods': e.g. power, possessions, reputation, offices, honours, children, brothers, friends, clothes or houses. Diogenes exemplified his Cynic philosophy in his life: scandalously taking up residence in a barrel and famously mocking the glory of Alexander the Great. Like Diogenes, Nietzsche identifies a technique or exercise of enduring and domesticating his pain: Diogenes inured himself to pain through constant exposure, Nietzsche comically deflates its significance.[7] Nietzsche shows how he domesticates his own pain by training it to be obedient or doglike.

Framed this way, we can see that even such seemingly minor personal diversions key into Nietzsche's overarching project of experimenting with and reclaiming the ancient model of the philosophical physician. In Nietzsche's aphoristic texts what appears marginal is central to his project of rejuvenating ancient philosophical wisdom. "What ultimately marked Nietzsche's affinity with ancient Cynicism", as Charles Bambach observes, "is his rejection of philosophy as knowledge in favour of *philosophia* as a discipline of and for *life*. Taking up the Cynics' understanding of their craft as *therapeia*, Nietzsche defines philosophy as therapy, as 'a spiritual cure' for the maladies that beset European culture" (Bambach 2010: 442–443).

---

[7] Nietzsche commentators tend to pass over such sections in silence, but for one exception see Higgins (2000: 167–169).

In fact, Nietzsche describes the free-spirit trilogy as a philosophical therapy through which he overcame "the pessimism of weariness with life" partly through precisely Cynic therapy:

> Just as a physician places his patient in a wholly strange environment . . . so I, as physician and patient in one, compelled myself to an opposite and unexplored *clime of the soul*, and especially to a curative journey into strange parts . . . A *minimum* of life, in fact, an unchaining from all coarser desires, an independence in the midst of all kinds of unfavourable circumstances together with pride in being *able* to live surrounded by these unfavourable circumstances; a certain amount of cynicism, a certain amount of 'barrel'. (*HH* 2 P 5)

On the most general level, then, the significance of *GS* stands or falls with this controversial 'meta-philosophical' assumption that philosophy can and ought to be analogous to medicine. Can the philosopher once again reclaim the mantle of the cultural physician and physician to the soul? That philosophers can or should do so is a highly controversial claim. "Can we really believe", as Williams once asked in another context, "that philosophy, properly understood in terms of rigorous argument, could be so directly related to curing real human misery, the kind of suffering that priests and doctors and – indeed – therapists address?" (1994: 25–26). Is the truth necessarily consoling or life enhancing? Williams, for his part, answered this question with a decisive 'no': rigorous philosophy cannot be therapeutic.[8]

Nietzsche himself recognised the difficulties of these grand claims about the philosopher as physician or therapist. In *HH* he bluntly identifies what he calls a "fundamental insight": "there is no preestablished harmony between truth and human flourishing or wellbeing" (*HH* 517). "What", he asks in *D*, "have [known truths] in common with the inner states of suffering, stunted, sick human beings that they must necessarily be of use to them?" (*D* 424). "It may turn out", as John Sellars puts it, "that truth is no consolation at all" (Sellars 2017: 48). Yet in the very same works where Nietzsche recognises that it is problematic to draw any connection between truth and flourishing, he also explicitly calls for the renewal of the philosophical physician. Nietzsche also claims that through his own

---

[8] Richard Sorabji (1997) contests Williams' claim. See also Williams' reply (1997).

philosophical experimentations he successfully cured himself of a pessimistic malady endemic to modern culture. As we shall see, in *GS* Nietzsche struggles with the question of the utility and value of truth for life, but he does not resile from the idea that the philosopher can play the role of physician. Nietzsche's revaluation of values aims not just to change our theoretical beliefs, but is guided by his "therapeutic" ambition "of bringing about revised affective habits" (Janaway 2007: 48).

Indeed, both in earlier unpublished drafts and notes and in the free-spirit trilogy books themselves, Nietzsche explores the merit of recalibrating philosophy so that it might once again take its lead from the medical analogy that structured the Hellenistic philosophies, especially Epicureanism and Stoicism. It is in this vein that Nietzsche asks in *Schopenhauer as Educator* (1874), "Where are the physicians for modern mankind who themselves stand so firmly and soundly on their feet that they are able to support others and lead them by the hand?" (*SE* 2). In *Daybreak* he imploringly repeats this question: "*Where are the new physicians of the soul*"? (*D* 52). *GS* revives the ancient idea of philosophy as a medical art by attempting to put it into practice. In texts and unpublished notes prior to the free-spirit trilogy Nietzsche surveyed the ancient model of philosophy and lamented its demise. In *GS* in particular he attempts to apply and develop it, acting as both the cultural physician to the modern age and physician to his own soul. *GS* is the culmination of Nietzsche's decade-long attempt to reconceive philosophy as an art of living and therapeutic practice.

Yet, and this is my second central claim in this book, *GS* does not simply recycle the ancient model of philosophy but rather Nietzsche aims to develop a *rival*, post-classical philosophical therapy. Nietzsche highlights how in *HH* and *D* he had applied the classical philosophical therapies to cure himself of his romantic or Schopenhauerian pessimism. Nietzsche had also drawn on enlightened scientific scepticism, especially the newly emerging methods of natural history, to liberate himself from the turmoil of irrational moral emotions and religious feelings. We can use 'science', as he puts it "to deprive man of his joys and make him colder, more statue-like, more stoic" (*GS* 12). This is what Nietzsche had sought to do in *HH* and *D*. In these first two instalments of his free-spirit trilogy,

Nietzsche's "anti-romantic, scientific regimen", as Paul Franco aptly called it (Franco 2011: 206), was an integral part of his cure for his own "pessimism of weariness with life" (*HH*2 P 5). It is this employment of science to make one more stoic, colder, or 'wintry' that he repudiates in *GS*.

In *GS* Nietzsche continues to conceive his philosophy as consistent with the Hellenistic medical model of philosophy and the book itself as a means to his own cure. In this respect, *GS* is continuous with the general philosophical framework of the free-spirit trilogy. However, the singular importance of *GS*, and one of the reasons it has greater intellectual significance than *HH* and *D*, is that it marks an important turning point in Nietzsche's philosophy. It is the precise point at which he begins to formulate an ethical project and a new ideal of happiness and health that radically breaks with the values motivating the classical philosophical therapies. It is therefore worth considering this shift from *HH* and *D* to *GS* in greater detail.

In the mid- to late- 1870s, Nietzsche drew upon ancient philosophical therapies, especially Cynicism, Epicureanism and Stoicism, to cure himself of pessimism. Nietzsche describes how in the free-spirit trilogy he turned his "perspective *around*" from pessimism, which condemns the world on the basis of the painfulness of life, to "optimism for the purpose of restoration so that at some future time I could again have the *right* to be a pessimist" (*HH* 2 P5). Nietzsche's 'optimism' took the form of the general Hellenistic commitment to the tranquil endurance and acceptance of misfortune and suffering. On this 'optimistic' view the exercise of philosophic reason necessarily secures tranquillity. In *HH* and *D* Nietzsche experimented with variations on the classical philosophies of rational self-mastery or self-tyranny to treat his weariness with life. He freely admits in both his published works and private letters that he had recourse to these ancient therapies to cure himself of romantic pessimism. In the late 1870s his own bodily "torture" reached its worst point and he was therefore deeply in need of treatment for precisely the kind of emotional turmoil that Greek philosophy was designed to overcome or extirpate. "The aim of wisdom", as he puts it in his notebooks, "is to enable man to face all the blows of fate with equal firmness, to arm him for all times" (*PT* 49). Since, as he put it, "the consolations of Christianity" are becoming an "antiquity", "the means of comfort provided by ancient philosophy come once again to the fore with a renewed radiance" (*KSA* 8: 41 [32]). And speaking in a directly personal way, he remarks in 1878: "I need the ointment boxes and medicines of <u>all</u> ancient philosophies", which leads to the self-directed injunction, "Become ancient!" (*KSA* 8: 28 [41]; *KSA* 8: 28 [40]).

Nietzsche acknowledges the value of classical and Hellenistic exercises in self-tyranny: they made it possible for him to overcome romantic pessimism. In the Preface to *GS* he observes they proved successful in his battle against the "tyranny of pain" by surpassing it "with a tyranny of pride that refused the *conclusions* of pain" (*GS* P 1). Following the classical philosophical therapies and cultivating self-sufficiency made it possible for him to refuse the conclusions of pain, or the pessimistic judgement that denies the value of life and devalues passionate commitments and evaluations. Through these philosophical therapies Nietzsche sought to make himself immune or indifferent to the "blows of fate". Nietzsche suggests that through a combination of ancient philosophical therapy and cold modern scientific scepticism he learnt to endure his suffering, or "to preserve an equilibrium and composure" in the face of misfortune (*HH* 2 P 5).

By the time of *GS*, however, Nietzsche had reassessed the therapeutic benefits of the ancient philosophies and modern positivism. *GS* has a distinctive importance because in this text he attempts to formulate a rival to the ancient therapies. In *GS* Nietzsche aims to treat not only the illness of romantic pessimism, but also the maladies that derive precisely from these ancient 'therapies'. He now targets as illnesses both 'romantic' pessimism *and* the Hellenistic 'petrification' of life that earlier in the free-spirit trilogy he had drawn on as a cure of or counterweight to his own case of romantic pessimism. That is to say, in *GS* he comes to see that the ancient forms of 'optimism' are not remedies, but continuations or refractions of the illness of weariness with life. Against their 'optimistic' notion of self-sufficiency, he seeks to define a new type of healthy, strong pessimism. In *GS* Nietzsche formulates a philosophical therapy that does not aim to cultivate merely the endurance of life, but to realise the affirmation or love of life. We should not confuse tranquil endurance or fortitude, he cautions, with human flourishing.[9]

---

[9] *Cf.* Augustine: "That virtue which goes by the name of fortitude is the plainest proof of the ills of life, for it is these ills which it is compelled to bear patiently" (*civ.* 19.4). Nietzsche, as it

For this reason *GS* criticises rather celebrates Cynic and Stoic pride as a sickness rather than cure, a form of self-tyranny rather than self-enhancement. Nietzsche came to see the Hellenistic ideal of *ataraxia* or *apatheia* as a symptom of the "petrification" or "fossilization" of life (326). To borrow from Diogenes Laertius, we might say that in *GS* Nietzsche laments the Stoic injunction to "take on the colour of the dead".[10] He now treats Hellenistic therapies as *objects* of therapeutic treatment and evaluation, rather than as *mediums* of diagnosis and treatment. From the vantage point of a post-classical philosophical physician, he claims, we must develop a therapy to cure the diseases expressed or engendered by these ancient therapies (Ure 2008, 2009; Ure and Ryan 2014; Faustino 2017). As Marta Faustino succinctly states, Nietzsche formulates "a therapy of therapies" (Faustino 2017: 98).

Nietzsche marks out *GS* from the earlier books in the trilogy by what we might call its anti-Hellenistic erotic pedagogy. "*One must*", as he puts it, "*learn to love*" (334). Nietzsche's chosen title flags the significance of this erotic pedagogy as a counter to classical rationalism and scientific positivism: it is a German translation of the Provençal subtitle "La gaya scienza", which the twelfth-century troubadours used to refer to the art of love poetry. The troubadours sought to revalue mortal *eros* against its philosophical stigmatisation or depreciation. Nietzsche's conception of poetic idealisation resonates with the troubadour's conception of love as a form of devotion and service to a perfect, if unattainable ideal.[11] Nietzsche will later identify devotion to a higher ideal as the hallmark of the Provençal troubadours' conception of love: "artful and enthusiastic reverence and devotion are the regular symptom of the aristocratic way of thinking. This makes plain why love *as passion* – which is our European specialty – simply must be of noble origin: as is well known, its invention must be credited to the Provençal knight-poets, those magnificent and inventive human beings of the 'gai saber' to

---

were, rewrites Augustine's diagnosis of Hellenistic philosophies: the virtue of fortitude is not the proof of the ills of life, but of the illness of those who need this virtue.

[10] Diogenes Laertius reports this as the Delphic Oracle's answer to the Stoic Zeno's question about how to attain the best life: "It is stated by Hecato and by Apollonius of Tyre in his first book on Zeno that he consulted the oracle to know what he should do to attain the best life, and that the god's response was that he should take on the complexion of the dead" (*DL* 7.1).

[11] On the troubadours' concept of courtly love, see De Rougemont (1983: 74–80) and Singer (2009: 19–36).

whom Europe owes so many things and almost owes itself" (*BGE* 260). As we shall see, *GS* is an attempt to rechannel all the force of *eros*, all its poetic powers of idealisation, into precisely those fleeting appearances that the ancient and Christian traditions devalued.

GS also gradually begins to take a sceptical view of the scientific positivism that Nietzsche had extolled in *HH* and *D*. Scientific positivism, he claims, "is the *stupidest* of all possible interpretation of the world, i.e. one of those most lacking in significance" (373). Like Odysseus' sailors, classical philosophers and modern positivists, he claims, are deaf to the 'music' of life. Clearly Nietzsche believes that "something important lies beyond the 'horizon' of science", as Clark puts it, but that the scientist does not know what it is (Clark and Dudrick 2012: 121). Alluding to his friend Paul Rée's commitment to disinterested, positivistic methods of inquiry, Nietzsche observes,

The lack of personality always takes revenge: a weakened, thin, extinguished personality, one that denies itself and its own existence, is no longer good for anything – least of all philosophy. 'Selflessness' has no value in heaven or on earth; all great problems demand *great love*. It makes the most telling difference whether a thinker has a personal relationship to his problem and finds in them his destiny, his distress, and his greatest happiness, or an 'impersonal' one, meaning he is only able to touch and grasp them with the antennae of cold, curious thought. In the latter case nothing will come of it, that much can be promised. (345)

Nietzsche disputes the positivistic commitment to disinterested, impersonal inquiry and its unconditional faith in truth as something divine. First, he argues that this conception of inquiry is destined to fail. By failing to engage their passions and affects, he claims, positivists cannot pursue philosophical investigations. Intellectually they are hamstrung by their faith in absolute, divine truths. In the matter of moral values, which are Nietzsche's central concern, to arrive at truth requires the activation of passions. Second, as a philosophical physician he diagnoses the positivistic commitment to the notion of truth as divine or absolute as a symptom of an "*instinct for weakness*": viz. "*a demand for certainty*" that betrays an inability to invent or command new values (347). On the other hand, he holds that what most distinguishes philosophical inquiry from selfless, disinterested models of science is that it engages the investigator's affects and drives. For Nietzsche, as we noted at the outset, philosophy must traverse the personal: it must proceed from and find its motivation in the philosopher's great love or passion.

In *GS* then Nietzsche's enthusiasm for the ancient Hellenistic schools turns into contempt as he begins to diagnose the Hellenistic retreat from or contraction of life, the Christian flight from the world, romantic pessimism's weariness with life, and the positivistic *"demand for certainty"* (347) as merely different versions of weakness or illness. Though Nietzsche still endorses the model of the philosophical physician and shares the Cynics', Stoics' and Epicureans' goal of formulating a naturalistic ethics of human flourishing, his naturalistic ethics contests their belief that the good life necessarily requires the extirpation or minimisation of the passions. Nietzsche's ethics rejects the belief that individual flourishing requires the Stoic retreat from or Epicurean contraction of the passions that alone imbue life with value. To put it in positive terms, in *GS* Nietzsche argues that the suffering of the passions is an integral part of his new ideal of happiness, or what he calls "superabundant happiness" (326).

In this light we can see more clearly the importance of *GS* in Nietzsche's philosophical odyssey: it expresses the intoxicating recovery of health after his battle with romantic despair and his own temptation to overcome its pessimistic condemnation of the world through a retreat to the inner citadel.[12] *GS*, as he puts it, expresses the convalescent's delight in crossing the threshold from sickness to health. By contrast, the earlier books in the trilogy, he implies, only replaced his romantic pessimism with illnesses engendered by the Hellenistic therapies. In these works Nietzsche had 'cured' himself, but only by taking on the colour of the dead. Nietzsche describes the result of his experiments with these therapies as the "icing up in the midst of youth ... dotage at the wrong time" (*GS* P 1).[13] In the 1887 Preface he added to the second edition of *GS*, Nietzsche evokes the

---

[12] See e.g. Seneca: "The soul stands on unassailable grounds, if it has abandoned external things; it is independent in its own fortress; and every weapon that is hurled falls short of the mark. Fortune has not the long reach which we credit her; she can seize none except him that clings to her. Let us recoil from her as far as we are able" (*Ep.* 82.5).

[13] Michel Foucault shows how Hellenistic philosophers characterised their ideal of complete, untroubled self-sufficiency as analogous to "old age" (2005: 108). If the Hellenistic philosophers' ideal of self-sufficiency counsels that we achieve 'old age' even in our youth, in *GS* Nietzsche identifies his philosophical therapy with recovery from this onset of dotage at the wrong time.

"*experiences*" it expresses: "It seems to be written in language of the wind that brings a thaw: it contains high spirits, unrest, contradiction, and April weather, so that one is constantly reminded of winter's nearness as well as the *triumph* over winter that is coming, must come, perhaps has already come" (*GS* P 1).

In a moving letter to the great classicist Erwin Rohde, his old university friend and advocate, informing him that he will soon receive a copy of *GS,* Nietzsche proclaims the success of his post-classical philosophical therapy:

What years! What wearisome pain! What inner disturbances, revolutions, solitudes! *Who* has endured as much as I have? . . . And if now I stand above all that, with the joyousness of a victor and fraught with difficult *new* plans – and, knowing myself, with the prospect of new, more difficult, and inwardly profound sufferings and tragedies and *with the courage to face them*! – then nobody should be annoyed with me for having a good opinion of my medicine. *Mihi ipsi scripsi* – [I have written for myself] – and there it stands; and thus everyone should do for himself his best in his own way – that is my morality, the only remaining morality for me. (Middleton 1996: 187)

Why, though, we might ask, should Nietzsche's return to health bear any philosophical significance? Is Nietzsche's "experience", which he describes as "the history of an illness and recovery" merely, as he fears, his "personal experience alone", his "'human, all-too-human'?" (*HH* P6). Is *GS* simply an idiosyncratic exploration of a troubled life? "What is it to us", as he puts it self-mockingly, "that Mr Nietzsche has got well again?" (*GS* P 2).

Examining his own therapy from a third-person, spectator's per-spective, Nietzsche claims that his own struggles with pessimism are a microcosm that sheds light on the macrocosm, or more precisely on the crisis of modern European culture. In *GS* Nietzsche maintains that his curative journey from romantic pessimism through Hellenistic petrification and positivistic detachment to 'superabun-dant' health has profound significance for modern culture. Nietzsche claims that his readers, or at least the free spirits among them, can learn a great deal from his struggle to overcome his pessimistic condemnation of the world, his 'stoic' efforts to endure his misfor-tunes and suffering, and his final victory in recovering full health or flourishing. To his own question about whether "the history of an illness and recovery" he records in the free-spirit trilogy was merely a personal experience he answers: "Today I would like to believe the reverse; again and again I feel sure that my travel books were not written solely for myself, as sometimes seems to be the case – . May I now, after six years of growing confidence, venture to send them off again? May I venture to commend them especially to the hearts and ears of those burdened with any kind of 'past' and have sufficient spirit left still to suffer from the *spirit* of their past too?" (*HH* 2 P6).[14] Nietzsche claims then that as a physician to his own soul he also fulfils the role of cultural physician. Mr Nietzsche's therapeutic cycle displays modern culture writ small. His personal struggles crystallise all our struggles.

In *GS* he suggests that his psychological diagnosis of philosophies as symptoms of illness granted him an important insight into the way unconscious moral values orient and shape these philosophies. Nietzsche claims that through his therapeutic experiments with ancient philosophical remedies he discovered that all grand, meta-physical philosophies have been symptoms of illness masquerading as cures. He argues that this philosophical quack-doctoring, its so-called cures, have not served to enhance the highest forms of life, but have protected and preserved the weakest types of life. In particular, Nietzsche aims to show that moral values, which philosophers have enshrined as the 'highest' values, have only pre-served weak, decaying forms of life. Even modern scientists, in particular contemporary natural historians of morality, he suggests, have been nothing more than unwitting "shield-bearers" (345) of moralities that protect the weak and prey on the strong. Nietzsche comes to see morality not just as an 'error', but as a form of predation. In *GS* Nietzsche therefore expands the role of the philosophical physician: he shows that for the sake of comprehending the possibi-lities of human flourishing we need a therapy of the philosophical therapies and a diagnosis of their moral values as symptoms of illness or degeneration. Nietzsche's naturalistic project aims to devalue the currency of moral values.

---

[14] Cf. Seneca: "I am not so shameless as to undertake to cure my fellow-men when I am ill myself. I am, however, discussing with you troubles which concern us both, and sharing the remedy with you, just as if we were lying ill in the same hospital" (*Ep.* 27.1).

In *GS* then Nietzsche identifies a crisis unique to the modern age: viz. the death of God or the decline of European moral values. Nietzsche claims that the highest values that have given meaning and purpose to human life have all been symptoms of the denial of life, or what he later calls the ascetic ideal. Through his self-diagnosis and self-cure Nietzsche discovers that our *moral* values have been symptoms of life denial or weakness. Nietzsche identifies a terrible paradox in the ascetic ideal: it values or gives meaning to life only as the instrument of its own extinction. Nietzsche analysed the ascetic ideal as redeeming the will: it protected the species from "suicidal nihilism" by giving suffering a meaning. "The meaninglessness of suffering, not the suffering", as Nietzsche later put it "was the curse that so far blanketed mankind – and the ascetic ideal offered man a meaning!" (*GM* III.28). Up to now, he claims, philosophers, moralists and 'soul-doctors' have only valued the mortification or petrification of life. He identifies Platonism's ideal of the philosophical life as a preparation for dying as the original expression of the ascetic ideal (*Ph.* 67 c–e). Nietzsche identifies Stoicism and Epicurean as variations on the ascetic ideal insofar as they aim to extirpate or minimise the passions (respectively) to achieve tranquillity in this world. Christianity, he claims, paradoxically preserves an attachment to life by granting the highest value to slow suicide as the means to eternal redemption (131). Nietzsche holds that these variations on the ascetic ideal once made life worth living by conceiving the sacrifice of our strongest instincts or drives as a means to transcendent or immanent redemption. The ascetic ideal makes life denial the highest value. Despite all the important differences among our philosophical and religious traditions, Nietzsche believes they all express weakness or disease in this ascetic denial of life. They are all variations on a self-defeating will to nothingness.

Yet it is precisely the ascetic ideal, he suggests, that is now collapsing. According to Nietzsche, that this ideal must gradually wane is one of the unintended consequences of the unconditional will to truth, or faith in the value of truth, that underpins our metaphysical tradition. Without the meaning this ideal confers on life, he argues, the weak cannot sustain their faith or trust in life. For this reason, Nietzsche describes the death of God as "an eclipse of the sun the like of which has probably never existed on earth" (343). This event, he claims, does not, therefore, merely signal the collapse of certain religious beliefs, a cognitive correction that leaves everything else untouched, but a radical transformation of our form of life and ways of being in the world.

For Nietzsche *GS*' fundamental significance for modern philosophy and culture lies in its claim that the consequences of the death of God extend into the very fabric of our lives. He conceives this event as a potential turning point in history. Since the Platonic-Christian metaphysical orientation is deeply woven into the structure of our affects and the system of values through which we have hitherto oriented ourselves, it collapse must bring in its wake a profound spiritual and moral crisis. Nietzsche believes that it may take centuries for individuals to comprehend the gravity of this event – he confesses that even he only understands the "initial consequences" of the death of God (343). On his diagnosis, our capacity to endure life, indeed our very capacity to orient our lives and give meaning and value to existence has come to rely on metaphysical concepts to which we can no longer give our intellectual assent (110). In rejecting 'God', used here by Nietzsche as a synecdoche of all metaphysical views, we have deprived ourselves of the conceptual foundations required to sustain the conviction that transient, mortal life serves a transcendent purpose, that the sufferings of this life will be redeemed in another world, and for belief in objective or unconditional moral values and rules. It deprives us of both our existential and moral compass. We can no longer find justification for life or morality by interpreting them in terms of transcendent foundations.

Nietzsche figures the effects of the death of God as analogous to a spatial disorientation: we are now positioned in "empty space" (125) without any markers or signposts to position or orient ourselves. After the death of God it will become increasingly impossible to "view nature as if it were proof of the goodness and protection of God; to interpret history to the honour of a divine reason, as continual witness to a moral world order and its ultimate moral intentions; to explain one's own experiences, as pious peoples have for long enough explained them, as if everything were predetermined, everything a sign, everything designed to promote the redemption of the soul: that time is *past*, it has conscience *against* it" (357). In short, Nietzsche maintains that debunking of metaphysics must bring with it the spectre of what he later called nihilism – the sense of 'meaninglessness' or 'purposelessness' that ensues when our highest values are devalued: "As we thus reject the Christian interpretation and condemn its 'meaning' as counterfeit, *Schopenhauer's* question immediately comes at us in a terrifying way: *Does existence have any meaning at all?*" (357).

Unlike the melancholic madman of *GS* 125, however, Nietzsche does not lament the death of God, but conceives it as a potential historical watershed, a "new dawn" (343) for the few free spirits that he addresses. According to Nietzsche, after the death of God European culture may degenerate into what he later calls the passive nihilism of the last men, who merely seek 'happiness', a comfortable, banal secure life (*Z* I.5). For the many, he concedes, it will mean the demise of the moral values that have hitherto given a higher meaning or sense to their lives. Alternatively, he suggests that the collapse of "our entire European morality" opens up the possibility that a few free spirits might be able to forge a new kind of "superabundant health" (326), "*the great health*" (382), which does not deny, but affirms life or nature. Against the ascetic idealisation of nothingness that he believes lies at the heart of European morality, Nietzsche exhorts free spirits to discover, explore, and experiment with new values that facilitate the emergence of higher human or 'overhuman' types who will enjoy an as yet unknown "divine happiness" (337), or an "ideal human, superhuman well-being" (382). In *GS* Book 5, as we shall see, he etches much more clearly the aristocratic politics that he believes necessarily flows from this diagnosis of modern culture.

Nietzsche could hardly have made the stakes higher in *GS*: his claim is that up to now European culture has suffered under the curse of an ascetic ideal that values and reinforces sickness, but that free spirits might formulate an affirmation of life that will radically transform their condition and open up the possibility of "superhumanity" (382). If his diagnosis is correct, in modern culture we are "stretched on a rope between today and tomorrow" (343), or as Zarathustra, the protagonist of his next book put it much more evocatively, "the human is a rope stretched between beast and Overhuman [*Übermensch*] – a rope over an abyss" (*Z* 1.4). In *GS* Nietzsche's principal goal is to ensure that as a philosophical physician he properly diagnoses the many masks of illness, the old and new guises worn by life-denying values, and identifies the possibilities of creating new life-affirming values so the free spirits can cross over to the other shore.

CHAPTER I

Nietzsche's Tragicomedy

In the opening section of *GS*, Nietzsche establishes the basic parameters of his analysis of modern culture (1). Nietzsche claims that it is a significant moment in the eternal ebb and flow of tragedy and comedy. He argues that modern culture is on the verge of becoming conscious of what he calls the "comedy of existence", viz. the recognition of the purposelessness of natural existence (1). Yet this newly recovered insight, he claims, is also the basis for the hope or expectation that free spirits might invent a new tragedy that will once again promote faith or trust in the value of life. In this context, he uses the term 'tragedy' as synonymous with moral teachings that existence has a "purpose" (1). In *GS*, Nietzsche's central aim is to forge a new tragedy or moral horizon.

To this end, in the opening section, Nietzsche sets out first to illuminate how modern science or naturalism is currently undermining the moral teachings that have underpinned our trust in life. Modern naturalism, he argues, renews our sense of the comedy of existence. On the basis of this naturalism, Nietzsche sketches the possibility of a new aristocratic moral horizon that might cultivate 'noble' individuals and explores the way our old moralities systematically create herd animals at the price of such individuals. We can explore Book 1's main claims by addressing the following two questions: How does Nietzsche think modern naturalism exposes the comedy of existence? What is his alternative moral horizon or tragedy?

Why then does Nietzsche believe modern free spirits are close to becoming conscious of the comedy of existence? Nietzsche arrives at this view through his idiosyncratic synthesis of Schopenhauerian philosophical pessimism and various strands of contemporaneous evolutionary theory. Together, he argues, they show first that a species' preservation has always taken priority over and determined individual members' desires and goals and second that a whole range of 'immoral' or 'evil' drives belong among the necessary means to its preservation.

Nietzsche opens section 1 by stressing the first point:

> Whether I regard human beings with a good or an evil eye, I always find them engaged in a single task, each and everyone of them: to do what benefits the preservation of the human race. Not from a feeling of love for the race, but simply because within them nothing is older, more inexorable and invincible than this instinct – because this instinct constitutes the essence of our species and herd. (1)

We can see here how Nietzsche entwines Schopenhauerian and Darwinian strands into his analysis of modern culture. Nietzsche recycles Schopenhauer's claim that "the species" is the "root of our true nature" and as such "has a closer and prior right to us than has the individual; hence it takes precedence". All the human species' instincts, Schopenhauer explains, "[are] directed to what is best for the species", and it is the good of the species that "always sets the individual in motion" (*WWR* 2: 539). "The interest of the species", as he puts it, "is infinitely superior to any interest of mere individuals" (*WWR* 2: 552). Schopenhauer adds that the instinct of the species treats individuals as merely instruments serving its reproduction. "The individual", he asserts, "has for nature only a indirect value, insofar as it is a means for maintaining the species. Apart from this, its existence is a matter of indifference to nature; in fact, nature herself leads it to destruction as soon as it ceases to be fit for that purpose" (*WWR* 2: 351). Nietzsche follows Schopenhauer's view that individuals are compelled by a species' instinct to serve its reproduction.

Nietzsche also shares Schopenhauer's view that species preservation largely hinges on what Schopenhauer calls the two anti-moral incentives: *egoism*, the source of greed, selfishness, covetousness and pride, and its off-shoot, *ill will*, the source of envy, *Schadenfreude*, malice, cruelty and so on (*BM*: 78–79). Nietzsche argues that from the perspective of the grand economy of the species' preservation, altruistic morality, which values compassion and selflessness, is myopic. If altruistic morality is taken as the *only* action-guiding principle, he maintains, it will necessarily cripple this economy:

Hatred, delight in the misfortunes of others [*Schadenfreude*], the lust to rob and rule, and whatever else is called evil: all belong to the amazing economy of the preservation of the species, an economy which is certainly costly, wasteful, and on the whole most foolish – but still *proven* to have preserved our race so far. (1)[1]

Nietzsche's naturalistic defence of 'evil' rehabilitates drives which motivate individuals to harm others for the sake of the advantages they derive from such actions and those that motivate them to enjoy seeing others suffer. Provocatively, Nietzsche singles out *Schadenfreude*, which Schopenhauer describes as "diabolical", as essential to nature's economy.[2] Nietzsche's image of this grand economy deliberately targets Paul Rée and Herbert Spencer's naturalistic defence of altruism and selflessness. We can illuminate his polemic by briefly outlining their moral theory.

Spencer and Rée argued that 'good' equates with the useful and 'evil' with the immediately harmful or disadvantageous to the species. Rée held that the morality of good (unegoistic) and evil (egoistic) sums up the species' utility: "The good person is a useful animal, the bad person is a harmful animal" (Rée 2003: 123). Rée maintained that the morality of compassion or selflessness has naturalistic, not metaphysical, foundations. The Darwinian theory of evolution, he argued, was sufficient to explain its origin and purpose: altruistic morality preserves groups by giving them a slight edge in the struggle for existence. Rée's argument hinges on two premises: firstly, that moral judgements are utility judgements, and secondly, that altruism and compassion have proven themselves the most useful practices in terms of the species' preservation. In the species' evolution, he

---

[1] Nietzsche later repeats this claim in *BGE*: "If, however, a person should regard even the affects of hatred, envy, covetousness and the lust to rule as conditions of life, as factors which, fundamentally and essentially, must be present in the general economy of life and must, therefore, be enhanced if life is to be further enhanced – he will suffer from such a view of things as from seasickness" (23).

[2] "There is no sign more infallible of a thoroughly bad heart and profound moral worthlessness than an inclination to sheer and undisguised enjoyment of this kind. The man in whom this trait is observed should be shunned forever ... Just as *Schadenfreude* is only theoretical cruelty, so cruelty is *Schadenfreude* put into practice, and such joy will appear as cruelty as soon as the opportunity occurs" (*BM*: 79).

asserted, co-operative drives have been selected and accumulated because they are useful to the species and egoistic drives deselected because they are disadvantageous in the context of the species' struggle to survive. In this Darwinian vein, Rée argued that we can explain the emergence and success of the morality of selflessness or the unegoistic through the selection for success of those communities that habitually associated feelings of approval with altruistic acts. Rée drew on Darwinian naturalism to secure a morality that applauded the 'un-egoistic', which he identified with compassion, benevolence, sacrifice, selflessness and neighbourly love, and maligned the egoistic, which he identified with envy, hatred, revenge, cruelty and *Schadenfreude*.[3] In Rée's view, co-operation and altruism are among those random natural variations that are selected because of their contribution to group survival. Altruistic morality embodies, so to speak, the practical wisdom of evolution.

Nietzsche flatly rejects Spencer and Rée's defence of altruism on the basis of its species' utility. Nietzsche implies that they are mistaken in using Darwinism to justify this morality. If we are to remain true to the naturalistic turn, he maintains, we must reject this morality as the sole measure of value. As we have seen, Nietzsche seeks to explain the value of motives and actions in terms of their contribution to the species' evolution. He appears to assume that Darwin's notion of an economy of nature regulated by the mechanical principle of natural selection gives us the appropriate vantage point to assess the value of these motives. On the Darwinian theory of evolution, drives that do not contribute to or hinder the species' preservation are gradually extinguished through the cycle of variation, selection and accumulation. The natural history of the species, he suggests, demonstrates that the so-called evil drives have not been extinguished (*D P*: 3). According to Nietzsche, the natural history of the species, which is a long catalogue of violence, conflict and conquest, is proof that so-called evil is a prerequisite of the species' survival. For Nietzsche, the only logical conclusion we can draw

---

[3] Rée uses the following German terms: *Mitleid, Wohlwollen, Aupoferung, Selbstlosigkei*t, *Nachstenliebe*, on one hand; *Neid, Hass, Rachtsucht, Grausamkeit, Schadenfreude*, on the other. These are essentially the same 'drives' Schopenhauer uses to distinguish between moral and anti-moral incentives.

from this fact is that 'evil' benefits the species. The value of altruism, he asserts, in his notebooks is not therefore "the conclusion of science; but the man of science lets himself be misled by the currently predominant drive to believe that science confirms the wish of his drive! Cf. Spencer" (*KSA* 9:8 [35]).

Nietzsche maintains, therefore, that evil drives must have long-term utility value for the species. Nietzsche bluntly states this point in two notes from this period:

All evil drives are as expedient and species-preserving as the good ones! Against Spencer. (*KSA* 9:6[456])

These glorifiers of selection on the basis of expediency (like Spencer) believe they know what the most favourable conditions for development are! And they do not count evil among them! (*KSA* 9:11[43])

On this basis, Nietzsche turns Rée's proposition on its head, I claiming that the bad (egoistic) person is in many cases a useful animal and the good (unegoistic) person is in many cases a harmful animal. From this large-scale evolutionary standpoint, Nietzsche maintains, the fact that an action causes others to suffer is not a valid objection. "Even the most harmful person", as he argues, "may actually be the most useful when it comes to the preservation of the species; for he nurtures in himself or through his effects on others drives without which humanity would long since have become feeble or rotten" (1). If, on the other hand, nature regulated the species exclusively in terms of altruistic moral principles, Nietzsche supposes counterfactually, it may well have become extinct long ago. "The dominance of altruism", he remarks in his 1880 notebook, "seems to me to ruin humanity – a process of dying off" (*KSA* 9:6 [74]). A morality of altruism put into practice would seriously weaken or enfeeble the species. It needs 'evil' drives to survive. 'Evil', in short, has its evolutionary uses. The new science of evolution, he maintains, does not confirm the unconditional value of altruism.

Nietzsche draws on his Darwinian-inspired analysis of nature's grand economy to make a broader point: this naturalistic explanation fatally undermines theological and metaphysical commitments. After the naturalistic turn, God is dead. Nietzsche makes this point by mocking God's impotence: "What *might* have harmed the species may have become extinct many thousands of years ago and may now belong to the things that are no longer possible even for God" (1). Nietzsche assumes that there is no metaphysical agency that could undo or alter natural selection. God is impotent. On this scientific view, the blind mechanism of natural selection replaces divine purpose or design as the sole explanation of natural phenomena. Nietzsche's first allusion in *GS* to his most famous *apercu* – "God is dead" – shows that it flows from his interpretation of evolutionary theory.

At this point, Nietzsche arrives at what will prove to be a provisional account of what he means by 'the gay science'. To comprehend Nietzsche's title, we need to examine briefly why he presupposes that we should connect an explanation of nature to a fundamental orientation or disposition. Why does Nietzsche see nature as a comedy or tragedy rather than simply explaining it scientifically? The answer to this question lies in the fact that *GS* is the meeting point of the ancient and modern streams of Nietzsche's philosophy.

Drawing on the classical and Hellenistic model of philosophy, Nietzsche assumes that our natural theories are in the service of a way of life. Pierre Hadot explains how Hellenistic philosophers connected physics and ethics:

> Among the Stoics and Epicureans physics (was) placed in the service of a way of life: a life of pleasure unmixed with pain for Epicurus; a life of rational coherence for Chrysippus. Ultimately, their physics were intended to justify moral attitudes . . . The physical theories proposed in the schools were . . . intended to deliver man from the anguish he feels in the face of the enigma of the universe. (Hadot 2006: 188)

Following this ancient tradition, Nietzsche presupposes that how we conceive nature, our 'physics', must shape our ethical orientation. For Nietzsche, at stake here is our ethical and existential orientation to existence. In this respect, Nietzsche was attracted by the common ancient idea of surveying human life as if from above (see Halliwell 2008: 337). Hellenistic philosophers made physics serve their ethics by taking a 'view from above'. By assuming the higher vantage point offered by 'physics', Hellenistic philosophers aimed to realise the ethical goal of philosophy, i.e. *ataraxia* or *apatheia*. By taking the view from above, for example, ancient Stoics and Epicureans engaged in a spiritual exercise through which they aimed to remain untroubled in the face of suffering and affirm fate. Nietzsche's engagement with Darwinian and other evolutionary strands of thought made it impossible for him to base his own exercise or *askesis* on ancient cosmologies or materialist doctrines. "By 1881", as Robin Small observes, "the Stoic approach, relying as it does on assumptions about the rationality of the natural order that it recommends as a guide to life, seemed inadequate to Nietzsche. The necessity of a world of becoming without any governing logos was far harder to confront" (Small 2005: 97).

Nietzsche's higher viewpoint is the magnificent economy of nature.[4] He takes a view from above informed by modern evolutionary naturalism as an exercise that shapes our ethical orientation. *GS* is Nietzsche's experiment in 'incorporating' this new naturalism into our ethics. He ascends to Olympian heights to see the comedy of existence.[5]

Why does Nietzsche believe we will experience comic relief by surveying nature from this view from above? After all, Charles Darwin admitted that we might suffer despair and horror from seeing nature from the evolutionary standpoint. "What a book a devil's chaplain might write", he observed, "on the clumsy, wasteful, blundering, low and horribly cruel works of nature!" (13.7.1856).[6] By contrast, Nietzsche takes the same naturalistic perspective as an exercise that engenders joy in nature as a comic burlesque. Nietzsche connects 'physics' with 'ethics' by viewing all natural events from the standpoint of the magnificent economy of nature rather than from

---

[4] In *NCW*, Nietzsche stresses the importance of this view from above: "As my inmost nature teaches me, whatever is necessary – *as seen from the heights and in the sense of a great [grossen] economy* – is also the useful par excellence: one should not only bear it, one should love it. *Amor fati* – that is my inmost nature" (*NCW*, Ep. 1, emphasis added).

[5] Stephen Halliwell shows that the idea of surveying life from above became embedded in Greek cultural consciousness as a result of the picture of the Olympian gods who view human existence from a certain distance as a kind of spectacle for their own interest and consumption. The Olympian view was then taken up by Greek philosophy and incorporated into its notion of the human mind's own capacity for comprehensive contemplation or *theoria* (literally, 'viewing'). Greek philosophy converted the Olympian's external spectatorship into the spectatorship that takes place inside the philosopher's soul and places it cognitively 'above the world' (Halliwell 2008: 337).

[6] From Charles Darwin's letter to J. D Hooker in Darwin Correspondence Project, "Letter no. 1924", accessed 18 June 2018, www.darwinproject.ac.uk/DCP-LETT-1924.

the standpoint of individual phenomena. If we practise seeing nature from this standpoint, he suggests, we can delight in the "eternal comedy of existence" (1).

How does nature look if we undertake this 'spiritual' exercise and see individual phenomena from the higher standpoint of nature's "magnificent" economy (1)? As we have seen, Nietzsche maintains that nature is a "wasteful" and "foolish" economy geared exclusively towards the species' preservation (1). Nietzsche's personification of nature as a wasteful spendthrift encapsulates an important aspect of Darwin's anti-teleological theory of evolution. It captures the way nature produces countless random variations, many of which prove superfluous or dangerous from the point of view of the species' successful adaptation. It also identifies nature with a profound indifference to human suffering insofar as its general economy requires the drives or affects of hatred, envy and lust to rule. On Nietzsche's neo-Darwinian view, we must reject the Aristotelian idea of nature as teleological and economical; it does not act with an end in view or conduct itself according to the principle of the least action. If nature were parsimonious, Nietzsche implies, it would certainly not generate innumerable useless variations. Likewise, if nature were guided by a 'moral' intention or purpose, it would certainly not generate countless superfluous or dangerous variations. In nature's economy, as Nietzsche conceives it, individuals only serve the species' preservation, and in this context, some individuals will be superfluous, worthless or counter-productive. If other individuals do have value, it is only insofar as they embody variations that contribute to the species' future success, and even in such cases, because of nature's wastefulness, many of these will perish without trace.[7] From this higher standpoint, then, we can see individuals as

---

[7] Cf. Tennyson, *In Memoriam*: "Are God and Nature then in strife/That nature lends such evil dreams?/So careful of the type she seems . . . / So careless of the single type". John Cottingham comments, "Nature, as Tennyson puts it seems to careful of the type, yet so careless of the single life" – but he goes on despairingly to add that even that is true: she is not even careful of the type, since the archaeological evidence reveals hundreds and thousands of extinct species. Everything seems grist for the remorseless evolutionary mill. In the face of this, how can we possibly say that "love [is] creation's final law?" (Cottingham 2003: 51).

superfluous, insignificant pawns who merely serve to reproduce the purposeless and wasteful economy of nature:

Pursue your best or your worst desires, and above all, perish! In both cases you are probably still in some way a promoter or benefactor of humanity and are thus entitled to your eulogist – as well as your mockers! But you will never find someone who could completely mock you, the individual, even in your best qualities, someone who could bring home to you as far as truth allows your boundless, fly- and frog-like wretchedness! (1)

Nietzsche first identifies the gay science or joyful wisdom with surveying individual phenomena from the heights of this grand economy. If we view them from this higher standpoint, he suggests, we see individuals as minute, superfluous variations that perish in sacrificing themselves for the species. Once we take this view from above,

perhaps even laughter still has a future – when the proposition 'The species is everything, an individual always nothing' has become part of humanity and this ultimate liberation and irresponsibility is accessible to everyone and at all times. Perhaps laughter will then form an alliance with wisdom; perhaps only 'gay science' will remain. (1)

In this first, provisional account, Nietzsche defines the gay science as an exercise in seeing things from above so that we can enjoy the eternal comedy of existence. Nietzsche conceives this joyfulness in terms of a godlike laughter that expresses the comic incongruity between individuals' delusion that they have great value and pursue their own individual ends and the truth of their evolutionary insignificance and their complete subservience to the species' reproduction.[8] If we survey individuals from above, Nietzsche suggests, we must laugh at the incongruity between their delusions that they rationally pursue their own individual ends when they merely unconsciously or instinctively serve the species' end. From the perspective of nature's economy, he suggests, we can see how individuals appear in their fly- and frog-like wretchedness, or their evolutionary

---

[8] In *WS*, Nietzsche identifies the comedy of human existence with humanity's deluded belief that it is the purpose of existence. From the higher point of view of 'physics', he suggests, this human conceit is as ludicrous as "the ant in the forest" imagining that "it is the goal and objective of the forest" (14).

insignificance as a random variation subject to the blind, purposeless mechanism of natural selection.

In this respect, Nietzsche borrows from Schopenhauer's account of the comedy of existence. Schopenhauer argues that the species sacrifices its individual members' interests and happiness in order to propagate itself (*WWR* 2: 552–56). The interest of the species, he claims, is infinitely superior to any interest of mere individuals. "In fact, the genius of the species", he explains, "generally wages *war* with the guardian geniuses of individuals; it is their pursuer and enemy, always ready ruthlessly to destroy personal happiness in order to carry out its ends" (*WWR* 2: 556). The species' end is its own propagation. Schopenhauer uses Cupid, the Roman god of sexual love, to personify the 'genius of the species'. Cupid, he argues, tramples underfoot the rights and interests of the individuals in order to propagate the species (*WWR* 2: 553). Cupid wages war against individuals by means of the sexual passions. Cupid, Schopenhauer argues, exploits individuals for collective ends that are contrary to their own purposes and happiness. Schopenhauer maintains that the comic genres express the way 'the genius of the species' dupes individuals to believe they are pursuing their own interests when in fact they are realising the species' interests to their own detriment. "The fundamental theme of almost all comedies", he writes, "is the appearance of the genius of the species with its aims. These run counter to the personal interests of the individual who are presented in the comedy, and threaten to undermine their happiness" (*WWR* 2: 553).

Surveyed from the Olympian heights of nature's grand economy, Nietzsche suggests, we can mock humanity and individuals as vain, deluded and risible figures in a purposeless play. Nietzsche's exercise of taking the view from above engenders a mocking laughter, or "*schadenfroh* ... with a good conscience", as he later puts it (200). Nietzsche stresses that this comic view from above is accompanied by a liberating sense of irresponsibility. By taking this perspective, we can enjoy the comic spectacle, because we are careless of the suffering and turmoil individuals endure. Thanks to this perspective, we derive comic relief from the oppressive imperative to discover that human suffering serves a purpose (Higgins 2000: 165–66). Like Epicurean gods, he supposes, we can live carefree and unconcerned about this suffering. We can see why Gilles Deleuze describes "irresponsibility" as "Nietzsche's most noble and beautiful secret" (Deleuze 1983: 20).

We should foreshadow, however, that between 1882 and the publication of *GS* Book 5 in 1887, Nietzsche recasts the view from above. In this period, Nietzsche clarifies and develops his view that our moral perspectives have shaped the economy of nature by giving preference to particular types of individuals, drives and actions over others. Nietzsche maintains that, unlike other animals, the human species can regulate its existence through the invention of moral values that determine the selection, accumulation, intensification and use of its drives. Up to this point, he claims, Christian morality has done so in ways that systematically favour the cultivation and protection of herd animals. By 1886, he suggests, therefore, that if we survey nature from the higher perspective of an Epicurean god, we will see that Christian morality has geared the economy of nature towards the sacrifice of higher individuals for the sake of preserving and protecting the weakest and lowliest human types:

> Supposing one were able to view the strangely painful and at the same time coarse and subtle comedy of European Christianity with the mocking and unconcerned eye of an Epicurean god, I believe there would be no end to one's laughter and amazement: for does not seem that *one* will has dominated Europe for eighteen centuries, the will to make man a *sublime abortion*? (BGE 62)

As we have seen, in Nietzsche's first rendition, the Epicurean god mocks all individuals because they suffer from the delusion that they have intrinsic significance and serve their own ends when they are merely grist for the remorseless evolutionary mill. In this later period, however, Nietzsche's Epicurean god laughs in amazement over the insanity of European Christianity in creating a morality that stunts the human animal for the sake of protecting the species' lowest, weakest types. He sees the Epicurean mockery of European Christianity as merely comic relief from despair over this degeneration of the species. However, as we noted, by 1886, Nietzsche had come to believe that the human species might regulate its own existence through the creation of values. Nietzsche suggests that free spirits must look to a new kind of philosopher and commander who can "teach man the future of man as his *will*, as dependent on human will, and to prepare for great enterprises and collective experiments in discipline and breeding so as to make an end of that gruesome nonsense that has hitherto been called 'history'" (*BGE* 203). Nietzsche therefore opposes the Epicurean god with a very different god, one who does not delight in contemplating the species' degeneration from a distance but who takes on its "artistic refashioning":

But he who, with an opposite desire, no longer Epicurean but with some divine hammer in his hand, approached the almost deliberate degeneration and stunting of man as constitutes the European Christian . . . would he have not have to cry out in rage, in pity, in horror: "O you fools, you presumptuous, pitying fools, what have you done! Was this a work for your hands! How you have bungled and botched my beautiful stone!" (*BGE* 62)

Ultimately, Nietzsche's free spirits idealise not the philosopher who delights in the carefree, divine irresponsibility of an Epicurean god but the philosopher "as the man of the most comprehensive responsibility who has the conscience for the collective evolution of mankind" (*BGE*: 61).

After this preliminary account of the meaning of 'the gay science' Nietzsche turns to an examination of what stands in the way of our acknowledgement of the comedy of existence. "At present", he claims, "things are still quite different, the comedy of existence has not yet 'become conscious' of itself; at present we still live in the age of tragedy, in the age of moralities and religions" (1). Nietzsche suggests that we still live in the age of moralities because we witness "ever-new appearances of the founders of moralities and religions", ethical teachers of the purpose of existence (1). What, Nietzsche asks, is the "meaning" of the constant recurrence of these ethical teachers? (1)

We can begin to answer this Nietzsche's by examining his conception of these teachers as metaphysicians. By this he means that these "heroes", as he ironically calls the founders of moralities and religions, invent the idea of a second, different existence behind or beyond this world and by this means take the "old, ordinary existence off its old ordinary hinges" (1). We can turn briefly to Schopenhauer's account of the moral and 'existential' role of metaphysics to illuminate Nietzsche's own sense of this matter. Why do moral teachers invent a second (metaphysical) world and with what effect on the individual and the species?

Schopenhauer argues that metaphysics serves both a moral and 'existential' end: it acts as a guiding star of our actions and it consoles us for the deep sorrows of life (*WWR* 2: 167). On the first front, he maintains that since egoism and ill will are deeply ingrained in human nature, most individuals need to believe that they are serving some egoistic end in order to motivate themselves to act 'morally' (*BM*: 80). Metaphysics achieves this trick. It gives individuals a "motive" that makes it possible for them to act *against their nature*, which Schopenhauer conceives as chiefly egoistic (self-advantage) and malicious (harm others for its own sake). In order to ensure that humankind acts against these fundamental egoistic propensities or 'morally', he explains "it has been everywhere necessary to have recourse to *machinery from another world*" (*BM*: 80). "Gods", as Schopenhauer explains, "have been pointed to, whose will and command the required mode of behaviour [i.e. altruistic, compassionate behaviour] was said to be, and who were represented as emphasising this command by penalties and rewards either in this, or in another world, to which death would be the gate" (*BM*: 80). On the basis of this metaphysical machinery moral teachers compel individuals to act morally on the grounds that in the world behind or beneath the ordinary world they will be rewarded for their 'good' actions and punished for their 'evil' ones. Metaphysics stiffens our wavering moral resolve. "For the mass of mankind" Schopenhauer asserts "it will perhaps be always necessary to continue to appeal to incentives of this nature [i.e. egoistic incentives], and we know that such is the teaching promulgated by the different religions, which are in fact the metaphysics of the people" (*BM*: 80).

On the second front, Schopenhauer argues that because humans, unlike other animals, can become acutely conscious of both their mortality and nature's purposelessness they have a metaphysical need for belief in second world behind or above nature. For this reason Schopenhauer proclaims than "man is an *animal metaphysicum*" (*WWR* 2: 160). "[I]t is the knowledge of death, and therewith the consideration of suffering and misery of life", he explains, "that give the strongest impulse to . . . metaphysical explanation of the world" (*WWR* 2: 16). Schopenhauer's idea is that for human creatures this world, the world of nature, is unbearable or unlovable without the metaphysical belief in a second world that endows necessary natural, causal events with meaning or moral purpose. Our awareness of nature's purposelessness motivates the need for metaphysical conception of a second world that shows us that our suffering is not meaningless, but serves a final purpose. Metaphysics therefore makes it possible for moral teachers to proclaim that we ought to love life because it has a redemptive or moral purpose. For example, religion, as the metaphysics of the people, assures human creatures that their sufferings will be redeemed and offers them the consolation of immortality. Metaphysics makes the world appear worthy of our trust or love.

For Schopenhauer therefore moral teachers must resort to metaphysical errors firstly to morally guide human action; and secondly they must do so to offer the 'metaphysical animal' consolation for the purposeless suffering they must endure. Schopenhauer claims that human creatures need to believe that their actions fulfil some higher reason or purpose, yet objective knowledge shows that they act instinctively or mechanically and in doing so they ensure the eternal repetition of a purposeless whole. Metaphysical errors console the species by deluding it that its actions serve some higher purpose. They do so by introducing a teleological view of the natural world. In the metaphysical picture, natural events happen for a reason or purpose; they are not merely a chain of causal necessities. The essential problem metaphysics addresses is the pain human creatures suffer from their awareness of senselessness and futility of their suffering. Unlike other animals, Schopenhauer observes, even the most insensitive or dullest human creature can become aware of the fact that its suffering is meaningless or senseless; the basic, creaturely sufferings we share with other animals is profoundly exacerbated by the fact that we know that these sufferings serve no final purpose. Metaphysics is needed to ward off the terrible idea that our suffering is simply a matter of blind causal necessity. We give our suffering some meaning or purpose, for example, through the metaphysical fantasy that it serves God's purpose or that it is a sign of redemption.

Nietzsche agrees with Schopenhauer's account of meaning of metaphysics. He claims that the founder of religions and moralities wrongly think of themselves as "God's emissaries" when in fact they work in the interests of the species. Nietzsche gives a naturalistic explanation of moral and religious founders: their inventions serve the species' preservation, not divine or metaphysical interests. They preserve the species by sustaining its trust in life. As Nietzsche puts it,

They, too promote the life of the species *by promoting the faith in life*. 'Life is worth living' each of them shouts, 'there is something to life, there is something behind life, beneath it; *beware*!' (1)

Like Schopenhauer, Nietzsche supposes that the meaning of the recurrence of moral teachers is that without the consoling belief that we act for a redemptive purpose or reason, not merely from blind, purposeless necessity, we cannot sustain our faith in life. By supplying us with metaphysical consolations, these ethical teachers of purpose sustain our trust in life. Thanks to these moral teachers we think we act as we do because we are pursuing moral or rational ends or goal:

Life *ought* to be loved, *because* – ! Man *ought* to advance himself and his neighbours *because* – ! . . . The ethical teacher makes his appearance as the teacher of the purpose of existence in order that what happens necessarily and always, by itself and without a purpose, shall henceforth seem to be done for a purpose and strike man as reason and ultimate commandment; to this end he invents a second, different existence and takes by means of his new mechanics the old ordinary existence of its old, ordinary hinges. (1)

Nietzsche suggests that moral teachers change the way existence *appears* to species: they make nature's purposelessness seem purposeful. Yet the real lever of the action is the blind drive to species' preservation. Nietzsche claims that due to the repeated appearance of moral teachers the species' trust in life has come to hinge on the false belief that nature itself and the species' actions serve a purpose. Moral teachers persuade us that we act as we do in the physical world order not from blind necessities that reproduce a purposeless existence, but to realise a metaphysical purpose. As Schopenhauer suggested metaphysics makes it possible for moral teachers to proclaim that we ought to love life *because* it serves a moral or redemptive purpose. Metaphysics makes existence seem trustworthy insofar as it embodies a moral purpose. Nietzsche also emphasises how metaphysics serves the species' need for consolation for the suffering that derives from the human animal's awareness of nature's purposelessness. Nietzsche's moral teachers assume that life is worth living only because of what seems to lie beneath or behind it; that is because it appears to be linked to a second, metaphysical world. In other words, moral teachers assume that without this belief in a metaphysical world the species would experience existence as bereft of value or worth; they assume, in other words, that the species cannot experience nature or life as sufficiently satisfying on its own terms to make it worth living. They conceive nature's economy as intrinsically or morally flawed and maintain that it can only be redeemed if it serves a metaphysical purpose.

Yet, Nietzsche emphasises that by "inventing a second, different existence" moral teachers sustain the species' faith in life, but they do so in a way that threatens to take "the old ordinary existence of its old, ordinary hinges". In what sense does Nietzsche think moral teachers 'unhinge' ordinary existence?

Nietzsche implies that moral teachers take old ordinary existence off its hinges by conceiving every individual as intrinsically important rather than as subservient to the species' preservation. Rather than acknowledging the comedy of existence, and mocking individuals as meaningless, valueless pawns in the great economy of nature, moral teachers elevate individuals above the species:

Indeed in no way does [the moral teacher] want us to *laugh* at existence, or at ourselves – or at him; for him, an individual is always an individual, something first, last and tremendous; for him there are no species, sums or zeroes. Foolish and fanciful as his inventions and valuations may be, as badly as he may misjudge the course of nature and deny its conditions – all ethical systems hitherto have been so foolish and contrary to nature that humanity would have perished from everyone had it gained power over humanity – all the same! (1)

In what sense does Nietzsche believe all ethical systems have been contrary to nature? In what respect do they deny the conditions of nature? As we have seen, Nietzsche argues that these teachers console the species by making it appear as if what happens of necessity seems to be done for a metaphysical purpose. Moral teachers' false representations of a metaphysical purpose operating behind nature serves humanity's desire to see meaning in the purposeless, necessary events of nature. Yet, he maintains, if humanity took these purposes seriously, that is if it acted on these teachers' principle that an individual is "something first, last and tremendous" they would undermine nature's great economy, which rests on the proposition "the species is everything, the individual nothing" (1).

In nature's great economy, as Nietzsche sees it, individuals perish if they impede the species' preservation. The species' evolution turns on the continual elimination of countless useless or damaging variations, the 'zeroes' in nature's equation. Instead of accepting this principle of the nature's economy (i.e. natural selection and its consequences), Nietzsche argues, moral teachers defend the equal value of every individual regardless of their contribution to the species' preservation. If this were put into practice, Nietzsche claims, it would preserve individual variations that, for the sake of the species' preservation, ought to perish. We should note in advance that Nietzsche later revises his account of the way in which he claims our ethical systems have been "contrary to nature" (1) Nietzsche later maintains that humanity will not perish if we put into practice the religious or moral commitment to preserving all individuals, regardless of their strength or weakness, health or sickness, but rather in doing so we will protect sickly herd animals and undermine the possibility of cultivating higher individuals (e.g. *BGE* 62; *GM* III. 11/13). Morality, Nietzsche laments, has reorganised the "total economy of mankind" so that it is oriented towards the preservation of the "surplus of unsuccessful cases" rather than cultivation of the species' highest, as yet unrealised individual possibilities (*BGE* 62). In short, Nietzsche's revised view is that that morality threatens the species' highest individual exemplars rather than humanity as a whole.

Nietzsche argues that the continual emergence of these teachers of the purpose of existence has fundamentally transformed the human species:

Man has become a fantastic animal that must fulfil one more condition of existence more than any other animal: man *must* from time to time believe he knows *why* he exists; his race cannot thrive without a periodic trust in life – without faith in the *reason in life!*"

Since we have become this fantastic animal, Nietzsche reasons, it follows that even if in the long run our 'tragic' teachings will be vanquished by the eternal comedy of existence, we must always create a new tragic teaching of purpose. Nietzsche seizes on this transformation of the human animal as an opportunity for free spirits to invent a new tragedy:

And ever again the human race will from time to time decree: 'There is something one is absolutely forbidden henceforth to laugh at' And the most cautious friend of man will add: 'Not only laughter and gay wisdom but also the tragic, with all its sublime unreason, belongs to the means and necessities of the preservation of the species'. And therefore! Therefore! Therefore! Oh, do you understand me, my brothers? Do you understand this new law of ebb and flood? We, too, have our time! (1)

Nietzsche's project in *GS* then is to vanquish through "laughter, reason and nature" all past ethical systems, which he claims are contrary to nature, for the sake of establishing a new tragedy (1).

CHAPTER 2

Nietzsche's New Nobility: Book 1

After establishing the architecture of *GS* in the opening section, Nietzsche devotes the remainder of Book 1 to preparing the ground for his own ethical naturalism. Nietzsche aims to expose the limitations and prejudices of older moralities, including both metaphysical and naturalistic moralities. Second, Nietzsche begins to formulate his ethical motif 'become who you are' as the basis of his ethical naturalism. Nietzsche's new ethical naturalism values 'noble' individuals who create and transform themselves through the cultivation of their own unique '*physis*' or nature.[1] We can get an anticipatory glimpse of Nietzsche's naturalistic ethics of self-cultivation through his surprising defence of Wagner as a model of how to become who one is in Book 2:

Our life, too, shall be justified before ourselves! We too shall freely and fearlessly, in innocent selfishness, grow and blossom from ourselves! And as I contemplate such a person, the following sentences still comes to mind today as they did before: 'That passion is better than Stoicism . . . that being honest even in evil is better than losing oneself to the morality of tradition; that the free man can be good as well as evil, but unfree man is a disgrace to nature and has no share in heavenly or earthly comfort; finally that *everyone who wants to become free must do so through himself*'". (99)[2]

---

[1] Nietzsche rarely uses the Greek term *physis*, which is the origin of English words such as *physics, physical* and *physiology*. Nietzsche's choice of the original Greek word indicates that he specifically intends to convey the ancient resonance carried in its root, the transitive verb *phyein*, "to bring forth, produce, put forth" (Desmond 2006: 133). In its earliest sense, *physis* means the growth of something into its peculiar way of being. On the history of the ancient notion of *physis*, see Hadot (2006: 17–28)

[2] Nietzsche quotes these three propositions from *RWB* 11, which he describes as "the language of nature restored in the world of man".

In formulating this ethical naturalism Nietzsche moves beyond the Hellenistic, often Stoically inflected ethics of self-mastery that he had used to criticise the Christian and Schopenhauerian morality in *D* (see Ure 2009). Nietzsche's noble ethics does not value tranquil self-mastery, but individuals "who have the courage to own up to their *physis* and to heed its demands down to its subtlest tones" (39). Nietzsche begins to sketch this noble morality as his alternative to the Christian and secularised Christian moralities of selflessness, which, as we have seen, he claims stunt the human animal and prevent the cultivation of its as yet unrealised highest possibilities for the sake of protecting the species' lowest, weakest types.

In Book 1 Nietzsche aims to sketch this new ethical naturalism and to identify and criticise the moralities or conventions that stand in the way of this project. In developing his ethics he draws on a mix of the old and the new theories and concepts of nature. Nietzsche leans on some contemporary biological theories to reconceptualise humans as animals who can transfigure their own particular *physis* rather than merely preserve themselves through adaptation to their circumstances. In this respect, Nietzsche believes he exposes and overcomes the prejudices that, so he alleges, shape moral and political theories that defend unconditional duties and/or selflessness. Nietzsche surveys and leans on a range of ancient concepts of nobility, including the ancient sophists' defence of *physis* (nature) against *nomos* (convention), to criticise contemporary moralities and to develop his own ethics of a 'higher' or noble individuality. Nietzsche identifies European morality as engaged in a hidden war with his own noble ethics.

We can see how Nietzsche sketches his noble ethics of self-cultivation by examining his account of the place of science and truth in this new way of life, the conditions that make it possible for the most fruitful individuals to create themselves as great, singular works of art and the moral conventions that systematically prevent the generation of such nobility.

Nietzsche flags his attempt to establish a noble ethics at the outset of Book 1. In *GS* 2 and 3 he develops a sharp contrast between noble and common forms of life. Nietzsche's first concern is with evaluating the role and value of truth seeking as a condition or expression of this higher way of life. As we shall see, Nietzsche betrays a profound and enduring ambivalence about the value of truth in *GS* and later works. If in *HH* Nietzsche endorsed ascetic positivism, or the detached, dispassionate pursuit of scientific truth, in *GS* he interrogates the origins, motives and value of the drive to truth. In *GS* Book 1 Nietzsche begins to cast a critical eye on his earlier commitment to the ideal of the free spirit as one who "lives only so as to know better" (*HH* 34).

In *GS* 2 Nietzsche first aligns philosophical truth seeking with rare or higher individuals. Here he identifies a type of philosophical nobility exemplified by an "intellectual conscience" that seeks certainty without regard for conventional measures of good and evil (2). Nietzsche implicitly takes ancient philosophers like Socrates and Diogenes the Cynic as models of rare, divinely inspired philosophical questioners. In Plato's *Apology*, we might recall, the ancient Athenians accused Socrates of impiety and corrupting the youth on the basis of his divine mission of rigorously testing his Athenian interlocutors' moral beliefs to determine the meaning of the Delphic oracles' claim that none were wiser than Socrates. Diogenes took the Delphic oracles riddle that he should "deface the coinage" as a divine command to decommission the "coinage" of social custom (*DL* 6.20–21). In revaluating conventional values Nietzsche imitates these ancient moralists' impious philosophical questioning.

Unlike the great majority, Nietzsche claims only these rare exceptions practise the examined life and live according to values they assess in terms of "the final and most certain reasons pro and con" (2). The free spirit, as put it earlier "demands reasons, the rest demand faith" (*HH* 225). Nietzsche claims that higher human beings separate themselves from lower types by having as their "inmost craving and deepest need" what he calls "*the desire for certainty*" (2). Nietzsche stresses as his personal judgement that it is contemptible "to stand in the midst of this *rerum concordia discors* and the whole marvellous uncertainty and ambiguity of existence *without questioning*, without trembling with the craving and rapture of questioning" (2).

In *GS* 3 Nietzsche elaborates this distinction between the noble and common types. Nietzsche's account of the difference between noble and common sheds an interesting light on this high estimation of intellectual conscience. Nietzsche suggests that the rare, noble desire for certainty is motivated by the "unreasonable" or "odd reason of passion". Nietzsche identifies the distinguishing feature of nobility as the pursuit of a passion that silences or subordinates instrumental reason, or reason as the calculation of the best means to one's own preservation and advantage. By contrast, he suggests, "the higher nature is more *unreasonable*", in its best moments its "reason *pauses*" (2). Nietzsche conceives this noble irrationality as analogous to animals sacrificing themselves to protect their offspring at the price of their own extinction; "the animal", as he elaborates, "becomes stupider than it usually is – just like the person who is noble and magnanimous" (3).

Nietzsche adds an important qualification to this concept of nobility. It is only noble to succumb to a passion, he argues, for the sake of a taste for "exceptions" (2). One might give way to any number of passions, but for Nietzsche not all of them count as noble. Passions are noble only if they pursue an idiosyncratic or "singular value standard" that leaves most people cold (2, 55). "The passion that overcomes the noble one", he observes, "is a singularity and he fails to realise this: the use of a rare and singular standard and almost a madness; the feeling of heat in things that feel cold to everyone else; a hitting upon values for which the scale has not yet been invented; a sacrifice on the altar of an unknown god; a courage without any desire for honours; a self-sufficiency that overflows and communicates to men and things" (55).

Nietzsche identifies intellectual conscience or a "passion for knowledge", which demands certainty at any price, including health, honour, advantage, ultimately even life, as an example of this type of nobility. On this first examination of the ethical worth of passion for knowledge, Nietzsche stresses that he values it only because he conceives it as a singular, idiosyncratic pursuit that the majority hold in contempt. In other words, Nietzsche does not value intellectual conscience because he conceives it as useful, liberating or therapeutic, but simply because it is a passion through which truth seekers heroically and magnanimously distinguish themselves from the herd.

As we shall see, however, Nietzsche revisits and revises his high estimation of the unconditional pursuit of truth or the desire for certainty at any price. In the period between the first and second edition of *GS* he will come to reject his own heroic characterisation and high evaluation of this desire for certainty. In fact, in the final book of *GS* Nietzsche will come to indict the impetuous "*demand for certainty*" as a measure and symptom of the weakness of the masses who cower before the possibility of inventing their own values (347).

Even in Book 1 Nietzsche betrays his ambivalence about the value of science. In *GS* 46, Nietzsche argues that in the long period of the morality of custom, which chained the species' inner life with iron necessity, fantasies and fairy tales were experienced as a source of relief from these moral clamps. In our age, he suggests, when human laws and concepts seem to undergo continual change, science by discovering truths that stand firm grants relief from a 'seasickness' induced by this constant transformation. "Our bliss", as he explains, "is like that of a shipwrecked man who has climbed ashore and is standing with both feet on the firm old earth – marvelling because it does not bob up and down" (46). We seek relief from perpetually changing values, he suggests, in the certainty or iron necessity of science. It rescues us from being lost at sea. Nietzsche's point is not to validate science as the only source of truth or express his own commitment to it, but to identify the pleasure we moderns derive from science (cf. Ridley 2007: 69; Cohen 2014: 44). Nietzsche diagnoses the modern commitment to science as springing from a fear of and desire to escape from shifting values. Yet in moral and political matters Nietzsche opposes the commitment to or belief in eternal or unconditional value horizons. Against "socialists and state idolators" who aim to make life better and safer and bring to an end all forms of distress that motivate change, he applauds those whose incurable dissatisfaction propels "constant *transformation*" (24). In *GS* 12, as we will shortly see, Nietzsche aligns modern science precisely with the socialist political ideal that he vehemently opposes, the goal of seeking a comfortable, painless life for the masses at the price of creative transformation. Nietzsche's diagnosis of our commitment to science as an escape from changing, fluctuating values to eternal or fixed horizons will later form the basis of his scepticism about the value of our faith in science.

Indeed, in Book 1 Nietzsche explicitly calls into question that value of science on the grounds that in its current guise it diminishes rather than enhances life. Nietzsche dismisses as "errors" the motives that in previous centuries legitimated the pursuit of science: viz. the religious assumption that it brings us closer to understanding God; the ancient belief, which Spinoza revives, that scientific understanding brings us beatitude, and the Enlightenment belief in the absolute utility of knowledge (37). Nietzsche supposes that these 'errors' do not characterise the contemporary commitment to science. Turning to the present, he therefore asks two questions: 'what is the aim of contemporary science?' and 'what *should* constitute its final aim?' (12).

Nietzsche's answer to the first question is that modern science serves the 'Stoic' ideal of eliminating pain from life. By comparison with religion, as he earlier put it, science's ideal is the very modest one of a painless life. "Modern science", he explains in *HH*, "has as its goal: as little pain as possible, as long life as possible – thus a kind of eternal bliss, though a very modest kind in comparison with religion" (*HH* 128). Nietzsche issues a fundamental challenge to this modest 'Stoic' ideal, which he believes informs contemporary science and modern politics of all stripes. We should not, he urges, mistake human flourishing with Stoic impassivity. Nietzsche claims that the Stoic ideal of tranquillity does not encompass life's highest or noblest possibilities, it is rather a symptom of exhausted life.

We can illuminate Nietzsche's case against the 'Stoic' ethics of modern science by briefly examining the Schopenhauerian interpretation of Stoicism. Schopenhauer agrees with the Stoics' view that "excessive joy and very severe pain occur always in the same person, for they reciprocally condition each other".[3] Excessive joy, he claims, hinges on the human-all-too-human "delusion that we have found something in life that is not to be met with at all, namely permanent satisfaction of the tormenting desires or cares that constantly breed new ones" (*WWR* 1: 318). When we inevitably discover that this is a false dawn, Schopenhauer claims, we pay for our excessive joy with equally bitter pain. According to Schopenhauer, this delusory anticipation of a sorrow-less life explains wild oscillations between manic joy and melancholic despair.

---

[3] See e.g. Seneca *Ep.* 23 "Pleasure (*voluptas*) unless it has been kept within bounds, tends to rush headlong into the abyss of sorrow".

Schopenhauer then suggests that Stoic ethics aims to free us from this emotional rollercoaster through a philosophical therapy of the passions. The aim of Stoic ethics he asserts is "a life as painless as possible, and thus as happy as possible" (*WWR* 2: 158–159). By extirpating these passions, as he explains, Stoics believe it is possible to meet every event with equanimity; they experience neither pleasure or displeasure because, in Epictetus' famous maxim, they do not demand that things happen as they wish, but wish that they happen as they do happen" (Epictetus, 1995: 8). In Schopenhauer's words, the Stoic sage therefore "always holds himself aloof from jubilation and sorrow and no event disturbs his *ataraxia*" (*WWR* 1: 88). Seneca argues that Stoic *ataraxia* is "true joy" (*Ep.* 23.4). He distinguishes between true joy (*gaudium*), which we can only realise through reason or virtue, and pleasure (*voluptas*), which we pursue through the passions. Stoic 'joy', he observes, derives not from embodied pleasure (*voluptas*), or the satisfaction of passions, but from being "lifted above every circumstance" (*Ep.* 23.3).[4]

Nietzsche accepts this Schopenhauerian interpretation of the Stoic's ideal as a painless life. The Stoics, he suggests, recognised that we cannot have the highest pleasure without suffering the greatest distress. They acknowledged, in other words, that "pleasure and displeasure are so intertwined that whoever *wants* as much as possible of one *must* also have as much as possible as the other – that whoever wants to learn to 'shout with joy to the heavens' must also be prepared for 'grief unto death'" (12).[5] If we wish to realise a painless life, therefore, we must forgo the greatest pleasures. The Stoics, Nietzsche claims, were consistent in aiming to realise their ideal of a painless life by desiring as little pleasure as possible.

Nietzsche maintains that *we* still face the same choice as that which the ancient Stoics confronted: "either *as little displeasure as possible,* in short lack of pain … or *as much displeasure as possible* as the price for the growth of a bounty of refined pleasures and joys that hitherto have seldom been tasted" (12). Nietzsche poses an either/or: either Stoic tranquillity at the price of pleasure or the intensification of pleasure at

---

[4] On the Stoic conception of joy, see Seneca, *Ep.* 23.4–6; Nussbaum (1994: 398–401) and Graver (2007: 52–53).
[5] Nietzsche quotes from the Clärchen's *lied* in Goethe's storm and stress play *Egmont*.

the price of the greatest suffering (see also 302, 338). Nietzsche suggests
that modern science follows the Stoic path. Science, he explains, is
"better known for its power to deprive man of his joys and make him
colder, more statue-like, more stoic" (12). Yet, he claims, if contemporary science promotes the Stoic ideal, it might yet pursue the
opposite course. Science, Nietzsche suggests "might yet be found to
be the *great giver of pain*! – and then its counterforce might at the same
time be found: its immense capacity for letting new galaxies of joy flare
up!" (12). Nietzsche clearly endorses the view that this should constitute the final aim of science, but he does not explain here how we
might harness it to this counter-ideal. In Book 4 he will return to these
issues, firmly identifying his ethics with the anti-Stoic ideal of joy,
which pursues "the path to one's own heaven ... through the voluptuousness of one's own hell" (338).[6]

In Book 1 Nietzsche also interprets Epicureanism, Stoicism's
ancient philosophical rival, in light of this choice between a life of
the most intense joys or a painless existence. Nietzsche's interpretation of Epicureanism in *GS* marks an important shift in his attempt
to formulate a rival philosophical therapy. In *HH* 1 and 2 and
D Nietzsche had drawn on Epicureanism, along with Stoicism, as
alternatives to Christian metaphysics (see *WS* 7; 295; *D* 72).
Nietzsche valued both as examples of ancient naturalistic philosophies and arts of living that aimed to realise a tranquil life, a state of
ataraxia, free from pain and worry (see Young 2010: 279–281; Ansell-
Pearson 2013a).[7] The late Roman Epicurean Lucretius summarised
the Epicurean ideal in terms of the belief that nature seeks only two
things "a body free of pain, a mind released from worry and fear for
the enjoyment of pleasurable satisfactions" (Lucretius II: 18–19).

---

[6] In *EH* Nietzsche identifies this as his own personal ideal and experience in recounting his
   perilous encounter with Wagner's music: "The world is poor for him who has never been sick
   enough for this 'voluptuousness of hell'" (*EH* 'Clever' 6). Nietzsche echoes the romantic
   motif of excess, famously encapsulated in William Blake's *Marriage of Heaven and Hell*:
   "The road of excess leads to the palace of wisdom". As Blake expands this point: "Without
   Contraries is no progression. Attraction and Repulsion, Reason and Energy, Love and Hate,
   are necessary to Human existence. From these contraries spring what the religious call Good
   & Evil. Good is the passive that obeys Reason. Evil is the active springing from Energy. Good
   is Heaven. Evil is Hell".
[7] On Nietzsche's interpretation and evaluation of Epicureanism, see Knight (1933), Bett (2005)
   and Caygill (2006).

As noted in the Introduction, Nietzsche personally drew on Epicureanism (and the other ancient therapies) to treat his own suffering. "My health", as he wrote to his friend Peter Gast in 1879, "is disgustingly rich in pain, as formerly; my life much more severe and lonesome; I myself live on the whole almost like a complete saint, but almost with the outlook of a complete, genuine Epicurus . . . with my soul very calm and patient and yet contemplating life with joy" (quoted in Kaufmann 1974b: 110n). In *GS*, however, Nietzsche reverses his judgement of Epicureanism: he no longer interprets it as a mean of or signpost to an affirmative philosophy, but as a philosophical way of life that is symptomatic of life denial.

We can catch a first glimpse of Nietzsche's reversal in *GS* 45. Here Nietzsche does not dispute or even survey Epicurean philosophy, but diagnoses Epicurus' character. Nietzsche describes Epicurus' ideal as "the happiness of an eye before which the sea of existence has grown calm and which now cannot get enough of seeing the surface of this colourful, tender, shuddering skin of the sea. Never before has voluptuousness been so modest" (45). Why can Epicurus not get enough of seeing existence as if it were like the surface of a calm, tranquil sea after a storm? Why does Epicurus have this particular insatiable desire? Nietzsche suggests that only "someone who is continually suffering", could invent 'happiness' as a calm, lucid, untroubled view of existence. Epicurean happiness is a refraction of suffering. Nietzsche diagnoses it as a symptom of one who suffers from the storm of the passions, and who seeks and finds release in a state of undisturbed contemplation.

In doing so he interprets Epicureanism through the idealist notion of the beauty. In German idealist aesthetics, beauty is partly defined by its impact or effect on the subject; an object is beautiful if it calms or stills the constant surge of desires. Beauty is anti-erotic. It stills our desires. For Kant we cannot perceive beauty unless we can adopt a disinterested attitude towards the object; for Schopenhauer we seek out beautiful objects in order to experience this cessation of interest or desire. As Schopenhauer explains, contemplation of the beautiful yields "the painless state prized by Epicurus as the highest good and as the state of the gods, for that moment we are delivered from the miserable pressure of the will. We celebrate the Sabbath of the penal servitude of willing; the wheel of Ixion stands still" (*WWR* 1: 196).

Those who suffer from the "from the storm of the passions, the pressure of desire and fear, and all the miseries of willing", he maintains, find release through the disinterested, calm, tranquil contemplation of natural beauty (*WWR* 1: 197). Nietzsche himself elaborates just this understanding of Epicurean happiness. For those who suffer from internal strife, he argues, happiness "appears to him, in accord with a sedative (e.g., Epicurean or Christian) medicine and mode of thought, pre-eminently as the happiness of repose, of tranquillity, of satiety ... as a 'Sabbath of Sabbaths'" (*BGE* 200). For Nietzsche then Epicurus' view of nature acts as a sedative. Epicurus, he suggests, invents an "optimistic horizon" that satisfies the needs of those who suffer from the tumult of their own passions (370). Epicurean philosophy, he claims, is for those "who suffer from an *impoverishment of life* and seek quiet, stillness, calm seas, redemption from themselves through art and insight" (370).

Epicurus, Nietzsche suggests, seeks calmness and repose and does so through a philosophy that conceives nature in ways that aim to eliminate all fear and strong passions or desires. In doing so, he echoes a common modern criticism of Epicureanism: viz. that it sacrifices scientific investigation on the altar of happiness (Lange 1925: 95–96, 103). Epicureanism, as Nietzsche later explicitly states, belongs among the Greek philosophies that undertake a "general assault on knowledge for the good of morality" (*WP* 442). "Epicurus", he argues, "denied the possibility of knowledge, in order to retain moral (or hedonistic) values as the highest values" (*WP* 578).

However, Nietzsche goes well beyond this standard criticism by diagnosing Epicureanism as a symptom of illness and identifying an ethical alternative: not scientific materialism, but what he calls Dionysian or tragic insight. Nietzsche's Dionysian ideal is the antipodes of Epicurus' modest voluptuousness, a secure, calm, untroubled vision of nature. If, as Nietzsche maintains, "the secret from harvesting from existence the greatest fruitfulness and most enjoyment is – live dangerously!" or to build cities on the slopes of Vesuvius and send ships into uncharted waters, then it necessarily requires forgoing the safety of the Epicurean garden and Epicurus' calm, untroubled contemplation of nature (283). Nietzsche maintains that the highest form of self-cultivation requires extreme, not modest voluptuousness. "By the voluptuousness of hell", as he later puts it in a note, "no sage has yet gone" (*KSA*: 13:20[103]). In the final analysis, Nietzsche conceives the Epicurean philosophy as a refraction of illness, not a cure. He argues that what for the Epicureans constitutes 'pleasure' is merely the absence of pain, and that their ideal is motivated by a fear of the highest, tragic joy. Epicurean philosophy, he argues, does not aim at the highest form of joy, which entails the affirmation of tragedy, but a sedated, tranquillised life. Nietzsche later sums up his ultimate diagnosis of Epicureanism in the following contrast: "I have presented such terrible images to knowledge that any 'Epicurean delight' is out of the question. Only Dionysian joy is sufficient: *I have been the first to discover the tragic*" (*KSA* 11:25 [95]).

In the course of developing his ethics of self-cultivation in Book 1, Nietzsche explores the conditions that make possible the emergence of new values, especially the singular value standards that separate noble individuals from herd animals. In *GS* 4 he fleshes out the claim he made against Rée and Spencer in *GS* 1 that so-called evil or harmful persons may actually be the most useful when it come to the species' preservation. "The strongest and most evil spirits", he asserts, "have so far done the most to advance humanity" (4). What exactly are the *uses* of 'good' and 'evil' persons? Nietzsche claims that the good *conserve* the species; that is they ensure the species successfully adapts to its environment. However, he also claims the good achieve this outcome at the cost of inhibiting the species' capacity to evolve or transform itself. The function of the good drives, he argues, is to *preserve* the species' *status quo*; the function of the evil drives is to make it possible for the species to *advance* beyond the *status quo*, to transform its conditions of existence.

Nietzsche argues that 'evil' persons topple tradition by reawakening in themselves and others dormant passions. He conceives the relationship between evil and the species' development as analogous to relationship between the ploughshare and the field: it removes the detritus that prevents growth and in doing so makes it possible for the species to flourish anew. "In every age", he observes, "the good men are those who bury the old thoughts deeply and make them bear fruit. But the land is eventually exhausted and the ploughshare of evil must come time and again" (4). Nietzsche does not merely describe this evil, he advocates that free spirits practise it. In *D* Nietzsche had already identified his free spirits as the ploughshares of evil. Like states and princes who have sacrificed one citizen for another in pursuing the general interest, "we too", he writes, "have general, and perhaps more than general interests: why may a few individuals of the present generation not be sacrificed for the coming genera-tions? their grief, their distress, their despair, their blunders and fears not be deemed necessary, because a new ploughshare is to break up the ground and make it fruitful for all (*D* 146).[8]

Nietzsche suggests then that 'evil' advances humanity by making it possible for the species to transform its values or conditions of existence, rather than merely repeat the past. Evil persons achieve this end by renewing in others their sense of "adventure" and their lust for new conquests. They hold out the possibility of a future that is much more than a mere continuation or repetition of the past. They do so, he claims by repeatedly reawakening "the sense of comparison, of contradiction, of delight in what is new, daring, unattempted; they force men to pit opinion against opinion, ideal model against ideal model" (4).

After elaborating his reasons for celebrating evil against Rée's Darwinian derived claim that altruism and compassion are the only necessary conditions of the species' health, Nietzsche immediately turns to briefly examine the moral rhetoric of unconditional duties. Against this moral rhetoric, which finds powerful expression in Kant's moral philosophy, he argues that moral scepticism is necessary to ensure that the strongest and most evil spirits can challenge "sublime commandments" or "categorical imperatives" (5). *Contra* all moral teachers, Nietzsche argues that moralists use the claim that the values they defend are unconditional as a rhetorical tool. Metaphysical claims about morality, he argues, are a sophistic trick. Metaphysical accounts of the groundwork of morality, he implies, only obscure the true significance of value claims. Instead, Nietzsche argues, the moralist's claim that his morality is unconditional expresses or serves particular social and psychological interests.

---

[8] Nietzsche originally wanted to call this book *The Ploughshare* (*Die Pflugschar*) (see Schaberg 1995: 77).

Nietzsche aims to engender scepticism about unconditional duties by showing how such claims derive from and serve mundane, sordid or strategic origins and purposes.

Nietzsche observes that a few rare spirits deploy the concept of a 'categorical imperative' to inspire themselves and others with the confidence that they are merely servants and instruments of the sublime (see also *D* 18). By presenting their imperatives as unconditional, sublime duties, Nietzsche suggests, these rare types appear to themselves and others as instruments of God, nature or pure practical reason. In so appealing to unconditional duties, Nietzsche suggests, they give their imperatives the greatest psychological and rhetorical force. By couching their morality in terms of unconditional duties they give it a "great *pathos*" it would lack if they presented their morality merely as a set of hypothetical imperatives (5). Taking aim at Kant, he implies that the idea of the universal moral law within is not analogous to starry sky above, but is a thing of this world, a rhetorical strategy that serves this-worldly ends. Nietzsche also suggests that many, ordinary individuals have much more banal reasons for endorsing the notion of unconditional duties: it enables them to present their craven, expedient submission to authority as a principled stance.

Nietzsche draws a lesson from this analysis of unconditional morality as a rhetorical ploy: moral sceptics and enlighteners, he suggests, should deprive duty of its unconditional character, but, he stresses, they should do not merely out of "decency" (4). Nietzsche does not explicitly state his other reason for rejecting "sublime commandments". We might surmise, however, that Nietzsche's concern is that moral preachers who aim to permanently enshrine one set of 'unconditional' values, threaten to put to sleep the many 'evil' passions that, as we have seen, he claims advances humanity.

Nietzsche maintains the moral sceptic can serve this end not simply by rejecting unconditional conceptions of moral duty, but by replacing the search for metaphysical groundwork of morality with patient historical research into the origins and evolution of different moralities and a program of ethical experimentation. In *GS* 7 Nietzsche frames his own historical research as an alternative and antidote to metaphysical speculation. What we require instead, he suggests, is a history of the way in different evaluative frameworks and passions have illuminated or 'painted' the world. Nietzsche maintains that our passions and evaluations paint or give colour to existence. Values colour the world.[9] Moralists are therefore painters of the world: how it appears to us, or the evaluative and emotional significance we grant it, turns on their colourations.[10]

In place of metaphysical speculation, therefore, Nietzsche proposes a history of all value systems that have given colour to existence. Instead of contemplating eternal forms or formulating 'timeless' truths, Nietzsche's science involves historically tracking the many values and practices that have given life a certain shape, appearance and direction, all of the different 'perspectives' on life. Nietzsche identifies these moralities as the "conditions of existence" that have shaped human life (7). Nietzsche conceives moralities as analogous to environments or climates: some moralities are 'temperate', zones, others 'tropical' zones, which enable very different flora and fauna to flourish (see *HH* 236). On Nietzsche's analogy, we can differentiate moralities as conditions of existence, or 'climates' that determine what type of life can flourish. Yet, he laments, because of the predominance of metaphysical approaches to morality we still know very little about the genesis and effects of moralities as conditions of existence.

Nietzsche sees this history as a prolegomenon to or preparation for other research questions. First, he maintains these histories should identify the effects or consequences of these values and practices. We might ask, for example, How has morality as a condition of existence, a so-called moral climate, nurtured or impeded the human drives? Nietzsche's idea of morality as a condition of existence opens up the possibility that we can measure the value of moralities in terms of the way in which they shape, nurture or develop human drives. In this context, Nietzsche stresses an important point that he will develop later in *GS*: viz. he claims that that human drives "still could grow" in

---

[9] Maudemarie Clark argues that 'colour' functions throughout *HH* and *GS* as a metaphor for value" (Clark 1990: 68); see also Clark and Dudrick (2007: 203).

[10] See also *HH* 16: "Because we have for millennia made moral, religious, aesthetic, demands on the world, looked upon it with blind desire, passion or fear ... the world has gradually becomes so marvellously variegated, frightful, meaningful, soulful, it has acquired colour – but we have been the colourists: it is the human intellect that has made appearances appear and transported its erroneous basic conceptions into things".

very different ways depending on their moral climate (7). Nietzsche maintains, in other words, that our species' drive structure is not yet fixed. Nietzsche's account of morality as a condition of existence, combined with his view that our species' drive structure is contingent and malleable, opens onto the question of what alternative moralities or 'climates' we might conceive.

Second, Nietzsche suggests that the new study of morality requires identifying the erroneousness "of moral judgements *to date*" (7). Nietzsche identifies at least two moral 'errors'. As we have seen, Nietzsche targets the metaphysical error that consists in the belief that good and evil are objective, independent properties of actions or drives. Our primary error, as he explains in Book 3, consists in taking our invented table of goods as "eternal and unconditioned" (115). Against this view, he holds that our moral 'errors' are conditioned as instruments of particular kinds of life and that our moral judgements are therefore necessarily temporary or contingent rather than eternal. In addition, as we have saw in *GS* 1, Nietzsche believes that contemporary naturalists like Rée and Spencer endorse a particular moral error: viz., they falsely argue that the morality of good and evil sums up what is useful for the species.

Third, and most importantly, Nietzsche believes this line of inquiry culminates in "the most delicate question: 'Can science not only eliminate morality as "error", but also furnish goals of action?'" (7). Nietzsche suggests that the addressing this question requires moral 'experimentation'. He envisages centuries of moral experimentation in which "every kind of heroism could find satisfaction" (7). If moralities are 'climates' that shape or regulate the conditions of life then we can find out how they do so by exposing ourselves to these different "clime[s] of the soul", as Nietzsche himself had done during his middle period (*HH* 2 P 5). We can experiment with moralities in order to test how they condition life, to determine what form/s of life they allow to flourish. Nietzsche then eschews the conventional philosophical approach of trying to give an a priori account of morality's foundations for the sake of experimenting with moralities to identify exactly how they shape or condition life.

In *GS* Nietzsche sketches a type of experimental scepticism as his alternative to metaphysical philosophies and their commitment to a priori reasoning about values:

I approve of any form of scepticism to which I can reply, "Let' s try it!" But I want to hear nothing more about all the things and questions which don't admit of experiment. This the limit of my sense of truth; for there, courage has lost its rights. (51)

Nietzsche's experimental scepticism is deeply at odds with ancient scepticism.[11] Ancient sceptics, we might recall, investigated the epistemic limits of evaluative judgements of good and bad, love and hate, by showing that there are equally strong arguments for and against all such judgements. As a result of discovering this 'equipollence', ancient sceptics were compelled to suspend all their evaluative judgements and in doing so they inadvertently realised the desired state of *ataraxia*, or tranquillity undisturbed by the passions, that they had thought they must attain from truth.[12] For the ancient sceptic the desired effect is *ataraxia* and he therefore celebrates its spontaneous emergence from the suspension of judgement that follows from equipollent arguments. In *HH* Nietzsche reluctantly comes close to endorsing a type of sceptical suspension of judgement. However, even here Nietzsche conceives the destruction of the passions as an unintended and unwanted effect of a sceptical assault on our

---

[11] On balance, it seems that Nietzsche opposed ancient Pyrrhonian scepticism's commitment to the suspension of judgement and idealisation of tranquillity. Katrina Mitcheson (2016) develops a very insightful analysis of Nietzsche's alternative experimental scepticism as an important exercise or practice in the art of self-transformation and self-cultivation. On the debate about Nietzsche's relationship to ancient Skepticism, see Parush (1976), Conway and Ward (1992), Mosser (1998), Bett (2000) and Berry (2004, 2005, 2010). Bett shows that between the very early and very late phases of Nietzsche's career, Nietzsche expressed little interest in ancient scepticism (2000: 67). In his late notes Nietzsche describes Pyrrho and Epicurus as "two forms of Greek decadence" (*WP* 437).

[12] Sextus Empiricus, the ancient champion of Pyrrhonian scepticism, captures the outcome of sceptical inquiry by means of a famous analogy: "Indeed, what happened to the Skeptic is just like what is told of Apelles the painter. For it is said that once upon a time, when he was painting a horse and wished to depict the horse's froth, he failed so completely that he gave up and threw his sponge at the picture – the sponge on which he used to wipe the paints from his brush – and that in striking the picture the sponge produced the desired effect. So, too, the Skeptics were hoping to achieve ataraxia by resolving the anomaly of phenomena and noumena, and, being unable to do this, they suspended judgment. But then, by chance as it were, when they were suspending judgment the ataraxia followed, as a shadow follows the body" (OP 1, 28–29).

evaluative judgements, not as an ideal outcome. Nietzsche claims that our ability to enjoy, affirm or value life depends upon belief in errors: we cannot have aversions or partialities, love or hatred, without evaluative judgements, yet all such judgements, he argues, are illogical and unjust. Nietzsche identifies the fact that we are illogical in this way, committed to aversions and partialities on the basis of erroneous judgements, as "one of the greatest and most irresolvable discords of existence" (*HH* 32). Nietzsche's recognition of this disharmony establishes an either/or: we can live in error for the sake of valuing life; or we can live in truth, but only at the price of no longer valuing or affirming life. After the free spirit's sceptical assault on metaphysics, Nietzsche concedes that a "free, fearless hovering over men, customs, laws and the traditional evaluations of things must *suffice* him as the condition he considers most desirable" (*HH* 34). In other words, in *HH* he only endorses this sceptical suspension of judgement as a '*faute de mieux*', not as the highest or most desirable state.

In *D* and *GS*, by contrast, Nietzsche judges the ancient sceptics' desire for tranquillity as an illness from which free spirits must seek redemption (*D* 477). Nietzsche conceives sceptical tranquillity as a symptom of illness or weakness: a flight from an impassioned life and the affirmation and denial that such a life requires. In contrast with ancient scepticism, Nietzsche outlines an experimental scepticism that aims to liberate the free spirit not from *all* values that stoke the passions or drives, but only from values that do not enable us to become who we are. Nietzsche aims to develop a scepticism out of which we can claim to emerge "more courageous and healthier than ever once more in possession of [our] instincts" (*D* 477). Indeed, the point of Nietzsche's scepticism is to experiment with ways of living so that one can cease being an unhealthy sceptic who flees from the strong evaluations that are a necessary basis of our passions or drives. Nietzsche conveys this point in his imagined dialogue between 'A' who has emerged from his scepticism able to recover his instincts and his critic B: "B: You have just ceased to be a sceptic! For you *deny*! – A: And in doing so I have again learned to *affirm*" (D 477).

Nietzsche explains this experimental scepticism by contrasting it with moral conduct. Rather than trying to conform with a moral law, and hence experiencing good or bad conscience depending on whether he succeeds or fails, the free spirit "sees his own action as experiments and questions, as seeking an explanation of something: to him, success and failure are primarily answers" (41). Nietzsche suggests that this experimental scepticism requires "courage" to test and find wanting a whole range of lives that give us comfort or that have collective moral approval and sanction (see *D* 61). Nietzsche stresses that we do not sacrifice these ways of life for nothing, or merely to attain a state of suspension: "Scepticism! Yes, but a scepticism of experiments! Not the inertia of despair" (*KSA* 9: 6[356]). Through experimentation, Nietzsche suggests, free spirits not only liberate themselves from conventional ways of life, they also invent and test out new evaluations, new moral horizons. Nietzsche's experimentalism requires the courage not only to overthrow moral conventions, but also to create and experiment with value horizons that are our *own* in a strong sense: viz. values that establish the conditions of existence for becoming who we are.

Nietzsche experimental scepticism aims to test how human drives might still develop in unknown or unprecedented ways, to test "every kind of heroism", as he puts it, and to make it possible for individuals to identify and experiment with ways of life that might realise their own singular value standards (7). In this respect, his experimental project requires self-knowledge; individuals must know their own particular kind of heroism. Yet, Nietzsche claims in the very next section, we in fact know very little about ourselves. Nietzsche suggests that we have not developed the tools to acquire self-knowledge, or knowledge of the "laws of development" of our own unique, distinctive individual virtues (8). Our self-knowledge, he asserts, is limited to our consciousness of those virtues that we have developed in order to safely navigate our social relationships. He suggests that these are qualities that serve to attract or repel others; they are, as he puts it, either "ornaments" or "weapons" (8). What we know of ourselves therefore are the 'virtues' or strategies that we have acquired by the demands of attracting or repelling others for the sake of self-preservation.

Yet Nietzsche suggests that there is an unexplored realm of "unconscious virtues", which follow entirely different laws of development to our conscious virtues (8; see also *D* 105, 115). Nietzsche conceives our known virtues as mechanisms of inclusion or exclusion that enable us to maintain and protect ourselves within a community. Nietzsche claims that we also have a range of as yet unknown or invisible 'virtues' that are not shaped by these necessities of social integration. He likens these invisible qualities to "the scales of reptiles" that have lines and forms that other creatures cannot see and so therefore cannot be explained in terms of socially adaptive functions (8). If our unknown, invisible virtues follow a completely different line of development this is presumably because they are not shaped by the necessity of signifying something to other members of the species. Nietzsche suggests that these invisible or, "unknown or badly known" qualities have "lines and subtleties and sculptures that might give pleasure to a god with a divine microscope" (8). Nietzsche view then is that individuals have unconscious virtues or "subtle sculptures" that are distinct from and independent of their adaptive needs. "For example", as he explains, "we have our diligence, our ambition, our acuteness – all the world knows about them – and in addition, we probably have *our* industry, *our* ambition, *our* acuteness; but for these reptile scales, no microscope has yet to be invented!" (8). Nietzsche stresses that those who merely acknowledge the *possibility* of these unconscious virtues are satisfied by far too little. Nietzsche implies that his project is much more ambitious: free spirits need to invent a "microscope" to see these "reptile scales" so that they can experiment with and cultivate their *sui generis* qualities.

In the next two sections Nietzsche implies that our atavistic traits might be the source of some of these unknown, hidden virtues. We harbour, as puts it, "hidden gardens and plantations" that "suddenly emerge into the light much later" or, mixing his metaphors, we are like "growing volcanoes approaching their hour of eruption" (9). Nietzsche suggests that by bringing back to life a whole range of traits that were once common, but are now rare, atavism makes possible individual grandeur or greatness: "These late ghosts of past cultures now seem strange, rare, extraordinary and whoever feels these powers in himself must nurse, defend, honour and cultivate them against another world that resists them: and so he becomes either a great human being or a mad and eccentric one unless he perishes too soon" (10).

Nietzsche argues, however, that contemporary morality systematically impedes the cultivation of great individuals. He develops this claim by arguing that we must conceive the morality of altruism and compassion as a value horizon that protects the community from 'higher' individuals by preventing them from pursuing their own singular ends and values. Nietzsche's exposé of the collective selfishness that he claims underpins the morality of altruism illustrates why he is often considered a "master of suspicion" (Ricoeur 1970: 149–150). Nietzsche builds his case first by collapsing the moral distinction between selflessness and selfishness, conceiving it as a mere foreground estimate that conceals the common motivational source of action, and second by diagnosing 'altruism' as the means by which collectives prey on higher individuals for the sake of their own security.

In *GS* 13 Nietzsche develops the first claim, arguing that altruistic morality (or selflessness) misrepresents individual motivation. Nietzsche investigates what it might mean for individuals to help or benefit others. What motivates them to benefit or harm others? To answer this question, Nietzsche introduces "the doctrine of the teaching of the feeling of power" (13). He claims that for agents their own 'feeling of power' is *the* criterion of value. According to Nietzsche, what we seek to achieve whether we help or harm others is to maximise our feeling of power.[13] As Nietzsche explains, "benefitting and hurting others are ways of exercising one's power over them – and that is all one wants in such cases!" (13). Nietzsche maintains that whether we benefit or harm another is a secondary concern; our only concern is which of these actions will best sustain our own feeling of power. Nietzsche's doctrine maintains that we are motivated by the desire to sustain the feeling of power, the feeling of being "'on top' that is, *above . . .* others", as he puts it (13), even at the price of sacrificing our happiness or life. Altruistic morality, he argues, short-circuits our understanding of human motivation. It evaluates actions merely in terms of their means – praising helpful

---

[13] Cf. Clark (1990: 210). She argues that Nietzsche could not have intended to explain all human behaviour as motivated by the desire for power because this necessarily prevents him from differentiating between power and other motives, or between, for example, rape and sex. Yet in this section Nietzsche does assimilate the desire to hurt and the desire to benefit others to one and the same desire to feel a sense of power.

actions and condemning harmful one – rather than in term of the end they serve: viz. our feeling of power. If it is true, Nietzsche's doctrine invalidates the moral distinction between egoistic and altruistic motivation. Instead we can only distinguish between different methods of satisfying the feeling of power. "Whether one prefers the slow or the sudden, the safe or the dangerous and daring increase in power", as he explains, "one always seeks this or that spice according to one's temperament" (13).

Nietzsche then seeks to differentiate between noble and common, strong and weak, versions of this common motivation. To this end, he distinguishes between two different ways of 'spicing' one's life: some make their feeling of power contingent on overcoming extreme resistance; others on overcoming minimal resistance. Nietzsche personifies these two temperaments in the figure of the knight and the female prostitute [*Freudenmädchen*]. Strong natures like members of a knightly caste, he suggests, only value the feeling of power when they derive it from overcoming significant opposition. They spice their lives with war or competition with equals. Knightly heroes therefore treat suffering, 'broken' individuals with contempt because there is no glory or pride to be had from conquering weaklings. On the other hand, he argues, weak natures like prostitutes derive their feeling of power from conquering "easy prey" (13). On Nietzsche's view, knights and prostitutes are both predators; the former prefers difficult conquests, the latter easy ones. Against the Schopenhauerian account of compassion as pure selflessness, which he takes as the mark of moral action, Nietzsche diminishes it as the 'virtue' of those who seek to satisfy their feeling of power through easy conquests. Through compassion, he implies, they take possession of those who can put up little opposition to this act of conquest. Nietzsche's polemical point is that far from being selfless, compassion is a weak, debased expression of the feeling of power. Nietzsche's conclusion is caustic: "Compassion is praised as the virtue of prostitutes" (13).

In *GS* 14 Nietzsche develops his argument that we are motivated by our desire for the feeling of power to take possession of others. Nietzsche once again challenges Schopenhauer's view that compassion is a purely selfless motivation. Schopenhauer maintains that Greek *eros* and Christian *agape* are polar opposites: "Selfishness (*Selbstsucht*) is *eros*, compassion (*Mitleid*) is *agape*" (*WWR* 1: 376).

"All love (*agape, caritas*) is pity [*Mitleid*]", Schopenhauer claims, and "all love that is not pity is selfishness [*Selbstsucht*]" (*WWR* I: 374; 376). Nietzsche aims to collapse this distinction between *eros* and *agape*. According to Nietzsche, *eros* and *agape* are not radically opposed forms of love, one selfish, the other altruistic. Rather Nietzsche recasts these along the continuum of the drive to possession. *Eros*, he argues, is merely an extreme form of this drive; compassion or *agape* a much weaker version. Nietzsche suggests that in fact *eros* or sexual love brings out much more clearly the craving for property that also motivates *agape* or compassion. Nietzsche claims then that Christian love or compassion, embodied in the principle love thy neighbour as thyself, is not distinct from, but an expression of *Selbstsucht* or self-seeking.[14] Or more precisely, he argues that compassion is an expression of 'greed' [*Habsucht*], a mania for having or possessing. "Our love of neighbour", he asks rhetorically, "is it not a craving for new *property*?" (14). Compassion, Nietzsche argues, far from being the only moral or purely altruistic motive, as Schopenhauer declares, is in fact a lust for possession: "When we see someone suffering, we like to use this opportunity to take possession of him, that is for example what those who become his benefactors and those who have compassion for him do, and they call the lust for new possessions that is awakened in them 'love'; and their delight is like that aroused by the prospect of a new conquest" (14).

Nietzsche argues that whether we morally disparage or praise the desire for possession that he claims characterises eros and agape, love and compassion depends on whether we wish to justify our own greed or undermine the greed of others. If we wish to justify our own greed to possess others, we will disguise it as a selfless act of love; if we wish to dissuade others from pursuing their own greed, we will diminish it as an expression of egoism. According to Nietzsche, 'the many' or the "have-nots" have used moral terms to justify their own drive to possession: in order to justify this drive they mask it as altruistic 'love'. Nietzsche recycles the ancient Greek sophist's argument that moral rules are prescribed by the weak to secure their own advantage. In Plato's *Gorgias*, Callicles famously expresses the sophist

---

[14] In the compound *Selbstsucht*, the German noun *Sucht* (seek) carries the primary meaning of passion, mania, rage or craze.

position that the law (*nomos*) is made by the weak to defraud the strong. "In my view", as Callicles put it, "those who lay down the rules and assign their praise and blame are the weak men, the many. And so they lay down rules and assign praise and blame with an eye on themselves and their own advantage" (*Gorg.* 483 b–c).

If, as Nietzsche claims, eros and compassion share the same motivation, how does Nietzsche evaluate or rank different expressions of the desire to sustain the feeling of power? Nietzsche criticises the morality of selflessness on the grounds that it prevents the cultivation and flourishing of great individuals. As we have seen, Nietzsche maintains that moral values ('good' and 'evil') are assigned on the basis of their utility or effects. When confronted with a specific morality, therefore, he asks: "*Who* derives advantages from its particular distribution of praise and blame?" In the case of the morality of selflessness, he argues, it is "society" or the "neighbour" that benefits from praising selflessness and condemning selfishness or 'self-seeking' (*Selbstsucht*) as bad/evil (21). However, Nietzsche maintains that while this morality of selflessness benefits society, it does so at the expense of rare individuals' capacity for greatness or nobility. The morality of selflessness, as he puts it "praises drives which deprive a human being of his noblest selfishness and of the strength of the highest form of self-protection" (21). As Nietzsche later explains, our reigning morality and its model of 'the good man' (unegoistic, self-denying, self-sacrificing) is "the most sinister symptom of our European culture", a "regressive trait", as the "danger of dangers" that will prevent the species from ever reaching its "*highest potential power and splendour*" (*GM* P 6). Nietzsche argues that the morality of compassion or selflessness is predatory insofar as it is an instrument that enables the weak to harm or exploit the strong for their own protection. Nietzsche conceives this morality as a mechanism that regulates individual and collective life to ensure maximal security for the herd. It is fear, not love of neighbour, he claims, that motivates the defence of selflessness (*BGE* 201).

In this respect, Nietzsche recycles the ancient sophist's argument that the law (*nomos*) is made by the weak to defraud the strong (see Barker 1918; Leiter 2015). Morality, on this view, enslaves the strong to the weak. Plato's Callicles expressed the point thus: "[The weak] terrorise the stronger men capable of having more; and to prevent these men from having more than themselves they say that taking more is shameful and unjust; and that doing an injustice is this, seeking to have more than other people; they are satisfied, I take it, if they themselves have an equal share when they're inferior" (483 c–d). Nietzsche also shares the Calliclean view that education is the means through which the individual is transformed into a mere function of whole; it cultivates drives in individuals that deprive them of their noble self-seeking. Callicles expresses the same point in arguing for the rule or law of nature against *nomos* (or convention): "we mould the best and strongest among us, taking them from youth up, like lions, and tame them by spells and incantations over them, until we enslave them, telling them they ought to have equal shares, and this is the fine and the just" (483e). "Callicles", as Barker explains, "treats conventional justice as a characteristic product of egalitarian democracy"; in line with the oligarchical circles of Athens, he regarded the democratic government of the city as "a species of mass selfishness" (Barker 1918: 74).

Nietzsche applies these Calliclean arguments to the contemporary morality of selflessness. In *GS* 21 he wants to show how the morality of selflessness, which condemns noble selfishness (*Selbstsucht*), is also a species of mass selfishness. It defrauds the strong and noble of their selfishness and in doing so protects the inferior at the expense of the superior. Nietzsche aims to expose the hypocrisy and baseness of altruism and compassion. The teachers of selflessness, he argues, are necessarily hypocrites: they fail to practice what they preach. Nietzsche's central premise is that "the 'neighbour' praises selflessness *because it brings him advantages!*" (21). If this is the case, he observes, the neighbour's *motive* for teaching selflessness contradicts the *principle* of this morality. Nietzsche attempts to hoist the 'neighbour' on his own petard: he aims to show that he preaches the morality of selflessness, not out of love for his neighbour, but out of a desire to prevent the best individuals from attaining their own heights and in doing so threatening the stability and well-being of the community or the herd. On the other hand, Nietzsche argues, if the neighbour were really committed to the morality of selflessness he must sacrifice himself to others' *Selbstsucht* rather than condemning their self-seeking as evil. "If the neighbour himself thought 'selflessly'", as he explains, "he would reject this decrease in strength, this harm for *his* benefit" (21). True selflessness, Nietzsche observes, would require the neighbour to encourage others to pursue their *Selbstsucht*, calling it good rather than evil, even if in doing so he brought harm on himself.

What advantage does Nietzsche think the 'neighbour' seeks by praising selflessness and condemning *Selbstsucht*? In what does his advantage consist? Nietzsche implies that the neighbour seeks his own advantage by establishing conditions of existence that protect a community of modest, average, herd-like animals. The best or most advantageous condition for the 'neighbourly' type is a community devoid of individuals who seek to grow to their own "proud height" (21). Neighbourliness, Nietzsche claims, requires the elimination or suppression of those individuals whose drives threaten the conditions that favour this modest herd animal. As he later expresses this point,

When the highest and strongest drives, breaking passionately out, carry the individual far above and beyond the average and the lowlands of the herd conscience, the self-confidence of the community goes to pieces, its faith in itself, its spine, as it were, is broken: consequently it is precisely these drive that are calumniated. Lofty spiritual independence, the will to stand alone, great intelligence even, are felt to be dangerous; everything that raises the individual above the herd and make his neighbour quail is henceforth called *evil*; the fair, modest, obedient, self-effacing disposition, the *mean* and the *average* in desires, acquires moral names and honours. (*BGE* 201)

Nietzsche argue that the herd seeks its own advantage by teaching higher individuals to sacrifice their *Selbstsucht*, or the application of their "entire strength and reason" to their own "development, elevation, promotion and expansion of power" (21). "'For society as a whole", the neighbour reasons, "the loss of even *the best individual* is merely a small sacrifice!'" (21). The neighbour's morality of selflessness demands the best individuals, as regards themselves, live modestly rather than grandly. It makes a virtue of levelling differences of rank and worth by compelling the best to sacrifice themselves for the 'common good' rather than pursing their own good (*Selbstsucht*).

In Nietzsche's view, therefore, the teachers of the morality of selflessness are the enemies of individual greatness or nobility. Against this morality, Nietzsche is adamant the noblest individuals must cultivate their own *Selbstsucht* to attain their heights and that to do so most effectively they require social conditions that endanger the herd. Nietzsche argues the most favourable conditions for the development of the best and most fruitful people are anathema to the herd. What conditions, he asks, makes it possible for the best individuals to "grow to a proud height" (19)? "Ask yourselves", Nietzsche demands, "whether misfortune and external resistance", or "evil", "belong to the *favourable* conditions without which any great growth even of virtue is scarcely possible?" (19). While misfortune and external resistance enable the best to flourish, he argues, they also ensure that the weak perish: "The poison from which the weaker nature perishes strengthens the strong man – and he does not call it poison" (19).[15] Nietzsche uses a parable to elaborate the sense in which great or noble individuals are harmful to others and their age. In sharp contrast to the Good Samaritan parable, Nietzsche identifies greatness with hard-heartedness or ruthlessness (*Unbarmherzigkeit*). "At times", he writes, "our strengths propel us so far ahead that we can no longer stand our weaknesses and perish from them. We may even foresee this outcome and still have it no other way. Thus we become hard against that within us that wants to be spared; and our greatness is also our mercilessness [or heartlessness]" (28). Nietzsche presents this as "a parable for the whole effect of great human beings on others and on their age": "precisely with what is best in them, with what only they can do, they destroy many who are weak, insecure, in the process of becoming, of willing, and thus they are harmful" (28). Nietzsche argues then that both the conditions of existence that facilitate nobility or greatness and the effects of nobility are incompatible with the conditions of existence that enable the weak to thrive. Nietzsche analysis of the morality of selflessness constructs the following dilemma: we can either promote noble greatness *or* democratic mediocrity.

Nietzsche makes aristocratic Greek antiquity the backdrop to his attempt to delineate and rehabilitate the concept of 'nobility' against modern democratic egalitarianism. Nietzsche aims both to define the concept of nobility and understand the conditions that might make possible the birth of *new* noble types and styles. Nietzsche examines

---

[15] On the collective plane, Nietzsche explains and illustrates how one and the same morality can act as a balm or poison in his analysis of the impact of Christianity on the Greco-Roman world and ancient German culture (*HH* 2, 224).

the conditions that gave nobility its specific colour in antiquity and that are absence in modern culture. Modern culture, he suggests, does not make pride in oneself contingent upon elevating oneself above others and it does not conceive dependence or servitude as contemptible. In *GS* 18 Nietzsche briefly examines one of the fundamental differences between the ancient and modern 'moral' sensibilities. He suggests that the contemporary world lacks the specific type of Greek nobility. The ancient Greek concept of nobility, he suggests, partly hinged on its aristocratic order of rank and slave economy. Noble Greeks measured their own majesty or height by the enormous distance between themselves and the utter baseness of slaves, or what he later extols as the condition of aristocracy: "the pathos of distance" (*BGE* 257). Ancient 'pride' was found on experiencing oneself as elevated far above others; it therefore required the debasement or enslavement of many. Nietzsche suggests that the Stoic sage exemplifies aristocratic Greek pride. On this view, the Stoic sage is the philosophical transfiguration of the Greek concept of nobility as being above and ruling over others. In one of their famous paradoxes the Stoics claimed that only the sage is truly free, though he be a slave; all others, though they be freeborn, are slaves in reality. In sharp contrast, Nietzsche observes that because we are accustomed to the doctrine of equality we moderns do not take pride in and through our elevation above others. We do not, Nietzsche suggests, derive our pride for being above and beyond others; and by the same token, we do not feel contempt for ourselves or others when we are dependent on or at the mercy of others. Nietzsche wants to underscore the point that for modern individuals it is not contemptible to be 'enslaved'. We are slavish. We lack pride – or at least 'ancient pride'.

Nietzsche acknowledges that perhaps the ancient notion of nobility or pride might be impossible for us, this does not preclude the possibility of a new type of nobility. His quixotic interest in promoting a new type of nobility obviously flies directly in the face of modern culture's democratic sensibility. In *GS* 20 he very briefly considers what might "spur a new kind nobility" (20). He suggests that if the current tyranny of prudence were to continue for a few millennia then it might compel even moderately aristocratically inclined individuals to react against it by praising folly. "To become noble might come to mean: to entertain follies" (20). Nietzsche stresses that 'noble' types form themselves as a reaction against the tyranny of common norms. While his own 'praise of folly' seems no more than a playful, opening gambit, it is important to stress that he is serious about identifying what makes it possible to spur a new kind of nobility.

Indeed he stresses that "noble style" is precisely what modern industrial culture lacks. Nietzsche indicts modern industrial culture as the "*most vulgar form of existence that has ever been*" (40). All military cultures are much higher than modern industrial culture, he claims, because the former have an order of rank based on the rule of the superior rather than on the contingency of wealth. Nietzsche argues that a truly noble class that legitimised itself as "higher, as *born* to command" would eliminate the socialist clamour for equality. The masses, he suggests, willingly submit to "any kind of *slavery*" as long as their superiors demonstrate signs that they belong to a "higher race" (40). If the masses were ruled by a nobility whose higher qualities derived from "the fruit of long ages", rather than by the "cunning, bloodsucking dog of a man" whose power is based on wealth, Nietzsche maintains, "there would not be any socialism of the masses" (40).

Nietzsche argues that it is noble individuals who cause cultural change or who transform "common taste" (39). He argues that cultural change is never *caused* by a change of opinion; on the contrary, changes of opinion are symptoms or results of a changed taste. As he argues in *GS* 39, it is not reason or opinion that explains the genesis or stability of moralities and religions. Moralities or religions were not originally adopted because our ancestors changed their opinions; rather, they adopted these religions and moralities because strong or great individuals tyrannically enforced them, and once established they became a habit and eventually a need of everyone. Great individuals cause significant cultural transformations or reformations by "tyrannically" enforcing the law of their own nature (*physis*) on common taste or customary practice (39). They do so, he argues, not for the sake of the herd but simply in order to establish conditions of existence that best suit their own '*physis*' (or nature). In an early note he identifies the meaning of this Greek word: "Return to the Hellenic meaning: art as *physis*" (*KSA* 19[290]). In his early use of this Greek term he qualifies it as "transfigured *physis*" (*SE* 3). For Nietzsche *physis* is not a passive natural activity but the art necessary to transfigure nature. As we shall see, Nietzsche's ethics values individuals who transfigure their own "*physis*", of who transform it into great works of art. "Nietzsche", as Bambach notes, "advocates the embrace of *physis* as the sphere of human creation and valuation" (Bambach 2010: 441). In *GS* 39 Nietzsche suggests that these individuals have "the courage to own up to their *physis* and heed its demands down to its subtlest tones". Great individuals' "aesthetic and moral judgements are (the) 'subtlest tones' of their *physis*" (39).

Nietzsche closes Book 1 with a parting shot at the politicisation of the morality of 'selflessness' and compassion. Nietzsche mocks those Europeans who cannot endure boredom and therefore "yearn to suffer something in order to make their suffering a likely reason for action, for deeds" (55). Nietzsche diagnoses modern politicians' desire to invent "monster[s]" so that they can fight "monster[s]" as a symptom of a failure of self-cultivation (cf. Reginster 2006: 234–235; Pippin 2008: 289). "They do not know what to do with themselves", he writes, so they "paint the unhappiness of others on the wall; they always need others! And continually other others! – Pardon me, my friends, I have ventured to paint my *happiness* of the wall" (55).

Nietzsche argues that because these modern Europeans "do not feel within themselves the power to do themselves good from within, to do something for themselves" (55) they seek to fill the world with their clamour about others' distress so that they have a motive for action. In other words, Nietzsche claims that in order to alleviate their own boredom they paint the unhappiness of others on the wall, and in doing so create real feelings of distress. The modern politicisation of compassion, he suggests, is symptomatic of their failure to know what to do with or for themselves, and it is responsible for aggravating rather than alleviating distress. As we have seen, Nietzsche diagnoses the morality of 'selflessness' as a greedy desire to possess weak individuals in order to sustain one's feeling of power and as a species of mass selfishness through which the 'herd' eliminates the best individuals for the sake of protecting its own conditions of existence. On the individual level, Nietzsche proposes an ethics of self-cultivation to counter the debilitating effects of compassion; on the political level, he proposes an aristocratic order of rank to counter the levelling effects of modern egalitarianism.

CHAPTER 3

Redeeming Art: Book 2

In Book 2 Nietzsche shifts his focus from morality to art. This book marks a small yet important step in his attempt to re-evaluate the value of art for life. Here Nietzsche begins a re-appraisal of the relationship between art and life that will trouble him for the rest of his philosophical career. As we stressed at the outset, as a philosophical physician, Nietzsche diagnoses our main philosophical and moral horizons as expressions and symptoms of life denial and explores the possibility of a new horizon that might enable free spirits to affirm life. Nietzsche's reflections on art are firmly anchored in this fundamental existential problem. They also inform his political anxieties about modern mass democracy. Nietzsche existential and political concerns about modern art come to the foreground in his analysis of the music-dramas of his mentor and friend the great German composer Richard Wagner. Nietzsche's deeply ambivalent relationship to Wagner and his grand vision of the total work of art forms the essential backdrop to Book 2's reflections on the meaning and value of art.

In this chapter, we will explore the significance of Book 2 by placing it in the context of his shifting evaluation of the value of art for life. Book 2 grapples with Nietzsche's two earlier, opposing positions: viz. his metaphysical enthusiasm for and positivistic disenchantment with art. As we shall see, against *HH*'s positivistic dismissal of the value of art, in *GS* Nietzsche restores one of the main claims of *BT*, his earliest work: viz. that art *is* our salvation. In *BT* and then again, though with more than a hint of scepticism, in *RWB* (1876), Nietzsche had lionised Wagner as a new Aeschylus whose music had the power to redeem modern culture. In late 1876, however, Nietzsche had become disenchanted with

Wagner's music after fleeing the inaugural Bayreuth Festival (1876) dedicated to Wagner's operas, and he found his worst fears later confirmed in early 1878 when he read a copy of Wagner's opera *Parsifal,* which he saw as a capitulation to Christianity. Nietzsche identifies his break with Wagner as an essential part of his own "spiritual cure", his "anti-romantic self-treatment" (*HH* 2 P 2). "At that time", as he reports, "it was indeed high time *to say farewell.* Richard Wagner, seemingly the all-conquering, actually the decaying, despairing romantic, suddenly sank helpless and shattered before the Christian cross ... " (*HH* 2 P 3). Nietzsche began his self-treatment by "forbidding" himself "totally and on principle, all romantic music, that ambiguous, inflated, oppressive art that deprives the spirit of its severity and cheerfulness" (*HH* 2 P 3). In an 1878 letter to his friend Malwida von Meysenbug, Nietzsche reports that having rejected "the art of Wagner", which, he confesses, had only made his romantic pessimism worse, he fled into solitude. "I now *live* my aspiration to wisdom", he writes, "down to the smallest detail, whereas earlier I had only revered and idolised the wise ... I live in solitude ... until once more, ripened and complete as a philosopher of *life,* I may associate with people" (Middleton 1996: 168).

Nietzsche describes his most positivistic work, *Human, All Too Human,* as a memorial to this crisis that compelled him to return to himself and to his goal of living wisely. In *HH* Book 4, 'From the Soul of Artists and Writers', Nietzsche begins what he calls his anti-romantic self-treatment by mercilessly criticising Wagner's romantic-Schopenhauerian conception of art and romantic music. Nietzsche's desecration of his former idol is swift and spectacular. Though Wagner is not attacked by name in the first volume of *HH,* Nietzsche's attempt to replace the metaphysics of art with a science of art is squarely targeted at Wagner's grandiose cult of the prophetic musical genius. In the late 1870s Nietzsche no longer praises him as the German artistic genius responsible for the rebirth of a new tragic age but gradually develops the view that he is merely an actor whose fame hinges on pandering to the needs of the democratic masses for theatrical intoxication. Whereas in his early works Nietzsche advanced a messianic and prophetic approach to the work of art that was endowed with a redemptive mission, he systematically erases this expectation in his texts from *HH* onwards (see Crépon 2009: chapter 16).

In *GS* Book 2, however, Nietzsche takes stock of his damning critique of romantic art and begins to consider whether and what kind of art might contribute to or form part of an affirmative life. We can therefore consider Book 2's analysis of art as a reassessment of his answers to his central questions: Does art help us to affirm, redeem or love life? Is there a life-affirming art? If so, how does it contribute to or express the affirmation of life? Even in the midst of his spiritual cure for his Wagnerian-Schopenhauerian pessimism, we might note, he later admits to harbouring the expectation that "a musician might come who was sufficiently bold, subtle, malicious, southerly, superhealthy to confront [romantic] music and in an immortal fashion take *revenge* on it" (*HH* 2 P 3).

We cannot doubt that, ultimately, Nietzsche answers these first two questions in the affirmative. At the close of Book 2 we find him in the midst of making one of his first attempts to redeem art from his own radical assault on the decadence of romantic art and artists. In *GS* 107 he claims that *without* art "our honesty" would lead us "to nausea and suicide" (107). Art, he claims, is a form of suicide prevention. On his view, then, we have the very best reason for offering our "*ultimate gratitude to art*" (107). However, since in *GS* Nietzsche rejects *BT*'s view that art can or ought to grant us metaphysical consolation, he must recalibrate his claim that the affirmation of life is essentially an aesthetic stance. How can art save us from despair if it does not offer us the metaphysical consolation? If we cannot be "'comforted metaphysically'" by art, as he later puts it, then what is the alternative "art of *this-worldly* comfort"? (*BT* ASC 7)

Nietzsche's commentators and critics discern several candidates for his answer: art saves us from despair by concealing all that is terrible in life; art redeems us by acting as a medium through which we can joyously confront and affirm the tragedy of existence; and art makes it possible to affirm existence by giving us techniques through which we transform our own lives into artworks. In the last case, Nietzsche implies that it is precisely by transforming ourselves into great works of art that we affirm the tragedy of existence. As *GS* develops, I suggest, he gravitates towards this ethics and art of self-cultivation. We can best make sense of Nietzsche's attempt to restore the value of art in Book 2 by tracking how he moves from his early defence of art as the source of metaphysical consolation, through his critique of metaphysics and his demotion of art to a handmaiden of science, to his redemption of the ethical ideal of the self as an artwork.

In *GS* Book 2 Nietzsche revisits the issue that he first addressed in *BT*: viz. the nature and role of art in the affirmation of life. It is in *BT*, as he later explained, that he first undertook the task of looking at art in the perspective of life (*BT* ASC 2). In the context of a scholarly investigation of the origins of Greek tragedy, Nietzsche proposed a radical reform of German culture based around the ideal of the rebirth of tragic myth. The young Nietzsche fervently hoped that Richard Wagner's total work of art might propel this revolution (see 370). In his preface to Richard Wagner, Nietzsche celebrated art as "the supreme task and real metaphysical activity of this life" against those who saw in it "nothing more than an amusing sideshow, a readily dispensable tinkling of bells to accompany 'the seriousness of existence'" (*BT* P). Nietzsche encapsulated his metaphysics of art in his famous claim that "it is only as an *aesthetic phenomenon* that existence and the world are eternally *justified*" (*BT* 5; see also *BT* 28).

Nietzsche developed this claim in response to a traditional philosophical quandary: How is it possible to derive pleasure from tragedy? How can "ugliness and discord, the content of the tragic myth", as he put it, "produce aesthetic pleasure?" (*BT* 24). How, he asked, did the ancient Greeks affirm existence through a tragic art that compelled them to "look boldly right into the terrible destructiveness of so-called world history as well as the cruelty of nature"? (*BT* 7) According to Nietzsche, the ancient Greeks drew from tragic art the metaphysical consolation "that life is at the bottom of things, despite all changes of appearances, indestructibly powerful and pleasurable . . . Art saves him and through art, life" (*BT* 7).

In *BT* Nietzsche entertains two distinct versions of the aesthetic justification of reality. Nietzsche develops a quasi-Homeric or 'Apollonian' conception that the Olympian gods justify human existence by living a transfigured form of it themselves. That the ancient Greek might endure the "terror and horror of existence", he claims, "he had to interpose between himself and life the radiant dream-birth of the Olympians" (*BT* 3). The Apollonian impulse, he explains, that "calls art into being, as the complement and consummation of human existence, seducing one to a continuation of life, was also the cause of the Olympian world which the Hellenic 'will' made use of as a transfiguring mirror. Thus do the gods justify the life of man: they themselves live it" (*BT* 3).

In *BT* Nietzsche develops a second tragic or 'Dionysian' account of the aesthetic justification of existence, which turns on the tragic insight into the world as the creation of an artist-god, the so-called artist's metaphysics he later lamented as "arbitrary, idle and fantastic" (*BT* ASC 5). Following his own artistic version of Schopenhauer's metaphysics of the world as will, he conceived individuals as the mortal, transient phenomena of an eternal "primordial artist of the world" who creates the whole tragi-comedy of existence for his own delight. In ancient tragedy, he argued, we look into the terror of individual existence, yet we derive metaphysical comfort

when we become one with the infinite primordial joy in existence, and when we anticipate, in Dionysian ecstasy, the indestructibility and eternity of this joy. In spite of fear and pity, we are the happy living beings, not as individuals, but as the one living being, with whose creative joy we are united. (*BT* 17)

Nietzsche argues that we can understand the pleasure we derive from tragedy in terms of Dionysian ecstasy. Through tragedy, he claims, we momentarily become one with eternal artist of the world who lies behind all phenomena and experience "its raging desire for existence and joy in existence" (*BT* 17). Tragedy is a delight in the eternal life of the will and its exuberant creation and destruction of countless phenomena. Tragedy enables us to take joy not in ourselves as individual phenomena, but in the eternal will that delights in perpetually creating and destroying phenomena. Nietzsche claims then that it is only as the aesthetic phenomena of this primordial artist that the world is eternally justified, and that we mortals can only experience this joy through momentary Dionysian ecstasy.

How then does tragic art produce in us pleasure in existence or the affirmation of life? "At this point", as Nietzsche sums up his final view, "we must make a bold leap into a metaphysics of art repeating our earlier assertion that existence and the world seem justified only as an aesthetic phenomenon. Accordingly, the tragic myth has to convince us that even ugliness and discord are an artistic game which the will in the eternal abundance of its pleasure, plays with itself" (*BT* 24). Nietzsche's metaphysical consolation is distinct from religious and moral justifications of existence. Unlike religious and moral justifications of the world, his aesthetic justification does not feed our hope that we might escape the discord of the eternal will to life or that we might improve the world by overcoming injustice and suffering. These religious and moral justifications of existence, he will later argue, must ultimately lead to the denial of the value of life or nihilism. Albert Camus glosses Nietzsche's point nicely: "Any attempt to apply a standard of values to the world leads finally to a slander of life. Judgements are based on what is, with reference to what should be – the kingdom of heaven, eternal concepts, or moral imperatives. But what should be does not exist: and this world cannot be judged in the name of nothing" (1981: 58).[1] Nietzsche's purely aesthetic justification of existence sanctifies the eternal creation and destruction of phenomena as the play of this artist-god. In this case, metaphysical consolation, which he claimed the Greeks experienced through tragedy and that we might recover through Wagner's music-dramas, is communion with the artistic process of life.

Under the pretext of a scholarly investigation of the origins of tragedy, Nietzsche's first book formulates this artist's metaphysics and then seeks to explain how modern German culture might reclaim the ancient Greek's Dionysian insight into existence. To the horror of almost all of his fellow philologists, who expected a conventional work of philology from a newly appointed Basel professor, Nietzsche took it upon himself to draft an aesthetic and political manifesto proclaiming Richard Wagner the champion of a rebirth of tragic culture in Germany. Nietzsche identifies Wagner as the new Aeschylus who might restore German culture, rescuing it from an excess of rationalism that had destroyed the mythical horizon necessary to its health (*BT* 23).[2] Wagner's '*Gesamtkunstwerk*', or

---

[1] "A nihilist: as Nietzsche explains "is a man who judges of the world as it is that it ought not to be, and the world as it ought to be that it does not exist" (*WP* 585)

[2] Cf. Allan Megill, who argues that a call for a "return to myth" is the central motif of Nietzsche's philosophy: "myth remains, for the later Nietzsche as for the earlier, an absolutely central element of culture – indeed, the only escape from the malaise from which he believed 'modern man' was suffering" (Megill 1987: 64).

total work of art, a synthesis of music, poetry and visual drama, which had for the first time since antiquity reclaimed the ancient Greek's Dionysian insight into existence, Nietzsche boldly asserted, could do nothing less than overcome modern decadence and lead the way to the rebirth of a tragic culture. Nietzsche's daringly unconventional use of philology to defend this sweeping project of cultural renewal singled him out as the target for the opprobrium of almost the whole philological community. The contemporary German philologist Hermann Usener summed up this animus. Nietzsche reports in a letter to his friend Rohde how Usener had revealed to his students that he regarded *BT* is "sheer nonsense" and pronounced its author "professionally dead" (quoted in Silk and Stern 1981: 105).[3]

Nietzsche's redemptive approach to art and his championing of Wagner as its prophet did not endure. In the mid 1870s Nietzsche in fact made a concerted effort to liberate himself from *BT*'s meta-physical doctrines and overblown Wagnerian fantasies that had – as he later avowed – marred his early writings. Nietzsche's free-spirit trilogy inaugurated a new period in his philosophy: a decisive move away from Wagnerian art and Schopenhauerian metaphysics to a form of philosophical naturalism, one informed by emerging currents of scientific and evolutionary discourse. "I want to declare expressly to the readers of my earlier works", as he explained in an 1876 note written during his lengthy stay in Sorrento, "that I have abandoned the metaphysical-aesthetic views that essentially domi-nated them: they are pleasant, but untenable" (*KSA* 23[159]).

Nietzsche identified *HH* as the "memorial of a crisis" that gave expression to this radical break in his life and thought (*EH* HH 1):

What reached a decision in me at that time was not merely a breach with Wagner. I noticed a total aberration of my instincts of which any particular blunder, whether it be called Wagner or the professorship at Basel, was only a symptom. I was overcome by *impatience* with myself; I saw that it was high time for me to recall and reflect on myself ... With commiseration, I saw myself utterly emaciated, utterly starved: my science entirely failed to

---

[3] *BT*'s publication triggered a bitter and prolonged attack on Nietzsche's scholarly reputation led by Ulrich von Wilamowitz-Moellendorf. On the so-called Nietzsche-Wilamowitz *Streit*, see Kaufmann (1967: 4–9), Musgrave Calder (1983: 214–254) and Silk and Stern (1981: 90–107).

include *realities*, and my "idealities" – who knows what the devil they were worth! – A truly burning thirst took hold of me: henceforth I pursued nothing other, in fact, than physiology, medicine, and natural sciences . . . It was then, too, that I first guessed the correlation between an activity chosen in defiance of one's instincts, a so-called "vocation" for which one does not have the *least* vocation, and the need for an *anesthetization* of the feeling of desolation and hunger by means of a narcotic art – for example, Wagnerian art. (*EH* HH 3)

Drawing inspiration from Paul Rée's natural histories of morality, in *HH* Nietzsche adopts a type of positivism, which he eponymously dubbed 'Réealism'.[4] In the winter of his positivistic discontent, Nietzsche vehemently rejected his earlier metaphysical interpretation of art, which was the basis of his claim that life is only justified as an aesthetic phenomenon. Instead in *HH* he examined art through the lens of science. In making the move from a metaphysics to a science of art, as we shall see, Nietzsche demotes art to the role of science's handmaiden.

Nietzsche's scholarly friend and advocate Erwin Rohde observed that coming to *HH* after experiencing Nietzsche's earlier writings was like being chased from the *calidarium*, the steamy waters, into an icy *frigidarium*, a "rather shocking experience" (quoted in Heller 1986: xi). Rohde's metaphorical description expresses the fundamental change Nietzsche made to the philosophical cast and style of his work in the late 1870s. The shocking drop in temperature that Rohde experienced in reading *HH* can be understood as the effect wrought on him by Nietzsche's coolly detached, scientific dissection of morality, religion and art. Nietzsche sought to show that they do not bring us closer to the metaphysical world, but answer to human, all too human needs and interests (*HH* 37).

In his new scientific guise, Nietzsche looked to modern science rather than tragic art as the instrument of cultural regeneration. Nietzsche pours cold water on his earlier romantic enthusiasms about the metaphysical significance of art and evaluates it strictly in terms of its place in the emergent scientific culture. One measure of this shift is his radical reinterpretation of Greek tragedy. Against the Aristotelian account of tragic catharsis, or the purging of emotions,

---

[4] Robin Small's *Nietzsche and Rée: A Star Friendship* (2005) is the locus classicus on this topic.

Nietzsche endorsed Plato's criticism of tragedy as an imitative art that intensifies fear and pity and in doing so cultivates "a gloomy, disheartened view of the world and a soft, susceptible tearful soul" (*HH* 212; see *Rep.* 606a-b). In *RWB*, Nietzsche's hollow-sounding eulogy to Wagner's 'music of the future', he had defended Wagner precisely against Plato's banishment of the tragic poets (*RWB* 7; *Rep.* 398a). In *HH*, in stark contrast, Nietzsche revived Plato's critique and sought to promote the emergence of a new higher, scientific culture rather than the rebirth of a tragic culture.

Nietzsche declares that in this new culture we must witness the "twilight of art" (*HH* 223). "Just as in old age one remembers one's youth and celebrates festivals of remembrance", he writes, "so will mankind soon stand in relation to art: it will be a moving recollection of the joys of youth" (*HH* 223). Science, he suggests, merely seeks knowledge and nothing further, whereas art wants to bestow on life and action the greatest possible profundity and significance, and does so with the aid of discredited metaphysical interpretations of existence (*HH* 6). The highest flights of our highest artists, he observes, have "raised to heavenly transfiguration precisely those conceptions which we now recognise as false: they are the glorifiers of the religious and philosophical errors of mankind" (*HH* 220). Our great art forms, he claims, glorify all the metaphysical errors that have made life "valuable, terrible, delightful" (*HH* 9). If, then, the significance of art has turned on satisfying a metaphysical need for a world beyond appearances, Nietzsche argues, the rise of science must spell its demise (*HH* 153, 223). Nietzsche diagnoses our difficulty in bidding farewell to art as nostalgia for a lost love, "whether she be called religion or metaphysics" (*HH* 153). Indeed, from this positivistic perspective, Nietzsche formulates a stronger objection to art: he maligns it as a retrogressive force that consoles us for life's sufferings by means of irrational dreams of eternal salvation and in doing so impedes the development of real improvements in the conditions of life (*HH* 108, 147, 159, 148). "This is", as Safranski correctly notes, "Nietzsche's most direct condemnation of the 'tragic perspective', which he had otherwise valued so highly, and his most explicit endorsement of utility and practical efficiency" (Safranski 2003: 197).

At most, he claims in *HH*, art can serve as a temporary handmaiden to science. Nietzsche's claim rests on the idea that the passage from a metaphysical-religious to a scientific culture is a violent and perilous leap. To sustain this great leap forward, he maintains, we need to enlist the help of transitional orders of ideas (*HH* 27). We require this help so that we can grow accustomed to satisfying ourselves with science's "little unpretentious truths", such as "the dietetics of health", for example, rather than hoping to realise metaphysical dreams of "the eternal salvation of the soul" (*HH* 3, 22). In the age of science, he suggests, we must give up our dreams in exchange for dietetics.

In this regard, Nietzsche claims that art might now serve a new purpose as one of the transitional means that enable our species to gradually relinquish its metaphysical illusions and embrace the austerity of scientific positivism (*HH* 27). In his positivist guise, Nietzsche sees the value of art merely as means of helping us set aside rather than satisfy our metaphysical need. "From art", he suggests, "it will be easier to go over to a truly liberating philosophical science" (*HH* 27). If, as he claims, art nourishes the metaphysical need far less than religion or metaphysical philosophy we can use it as weak substitute while we gradually adjust to the asceticism of the new, post-metaphysical culture (*HH* 27).

In making the move from *BT*'s romantic pessimism to *HH*'s scientific positivism, Nietzsche demotes art from "the highest task and truly metaphysical activity of this life" to a small dose of ersatz religion that we need to smooth our gradual transition to a scientific culture. Nietzsche judges that with the victory of science over metaphysics and art, we will attain a higher, more 'manly' culture concerned with "rigorous thinking" rather than with the "spinning out of forms and symbols" (*HH* 3). By means of rigorous methods that deliver little unpretentious truths, Nietzsche suggests, science can show us how to eliminate the causes of human suffering rather than, as art does, merely ameliorate the effects.

Yet, even in his so-called positivistic phase, Nietzsche does not entirely brush aside art as merely a lost love that hampers our willingness to pursue the goal of using scientific knowledge to eliminate human suffering. In the second volume of *HH* Nietzsche's radical scepticism about the epistemic and cultural value of art is already waning. Here Nietzsche's revaluation of art begins to take shape as his focus shifts from the works of art to the art of self-cultivation and self-transformation. In this context, Nietzsche argues in fact that the "true art" is the art of self-cultivation, not the creation of works of art. He gives priority to this art through which we make *our* lives beautiful, partly through reinterpreting as beautiful those passions, fears and torments that we might otherwise condemn as ugly and painful. Indeed, he argues *against* works of art where they are independent of the art of living. Nietzsche identifies this art of self-cultivation as the means to improve and transform our lives:

Against the art of works of art. – Art is above and before all supposed to *beautify* life, thus make *us* ourselves endurable, if possible pleasing to others: with this task in view it restrains us and keeps us within bounds, creates social forms ... Then art is supposed to *conceal* or *reinterpret* everything ugly, those painful, dreadful, disgusting things which all efforts notwithstanding, in accord with the origin of human nature again and again insist on breaking forth: it is supposed to do so especially in regard to passions and psychical fears and torments ... After this great, indeed immense task of art, what is usually termed art, *that of the work of art*, is merely an *appendage*. A man who feels within himself an excess of such beautifying, concealing, and reinterpreting powers will in the end seek to discharge this excess in works of art as well ... Now, however, we usually start with art where we should end with it, cling hold of it by its tail and believe that the work of art is true art out of which life is to be improved and transformed – fools that we are! (*HH* 2 174)

Nietzsche argues that that we ought to give priority to this art of living over the production or consumption of works of art if we are to achieve the artistic goal of beautifying life. In modern culture, he laments, what people desire of art is "that it shall scare away their discontent, their boredom and uneasy conscience for moments or hours at a time and if possible magnify the errors of their life and character into errors of world destiny" (*HH* 2 169). Against this modern need for art as an escape from boredom, Nietzsche contrasts the Greek, "to whom their art was an outflowing and overflowing of their own healthiness and well-being and who loved and viewed their perfection repeated outside themselves – self-enjoyment was what led them to art, whereas what leads our contemporaries to it is – self-disgust" (*HH* 2 169). For the Greeks, he claims, artworks, were only the beautiful excess of their self-enjoyment. Nietzsche suggests that we mistakenly assume that such artworks constitute the greater part of the domain of art. Yet the "great, immense task of art", as he sees it, lies in the art of the self, not in creation of artworks. A successful art of the self should result in the kind of self-enjoyment that can 'over-flow' into the desire to see its own perfection mirrored in a work of art. As we shall see, Nietzsche develops this ideal of the art of the self in *GS* as he reassesses his coldly positivistic dismissal of the value of art and formulates his own ethics of self-cultivation.

Against this backdrop, we can now turn to *GS* Book 2 to see how Nietzsche sets out to reassess his earlier claims about the role of art in life. In its opening section Nietzsche argues that we necessarily construct the way world appears to us on the basis of irrational passions. We are all similar to "artist[s] in love", he claims, insofar as we interpret or depict the world in ways that satisfy our passions, interests or needs (57). In our construction of the world of appear-ances we cannot, as he puts it, free ourselves from the intoxication of our passions.

Nietzsche develops this view not to criticise our artistic fabrication of the world of appearances but to correct the self-misunderstanding and self-delusion of sober realists who "insinuate that the world really is the way it appears [to them]" (57). We are all akin to "artist[s] in love", he holds, whether sober realists acknowledge it or not. They feel that they are armed against their own passion and fantasies, and therefore believe that before them "reality stands unveiled" (57). Yet far from seeing the world as it is in itself, naked or unveiled, even these realists, he argues, "still carry around the valuation of things that originate in the passions and loves of former centuries" (57). Nietzsche likens these so-called realists to the young Egyptian in the ancient story of the 'Veil of Sais' who in his feverish desire for the truth breaks a sacred prohibition on removing the veils covering a statue Isis beneath which he will see "truth one and indivisible". Nietzsche suggests that their attempt to see the world unveiled, or independently of our passions and fantasies, is necessarily destined to failure:

In every experience, in every sense impression there is a piece of this old love; and some fantasy, some prejudice, some irrationality, some ignorance, some fear, and whatever else, has worked on and contributed to it. That mountain over there! That cloud over there! What is 'real' about that? Subtract just once the phantasm and the whole human *contribution* from it, you sober ones! Yes, if you could do *that*! If you could forget your background, your past, your nursery school – all of your humanity and animality! There is no 'reality' for us – and not for you either, you sober ones. (57)

Nietzsche recalls here a section from Book 1 (54), "*The Consciousness of Appearance*" where he describes his insight that the world as its appears to him is shot through with all the earlier passions of human and animal life:

How wonderful and new and yet how gruesome and ironic I find my position *vis-a-vis* the whole of existence in the light of my insight! I have discovered for myself that the human and animal past, indeed the whole primal age and past of all sentient being continues in me to invent, to love, to hate, and to infer. I suddenly woke up in the midst of this dream, but only to the consciousness that I am dreaming and that I must go on dreaming lest I perish – as a somnambulist must go on dreaming lest he fall. (54)

Nietzsche suggests not only that we can become conscious of the way in which we construct the world of appearance on the basis of primordial passions and errors but that also that we must continue to construct our experiences in this way lest we perish. Nietzsche implies that just as somnambulists require their dream representa-tions to guide them so too he needs the world of "appearance" to orient and guide his judgements and actions.[5] Nietzsche suggests that "we men of today" are just such somnambulists:

We need only to love, to hate, to desire, simply to feel – *at once* the spirit and power of dreams comes over us, and we climb with open eyes, impervious to all danger, up the most dangerous paths, onto the roofs and towers of fantasy, without any vertigo, as though born to climb – we sleepwalkers of the day! We artists! (59)

Nietzsche conceives the world of "appearance" not as a veil or mask that conceals an unknown and radically different world, or in the language of metaphysicians, the world as it is in itself. Nietzsche jettisons the metaphysical assumption that there is a radically differ-ent 'true world' that lies beneath or beyond world of appearance:

[5] See also: "Our knowledge is no knowledge in itself . . . it is the magnificent result, developing over thousands of years, of necessary optical error – necessary because we generally want to live – errors because all laws must be perspectives, errors in themselves" (*KSA* 9:11 [9]).

What is "appearance" for me now? Certainly not the opposite of some essence: what could I say about any essence except to name the attributes of its appearance! Certainly not a dead mask that one could place on an unknown x or remove from it! (54)

Here Nietzsche rejects the coherence of the metaphysical idea of a 'true world', a world in and of itself that lies behind or beneath the 'apparent' world that is open to us through human thought, experience and sensation. In *HH* Nietzsche maintained that the idea of a metaphysical world is a logical possibility: "It is true, there could be a metaphysical world; the absolute possibility of it is hardly to be disputed. We behold all things through the human head and cannot cut off this head; while the question remains what of the world would still be there if one had cut it off " (*HH* 9). Nietzsche suggests, however, even if we could establish the existence of a true world beyond human experience we could only identify it negatively as "a being other, an inaccessible, incomprehensible being other" (*HH* 9). Such knowledge, he observes, would be practically useless, "more useless", as he explains it, "than knowledge of the chemical composition of water must be to a sailor in danger of shipwreck" (*HH* 9, see also *HH* 29).

In *GS* 54 Nietzsche appears to take one further step in his critique of metaphysics, one that later identifies in his famous account of the stages in the gradual demise of metaphysics, 'How the "Real World" at Last Became a Myth'. Here Nietzsche approaches the fifth stage in this history: he no longer conceives the metaphysical world as a logical possibility, but one that is a matter of practical indifference, rather he denies the existence of the "true world".[6] "The 'apparent' world", as he later explains, "is the only one: the 'real' world has only been *lyingly added*" (*TI* 'Reason' 2).

---

[6] There is broad agreement that the last three stages Nietzsche identifies in his account of how the 'true world' at last became a myth represent stages of his own thinking in *HH* and *GS* and beyond. However, two issues remain contentious: first, whether Nietzsche's rejection of metaphysics necessarily requires him to abandon his so-called 'falsification' thesis, the view that that all knowledge falsifies reality; second, whether after *BGE* he did in fact abandon this thesis and endorse the empirical sciences as the source of truth (Clark 1990: 95–125; Clark and Dudrick 2007: 369–385; see also Ridley 2007: 68–72). Against Clark's view, some commentators argue that Nietzsche's rejection of metaphysics does not entail the rejection of his falsification thesis and second that in fact he maintained this thesis throughout his career (see Anderson 1996: 316–322; Hussain 2004: 327–340; Hatab 2008: 182; Franco 2011: 236; Meyer 2011: 59–135).

Nietzsche rejects the very possibility of a true world beyond the world of experience and instead explains and diagnoses why we have invented another, second world. Against "so-called realists" who believe they unveil the world as it is in itself, independent of all human contribution, Nietzsche maintains that the only world we can know is the world of appearance that we construct on the basis of ancient prejudices, passions and errors. It is appearance, he suggests, "which lives and is effective", or that gives value or colour to the world and that therefore enables us to practically orient our lives. "Because we have for millennia made moral, aesthetic, religious demands on the world, looked upon it with blind desire, passion, or fear, and abandoned ourselves to the bad habits of illogical thinking", as he explained in *HH,* "this world has gradually become so mar-velously variegated, frightful, meaningful, soulful, it has acquired color – but we have been the colorists: it is the human intellect that has made appearance appear and trans-ported its erroneous basic conceptions into things" (*HH* 16).

Nietzsche's acknowledgement of the history of the passions and errors that we have knotted into the world of appearance, as we saw above, opens up the possibility of exploring "all that has given colour to experience" (7). In unpublished note, he explains this project as the effort to "look into the world through as many eyes as possible, to live in drives and activities so as to create eyes for ourselves" (*KSA* 9:11 [141]). In Book 3 Nietzsche conceives his own passion for knowledge as a greediness to see the world through as many eyes or perspectives as possible:

The sigh of the search for knowledge. – "Oh, my greed! There is no selflessness in my soul but only an all-coveting self that would like to appropriate many individuals as so many additional pairs of eyes and hands – a self that would like to bring back the whole past, too, and that will not lose anything that it could possibly possess. Oh, my greed is a flame! Oh, that I might be reborn in a hundred beings!" – Whoever does not know this sigh from firsthand experience does not know the passion of the search for knowledge. (249)

Nietzsche argues that it is our interpretations, evaluations or perspectives that constitutes the world of appearance. We must realise, as he explains, that *what things are called* is unspeakably more important than what they are. The reputation, the name, and appearance, the worth, the usual measure and weight of a thing – originally something mistaken and arbitrary, thrown over things like a dress and quite foreign to their nature and even to their skin – has, through the belief in it and its growth from generation to generation, slowly grown onto and into the thing and *has become its very body*: what started as appearance in the end nearly always becomes essence and *effectively acts* as its essence! (54)

Nietzsche's argument turns the metaphysical picture on its head: on his account 'essence' is merely the epiphenomenon of appearance. What we now conceive as the "essence" of a thing was originally an 'arbitrary' evaluation. Nietzsche maintains, for example, that our drives have no 'essence' independent of the evaluations we throw over or project onto them. Any given thing has no "essence", he argues, but is constituted through a series of arbitrary or random interpretations that gradually become incorporated into it.[7] We can illustrate this point with two of Nietzsche's examples. In *HH* he identifies "an art of idealisation" that the Greeks used to ennoble "reality"; the fact that they "saw in the aphrodisiac drive a divinity, and felt its operations with reverential gratitude has over the course of time saturated that affect with a series of exalted notions and actually very greatly ennoble it" (*HH* 214). Contrawise, Nietzsche suggests, "the passions become evil and malicious if they are regarded as evil and malicious. Thus Christianity has succeeded in transforming Eros and Aphrodite – great powers capable of idealisation – into diabolical kobolds and phantoms by means of the torments it introduces into the consciences of believers" (*D* 76).

If, as Nietzsche maintains, our perspectives and evaluations become incorporated into things, we cannot transform these things simply by exposing their origins:

What kind of fool would believe that it is enough to point to this origin and this misty shroud of delusion in order to destroy the world that counts as 'real', so-called 'reality'! Only as creators can we destroy! (58)

---

[7] Nietzsche foreshadows here the major point of his later historical method: "The development of a thing, a tradition, an organ ... is a succession of more or less profound, more or less mutually independent processes of subjugation exacted on a thing, added to this the resistance encountered every time ... The form is fluid, the 'meaning' even more so" (*GM* II. 12)

Nietzsche dismisses as naïve the belief that we can free ourselves from the weights and measures we inherit simply by means of a naturalistic investigation of their 'arbitrary' origins. The appearance 'artists' have given things is not like a veil or cloak we can easily discard, it has become part of their essence. It is at this point that he assigns a specific role to artistic creativity:

> But let us also not forget that in the long run it is enough to create new names and valuations and appearances of truth in order to create new 'things'. (57)

Nietzsche suggests that free-spirited philosophers must not only undertake a historical analysis of the genesis of the appearances that constitutes their 'reality', they must also create new values, appearances or measures. Without this 'artistic' creativity they will be powerless to alter existing values.[8] It is as artists, not analysts, he asserts, that they can create and transform what counts as our 'reality'. We see a significant shift in and broadening of Nietzsche's conception of art: it does not merely "lay a veil over reality" and make "the sight of life bearable by laying over it the veil of unclear thinking", rather as a type of value creation, an art of idealisation, as he calls it, it can fundamentally transform our drives, sensations and experiences.

After this examination of art as a means of constituting our reality and experiences, Nietzsche investigates and diagnoses how aesthetic concepts and artistic means and instruments are conceived and used in the context of what we now describe as gender relations (60–75). In the first of these sections, Nietzsche shows how 'beauty' has been conceived, or *mis*conceived, as he later argues, as a counterforce to the passions (see *GM* III.6). Schopenhauer, we might recall, claims that beauty, especially in the guise of musical melody, liberate us from the raging torment of our passions by granting us fleeting moments of detached, painless contemplation of the will to life:

---

[8] See *Z*, 'Of Self-Overcoming': "And he who has to be a creator in good and evil, truly, first has to be a destroyer and break values"; and *GM* II.24: "If a shrine is to be set up, a shrine has to be destroyed".

The inexpressible depth of all music, by virtue of which it floats past us as a paradise quite familiar yet eternally remote is due to the fact that it reproduces all the emotions of our innermost being, but entirely without reality and remote from its pain. (*WWR* 1: 264)

Schopenhauer argues that as long as we are driven by our passions we are condemned to suffer, but "as representation alone, purely contemplated, or repeated through art, free from pain" the will to life "presents us with a significant spectacle" (*WWR* 1: 267). If, in ordinary experience our individual will is aroused, "we are not then concerned with tones and their numerical relations; on the contrary, we ourselves are now the vibrating string that is stretched and plucked" (*WWR* 2: 451). By means of beauty, Schopenhauer suggests, we briefly escape from our ordinary empirical self, which is at the mercy of tormenting desires, painfully "stretched and plucked", as he puts it, to a second, serene, 'better' self that contemplates the world without desire (see also *BT* 6).

In *GS* 60 Nietzsche implicitly re-examines Schopenhauer's metaphysics of redemptive beauty. He aims to diagnose the Schopenhauerian claim that beauty is the promise of silence and distance, or "the silencing of the will", as he later puts it in explicitly Schopenhauerian terms (326).[9] He does so by examining his own desire to escape from the "hellish labyrinth" of his passions through the Schopenhauerian dream of serene, aesthetic contemplation of beauty (60). Writing in the first-person singular, he analyses his motivation for idealising beauty as a means of inducing a state of dreamlike contemplation:

Here I stand amidst the fire of the surf, whose white flames are licking; from all sides it is howling, threatening, screaming, shrieking at me ... Suddenly as if born out of nothingness, there appears before the gate of this hellish labyrinth only a few fathoms away, a large sailing ship, gliding along as silent as a ghost. Oh, this ghostly beauty! How magically it touches me! What? Has all the calm and silence of the world embarked here? Is my happiness itself sitting in this quiet place – my happier self, my second immortalised self? Not yet to be dead, but also no longer alive? As a spirit-like, silent,

---

[9] WWR 1: 390 "aesthetic pleasure in the beautiful consists ... in the fact that, when we enter that state of pure contemplation, we are raised for the moment above all willing, above all desires and cares ... we are, so to speak, rid of ourselves ... And we know that these moments when [we are] delivered from the fierce pressure of the will ... are the most blissful that we experience".

watching, gliding, hovering, intermediate being . . . To move *over* existence!
That's it! That would be it! – It seems as though the noise here has made me
into a dreamer? All great noise makes us place happiness in silence and
distance. (60)

Nietzsche closes this section by deflating this dream of a "better self"
that turns "life itself into a dream about life" (60). Nietzsche generalises his experience and suggests that men who suffer "amidst the
fire of the surf" imagine that their better selves live amongst women.
For them women are analogous to beautiful sailing ships that silently
glide over the sea of existence. Yet, Nietzsche observes, among
women "there is so much small, petty noise!" (60). The magic and
powerful effect of women, he 'cynically' concludes, is only possible at
a distance. Nietzsche's self-analysis shows how the image of women
as "silent, magical creatures" enchants him as way to escape from the
tumult of his own passions. As later explains this point: "'What does
it *mean* if a philosopher pays homage to ascetic ideals?' we get our first
hint: he wants *to free himself from torture*" (*GM* III.6). Nietzsche
exposes the ascetic desire that motivates his own conventional representation of women as beautiful objects. However, he does not
simply mock his own 'masculine' idealisation of beauty, in the
process he demeans women as petty. In the following sections
(61–75), Nietzsche develops his reflections on women.

Unsurprisingly, in post-war commentary, Nietzsche overall views
on relations between the sexes and on women have generated controversy and debate. They have done so because, among other things,
they controvert what have become widely accepted principles of
gender equality. Following Walter Kaufmann, one conventional
response to Nietzsche's embarrassing misogynistic perspective is to
dismiss it as a low point that is irrelevant to his philosophy as
a whole (Kaufmann 1974: 24).[10] "Nietzsche's prejudices about
women", he decreed, "need not greatly concern the philosopher"
(Kaufmann 1974: 84). First and second wave feminists, however,
condemn Nietzsche as profoundly misogynistic and patriarchal,

---

[10] Laurence Lampert is an exception to this rule. On the basis of the fact that *GS* 363 lies at the
numerical centre of *GS* Book 5 he infers that Book 5's discussion of each sexes prejudices
about love constitutes the central matter of his philosophy (Lampert 1993: 368–387).
Lampert's hermeneutic principle of interpretation is highly questionable.

while so-called postmodern or French feminists argue that his metaphorical representations of women are at cross-purposes with his
explicitly misogynistic comments and that feminist theorists can
make good use of his philosophy to 'deconstruct' essentialist gender
binaries (see Diethe 1989).

Very few commentators directly address Nietzsche's analysis of
gender and heterosexuality in the middle period. Among the exceptions, Kathleen Higgins charitably commends Nietzsche as
a "pioneer in gender theory" who prefigures the way contemporary
feminists challenge disempowering cultural constructions of gender
(Higgins 2000: 86, 85–89).[11] More plausibly perhaps, Ruth Abbey
shows that the charge that Nietzsche is misogynistic cannot be
sustained in view of his comments about women and gender in the
middle period (Abbey 1996; 2000). At the same time, however, she
shows that his views on these issues are little more than a "mélange of
rival ideas" (1996: 249). Since Nietzsche did not develop any coherent
perspective on these issues, she maintains, there is very little to be
gained from an in-depth examination of his various and "contra-
dictory" claims (1996: 249). However, even if we cannot dismiss
Nietzsche's middle works as misogynistic, this certainly applies to
his avowedly anti-feminist politics in the later works, including *GS*
Book 5. In his later works, as Abbey argues, "Nietzsche is seriously
disturbed by the rise of feminism, seeing it as both a symptom and
a source of socio-cultural decline and decay . . . the term feminism
becomes a shorthand for all the forces of decadence besetting modern
Europe, and, as with all campaigns for equality, Nietzsche sees the
push for female equality as driven by the ressentiment and self-
interest of the inferior" (Abbey 2000: 121). The late Nietzsche's
essentialist or naturalist conception of 'woman' as inferior to men,
and his account of 'woman's' 'virtue' as subordination and surrender
to men is on full display in *GS* 363:

I will never admit talk of *equal* rights for man and woman in love: there are
none . . . Woman wants to be taken, adopted as a possession . . . Woman
gives herself away; man takes more – I do not believe one can get around this

---

[11] Examining sections 60–75, Monika Langer demonstrates the weaknesses of Higgins' chari-
table interpretation (see Langer 2010: 78–89).

natural opposition through any social contract or with the best will to justice. (*GS* 363)[12]

If Nietzsche's slight and slighting comments on women and gender in Book 2 do not merit serious examination as gender theory or psychology, they do nonetheless illustrate how he thinks women create appearances to serve as a means of defence, seduction, or forgetfulness (e.g. 66, 67, 71). Nietzsche will later gather together these kinds of artistic stratagems to conceptualise a "will to appearance" as a fundamental "will of the spirit" (*BGE* 230). In other words, Nietzsche comes to identify a will to appearance, which includes a willingness to forget, deceive, dissemble, simplify, mask and so on, not as specific to either sex, but as a basic condition of existence.

Nietzsche devotes the rest of Book 2 (76–107) to a wide-ranging investigation of cultural matters, encompassing ancient Greek art and culture, a select range of literary figures and styles and finally contemporary German philosophy, music and language. We can discern several threads running through this section. First, in contrast to *HH*, Nietzsche argues that we have reasons to be grateful to art. In particular he moves beyond *HH*'s conception of art as a veil or illusion cast over reality. Instead he examines the relationship between art as perspective taking and our ability to revalue and affirm life. By strengthening and weakening our valuation, he implies it is this art of perspective that grants us the possibility of overcome life-denying values.

Following on from his analysis in Book 2's first three sections (57–59), he begins to explore exactly how art configures and reconfigures our evaluation of the world and ourselves through perspectives that select, strengthen, praise, simplify or magnify appearances. "Artists", he claims, "constantly *glorify* – they do nothing else – and in particular all those states and things reputed to give man the occasion for once to feel good, or great, or drunk, or merry, or well

---

[12] Referring to *GS* 363, Higgins attempts to get Nietzsche off the hook of feminist criticisms by claiming that he intended his comments about "woman" as descriptions rather than prescriptions (2000: 194). This is almost impossible to square with this emphatic rejection of equal rights for women based on an essentialist conception of 'woman' in terms of a natural propensity to male subordination that cannot be altered through any new social compact.

or wise" (85). In this section Nietzsche deflates artists' pretence of being the vanguard of new appraisals. Rather, artists, he claims, are merely the heralds of the real appraisers of new values, "the rich and the idle" (85). Yet we should not be distracted by Nietzsche's mockery of artists' vanity from his main claim, which he repeats and elaborates later in *TI*: that art is the great stimulus to life insofar as it praises, glorifies, chooses, prefers, and, in doing so, strengthens and weakens certain valuations. We cannot conceive art as purposeless or aimless, as he later put it, since its "basic instinct" aims at "a desirability of life" (*TI* 'Skirmishes' 24).

In aphorism 77 Nietzsche begins this section by illustrates his claim through an exploration of art forms that represent that antipodes of high, 'metaphysical' arts: the arts of Southern Europe such as Italian operas, Spanish picaresque novels, and the 'vulgar', ancient erotic art surviving in the public frescoes of Pompeii, which he had visited during his 1876–1877 sojourn in Sorrento. If, as he later argues, we moderns have become the most refined "artists in the field" of "conscience-vivisection and animal-torture", if we have viewed our natural inclinations with an 'evil eye', then these vulgar arts embody the opposite, "*the animal with a good conscience*" (77; *GM* II.24).

We need to understand Nietzsche's point about these arts in the context of his account of a Christian culture that for two millennia, so he will argue, has cultivated a bad conscience for "the *animal* man" or "the animalistic", in which any suggestion of our kinship with non-human is a matter of disgust and denial of our 'higher' nature (*GM* III.28). Nietzsche asks himself why he is not offended by the vulgarity of these ancient and modern arts that unashamedly and joyfully depict our 'animal' nature. "Is it because", he writes, "there is no shame and everything vulgar acts as confidently and self-assuredly as anything noble, lovely and passionate in the same kind of music or novel? 'The animal has its own right, just like the human being; let it run about freely – and you too, my dear fellow man, are still an animal despite everything!' That seems to me the moral of the story and the peculiarity of Southern humanity" (77).

Nietzsche conceives these arts as indications of and signposts to a good conscience that treats 'the human' *and* 'the animal' as worthy of artistic elevation and therefore induces feelings of delight rather than shame. In contrast with Northern works that he believes express

shame about our 'vulgarity', Nietzsche applauds Southern European
arts for artistically simplifying our 'animal' drives in the guise of
universally intelligible 'masks' or conventional personae. By giving
our animal 'vulgarity' a shared language or mask, he implies, they
purify, ennoble and elevate such drives. At the conclusion of both *GS*
Book 2 and 3, Nietzsche stresses that his alternative, affirmative ideal
carries with it this Southern European delight in the animal and
therefore entails liberation from shame and disgust over our 'animality' (107, 275).[13]

Nietzsche argues that art, especially theatrical art, can also extend
and refine our senses so that we can see and take pleasure in ourselves
as heroes. Our ability to see and value ourselves as heroes, he suggests,
depends on the invention of this particular art of perspective taking.
Nietzsche stresses that without the perspectives that theatrical artists
have created we would fail to see beyond our 'foreground':

> Only artists, and especially those of the theatre, have given men eyes and ears
> to see and hear with some pleasure what each himself is, himself experiences,
> himself wants; only they have taught us to value the hero that is hidden in
> each of these everyday characters and taught the art of regarding oneself as
> a hero, from a distance and is it were simplified and transfigured ... Only
> thus can we get over certain lowly details in ourselves. Without this art we
> would be nothing but foreground and would live entirely under the spell of
> that perspective [*Optik*] which makes the nearest and most vulgar
> [*Gemeinste*] appear tremendously big and as reality itself. (78)

Nietzsche implies that artists liberate us from the 'error' of seeing
ourselves entirely in terms of an optic that illuminates that which we
have in common with others. In this respect, he implies that artists
counter the tendency of consciousness and language to magnify our
herd nature (*D* 115; *GS* 354). In other words, Nietzsche conceives the
arts as counterforces to one particular perspective, what he calls the
herd perspective. In this herd perspective, we see in ourselves only
shared needs rather than seeing ourselves as individuals distinct from
our common traits. As Nietzsche explains in *GS* Book 5, "each of us,
even with the best will in the world to understand ourselves as

---

[13] Ruth Abbey shows how Nietzsche put his identification of the naturalistic, animalistic
origins of our drives and values to different uses. In some cases, he celebrates noble
individuals for being closer to animals (3), while at other time he praises our ability to
surpass our animal nature (see Abbey 2000: 8–9).

individually as possible, to know ourselves, will always bring to consciousness precisely that in ourselves which is 'non-individual', that which is 'average'; that due to the nature of consciousness the 'genius of the species' governing it – our thoughts themselves are continually as it were *outvoted* and translated back into the herd perspective" (354).[14] Nietzsche does not criticise arts that simplify and transfigure our view of ourselves as erroneous or falsifying. On the contrary, he maintains that they function as a liberation from the optic that compels us to see ourselves as nothing more than herd animals. Nietzsche claims then that we ought to be grateful to art insofar as it frees us from this herd perspective and enables us to see beyond our foreground to what "each himself is, himself experiences, himself wants" (78). Nietzsche values this art as a means of laying claim to our individuality.

In his characteristically ambivalent analysis of Wagner's music-dramas, Nietzsche elaborates one aspect of this artistic capacity that allows us to see ourselves beyond the foreshortened herd perspective.[15] In *GS* 87 he describes the vanity of those artists who over-estimate their talents and strive to create "great walls and bold frescoes" rather than cultivate the "small plants ... that are new, strange and beautiful and really capable of growing to perfection on their soil" (87). In *NCW* Nietzsche explicitly identifies Wagner as the specific target of this jibe (*NCW* 1). However, in mocking Wagner's over-reaching ambition and philosophical confusions, Nietzsche also confesses his admiration for Wagner as "our greatest miniaturist in music who crowds into the smallest space an infinity of sense and sweetness" (*CW* 7). Nietzsche's moving homage to his former friend is worth quoting at length:

Here is a musician who, more than any other musician, is a master at discovering the tones out of the realm of suffering, depressed, tormented souls and at giving speech even to dumb animals. Nobody equals him in the

---

[14] By means of this quoted phrase 'genius of the species', which is also the title of this section, Nietzsche refers to Schopenhauer's discussion of the way 'Cupid' or erotic passion deceives individuals into pursuing the species' best interests rather than their own highest ends. Nietzsche's point is that consciousness has an analogous function.

[15] Ridley gives a thumbnail sketch of the twists and turns in Nietzsche's appraisal of Wagner's music and cultural ambitions, noting that his criticisms are "shot to the core with ambivalence" (Ridley 2007: 141–155, 149).

colors of late fall, the indescribably moving happiness of the last, very last, very briefest enjoyment; he finds sounds for those secret and uncanny midnights of the soul in which cause and effect appear to be unhinged and any moment something can come into being 'out of nothing'! More happily than anyone else, he draws from the very bottom of human happiness – as it were, from its drained cup, where the bitterest and most repulsive drops have merged in the end, for better or for worse, with the sweetest. He knows how souls drag themselves along when they can no longer leap and fly, nor even walk; his is the shy glance of concealed pain, of understanding without comfort, of farewells without confessions. As the Orpheus of all secret misery he is greater than anyone, and he has incorporated in art some things that had previously seemed to be inexpressible and even unworthy of art, as if words could only frighten them away, not grasp them – very small, microscopic features of the soul: yes, he is the master of the very small. (87)[16]

We have seen in Book 1 how Nietzsche claims we have invisible qualities, which he likens to "sculptures on the scales of reptiles" (8). He describes these reptile scales as having "lines, subtleties, and sculptures that might give pleasure to a god with a divine microscope" (8). In *GS* 87 Nietzsche identifies Wagner with the Greek hero Orpheus, whom the Greeks venerated as the greatest poet and musician, and his music as analogous to this divine microscope. In this revised assessment Nietzsche ridicules his own former notion of Wagner as the new Aeschylus whose total work of art might drive a German cultural revolution and sees him instead as a new Orpheus whose music alone can express the "very minute and microscopic aspects of the soul, as it were the scales of our amphibian nature" (*NCW* I). Nietzsche redeems Wagner as "the Orpheus of all secret misery" who finds sounds for "those secret, uncanny midnights of the soul". In Book 4, as shall we shall see, Nietzsche claims that it is precisely our experience of "terrors, deprivations, impoverishments,

---

[16] Nietzsche elaborates here his claim in *RWB* that as a musician Wagner followed Beethoven in letting music speak the hitherto forbidden language of passion. "Before Wagner", as he writes, "music was a whole narrowly bounded; it applied to the steady, permanent states of mankind, to that which the Greeks calls *ethos*, and it was only with Beethoven that it began to discover the language of *pathos*, of passionate desire, of the dramatic events which take place in the depths of man" (*RWB* 9). Wagner, he writes, plunges into "woods, mist, ravines, mountain heights, the dread of night, moonlight and remarks in them a secret desire: they want to resound" (RWB 9). Roger Scruton observes of 87, which Nietzsche reproduces and slightly amend in *NCW* I, that it turns around his criticism of Wagner's drama as merely a theatrical display of emotions that intoxicate the weary, and acknowledges that it contains "sparks of lyrical insight without compare in the history of music" (Scruton 2014: 247).

midnights, adventures, risks, and blunders" that is necessary to the realisation of the highest joy. Without this Orpheus, he implies, it would be impossible to experience "the voluptuousness of one's own hell" that is, so he claims, "the path to one's own heaven".[17]

Nietzsche redeems art as a means of valuation and revaluation that can grant us a good conscience about ourselves as natural creatures and furnish us with the eye or perspective that enables us to see the singular, secret and otherwise inexpressible 'tones' and 'colours' of our souls. However, this leaves unanswered the question of why art, in particular tragic art, throws into high relief all that is ugly, hard and questionable in life? Why or to what effect do these artists bring suffering into the realm of art?

As we have seen, Nietzsche attempts to answer to this question through his analysis of Greek tragedy. In *BT* he argued against the Aristotelian tradition that tragedy has a moral purpose and effect: viz. to improve or clarify our ethical judgements or to stimulate and in the process purge our fear and pity.[18] According to his early view, Nietzsche speculates that tragedy granted the ancient Greeks a certain kind of metaphysical consolation: through tragedy they experienced the world's suffering as the creation and redemption of an eternal artist-god. By means of tragedy, as he explained, "we are happy to be alive, not as individuals, but as *the* single living thing, merged with its creative delight" (*BT* 17). In his 'colder' positivistic moment, Nietzsche entirely repudiates the idea we should learn to see suffering as beautiful. Instead, he argues that we should draw on science to figure out practical ways of alleviating human suffering. In this context, he again disagrees with Aristotle, but for different reasons. In *HH* Nietzsche argues that while tragedy might indeed aim to purge our fear and pity, as Aristotle had claimed, it achieves

---

[17] It is worth noting that while Nietzsche identifies Wagner with Orpheus' musical ability to move stones and to give speech to dumb animals, in 286 he admits that his own writings cannot succeed in their hopes unless his readers have "experienced splendor, ardour and rosy dawn in their own souls": "To move stones, to turn animals into humans – is that what you want from me? Oh, if you are still stones and animals, you had better look for your Orpheus first!" (286).

[18] Stephen Halliwell shows that commentators have subsumed every variety of moral, aesthetic and therapeutic effect under the word 'catharsis'. Aristotelian 'catharsis' has been conceived, for example, as a process of emotional purgation or alternatively as process of ethical attunement. See Halliwell (1998: 183, 350–356).

the opposite effect. Following Plato, Nietzsche argues that the danger of tragedy is that it feeds and waters the emotions, overwhelming us with suffering rather than alleviating it (*HH* 212).

In Book 2 Nietzsche once again addresses the problem of tragic pleasure, but from yet another perspective. He confronts this problem in the context of distinguishing between ancient tragedy and modern opera (80). Both, he suggests, allow us to take pleasure in artifice, or in convention's deviation from nature or reality. In modern opera, he suggests, we delight in the beautiful unnaturalness of music taking precedence over words; in Greek tragedy we enjoy the way the rhetoric counters the effects of images that arouse distressing emotions. Here Nietzsche again targets Aristotle's theory of tragedy. Nietzsche reverses his judgement in *HH*: he now argues that tragedians themselves "did everything in their power to counteract the elemental effect of images that arouse fear and compassion – *for fear and compassion were precisely what they did not want*" (80). What then were the tragic artists' aims and why did the Athenians enjoy the tragedies performed at the Great Dionysia state festival? Why might we too enjoy the tragic spectacle?

Nietzsche claims that ancient Greeks and we too can take pleasure in tragedy because it satisfies an acquired need to discover in art something that we cannot satisfy in reality. What makes us love tragic art, he asserts, is that it portrays heroes suffering *in extremis* yet nevertheless giving refined, articulate polished speeches. Nietzsche suggests that the narrow tragic stage and the stiff, conventional masks tragic actors wore served to deprive passion "itself of any deep background" and dictated to it "a law of beautiful speeches" (80). Ancient tragedy, he suggests, is an art form that banishes expressions of inarticulate terror or grief in the face of the "abyss", and gives us instead heroes who can, as it were, deviate from nature to the extent that they treat the very worst calamity as the occasion for refined discourse. "It delights us now", as he puts it, "when the tragic hero still finds words, reasons, eloquent gestures, and altogether a radiant spirit where life approaches a real abyss and a real human being would usually loses his head and certainly his fine language" (80). "The Athenians" Nietzsche emphatically declares "went to the theatre *to hear pleasing speech*!" (80).

Clearly, Nietzsche is not claiming that tragic heroes' articulate speeches alone explain the Athenians' desire to see tragedy. What they love in this art, he suggests, is that it satisfied their "pride" by portraying "a lofty, heroic unnaturalness" (80). Tragedy enabled the Athenians to delight in the idea that they might sustain "a radiant spirit where life approaches the abyss" (80). We too, Nietzsche implies, might also take pride in *ourselves* when we see how tragic heroes are not undone by their suffering, but are elevated to the highest rhetorical eloquence.

It is against this backdrop of Nietzsche's emerging appreciation of tragic art as a life-affirming art that he takes exception to modern theatre, or more particularly Wagnerian theatre. In GS Book 2 Nietzsche argues that modern theatre has altered the relationship between art and life. In *WS* he had already lamented that in an industrious age art no longer places grand demands on our time and energy, but is merely a form of distraction and intoxication for weary, everyday souls. Even great contemporary artists of opera, tragedy and music, he observes, administer to the needs of tired souls rather than addressing "expectant, wakeful, energetic soul[s]" (*WS* 170). "They have in their dispensary", he writes, "the mightiest means of excitation capable of terrifying even the half-dead; they have narcotics, intoxicants, convulsives, paroxysms of tears: with these they overpower the tired and weary, arouse them to fatigued overliveliness and make them besides themselves with rapture and terror" (*WS* 170).

In *GS* 86 Nietzsche repeats his criticism of the modern degeneration of theatre, which he identifies with Wagner's total work of art. In fact, this section is the chrysalis from which will emerge Nietzsche's later, full-blown polemic against Wagner's intoxicating "theatrocracy" (*CW* P1). Once again, Nietzsche frames his analysis in terms of his own personal experience:

This day I had strong and elevated feelings again, and if on its eve I could have music and art, I know very well what music and art I would not like to have, namely, the kind that tries to intoxicate its audience and *drive it to the height* of a moment of strong and elevated feelings – an art for those everyday souls who in the evening look not like victors on triumphal chariots but rather like tired mules who have been whipped somewhat too often by life. (86)[19]

Wagner's music, as Nietzsche presents it, aims to achieve precisely this of kind of intoxication. "The way Wagner's pathos holds its breath", as he later expresses it, "refuses to let go an extreme feeling, achieves a terrifying *duration* of states when even a moment threatens to strangle us" (*CW* 8).[20] Nietzsche objects to Wagner's music and theatre as a narcotic, "hashish-smoking", that compensates for the weariness suffered by those whose character and life lacks thought and passion (86). It enables these everyday theatre-goers, he suggests, to imitate "the high tide of the soul" when they have no knowledge or experience of these higher moods. These simulated intoxications, he maintains, do not redeem their lives but redeem them from themselves.

In this sense, Nietzsche derides theatre for producing in its audience "an effect without a sufficient reason", a simulacrum of the strongest thoughts and passions where there are no real grounds for them in their own lives (86). Wagner, as later put it, "wants effect, nothing but effect" (*CW* 8). Wagner's theatre, he claims, cultivates in its audience the actor's skill and taste for dramatic attitudes and poses that lack any substance.

Nietzsche explains the popular audience's desire for Wagnerian theatre as a hunger for intoxicating emotions that compensate for all that is lacking in their own lives. Wagner's theatrical art, as puts in Book 5, satisfies the dual needs of those "who suffer from *impoverishment* of life": viz. "quiet, stillness, calm seas, redemption from themselves" or, on the other hand, "intoxication, convulsion,

---

[19] In *CW* Nietzsche will identify Georges Bizet's music, especially his opera *Carmen*, as the alternative to Wagnerian decadence (CW 1–3). Referring to Bizet's *Carmen*, Nietzsche writes, "Has it been noticed that music gives wings to thought? That one becomes more of a philosopher the more one becomes a musician?" On Nietzsche's late and controversial preference for Bizet over Wagner, see Ridley (2014: 229–233). Adorno's analysis of Carmen shows why it appealed to Nietzsche: "In *Carmen*, which appropriates nature for itself without any sacral aura, one can breathe freely. The unsentimental, undiluted depiction of natural passion achieves what the inclusion of any consoling meaning would deny to the work' – it 'destroys the illusion that nature is anything more than mortal. This is the precise function of music in *Carmen*" (quoted in Ridley 2014: 233).

[20] Nietzsche seems to allude here to Wagner's famous Tristan chord. On Wagner and Nietzsche's relationship, see Magee (2001: 286–342).

numbness, madness" (370 and *NCW* 'We Antipodes'). Nietzsche's Wagnerian animadversions eventually lead him to take aim at theatre as a whole. "You will guess", as he explains in Book 5, "that I am essentially anti-theatrical – but Wagner, conversely, was essentially a man of the theatre and an actor, the most enthusiastic mimomaniac that also ever existed" (368).[21]

Clearly, Nietzsche's attack on Wagner is not simply a matter of aesthetic judgement. He conceives art criticism as a lens through which he perceives and diagnoses our political and cultural malaises. In Book 5 Nietzsche sharpens his critique of Wagner 'theatricalism' as a symptom and cause of modern democratic levelling. Theatre is the artistic analogue of demagoguery. Nietzsche explains this point by putting himself on stage delivering an address to a Wagnerian about theatre's corrupting effects:

Do be a bit more honest with yourself – after all we're not at the theatre! At the theatre, one is honest only as a mass; as an individual one lies, lies to oneself. One leaves oneself at home when one goes to the theatre; one relinquishes the right to one's own tongue and choice, to one's taste even to one's own courage . . . No one brings his finest senses of his art to the theatre; nor does the artist who works for the theatre: there, one is people, public, herd, woman, pharisee, voting cattle, democrat, neighbour, fellow man; there, even the most personal conscience is vanquished by the levelling magic of the 'greatest number'; there, stupidity breeds lasciviousness and is contagious; there, the 'neighbour' reigns; there one *becomes* a neighbour. (368)

Nietzsche uses a congery of derogatory synonyms for the undifferentiated masses – "the people, public, herd, woman, pharisee, voting cattle, democrat, neighbour, fellow man" – to direct our ire at theatre as an expression and instrument of democratic levelling. Nietzsche diagnoses Wagnerian theatre as both a cause and symptom of a decadent democratic culture whose romantic art, with its "theatrical cry of passion", panders to the needs of the masses for intoxication (*GS* P 4). Nietzsche objects to Wagnerian theatre as a 'demolatry', or the worship of the people. He argues that it both satisfies the hunger for intoxication of the many who lead impoverished, empty lives and that through participation in theatre one

---

[21] On Nietzsche's place in the long history of philosophical anti-theatrical prejudice that begins with Plato's *Republic*, see Barish (1985: 400–417).

"*becomes* a neighbour" in the strongly pejorative sense he gives this term. Nietzsche sees Wagnerian theatre as an extension of democratic levelling the results in the most extreme form of individual aliena-tion. Wagner's theatre, Nietzsche fears, overwhelms our personal conscience.[22] Wagner's popularity, as he later explains, signifies a "declining culture" in which "authenticity becomes superfluous, disadvantageous, a liability. Only the actor still arouses *great* enthu-siasm" (*CW* 11). With this diagnosis of Wagnerian theatre, Nietzsche completes his dramatic volte-face from fervent defender of Wagner as modern culture's redeemer to apostate who mocks Wagner as its democratic corrupter.

If Nietzsche rejects Wagner as the pied-piper of modern democ-racy, does he conceive an alternative to the Wagnerian art that satisfies the sick and exhausted with intoxication and madness? We can get some sense of his alternative from the invidious compar-ison he draws between ancient and modern artworks:

What do all our art of artworks matter if we lose the higher art, the art of festivals! Formerly, all artworks were displayed on the great festival road of humanity, as commemorations and memorials of high and happy moments. Now one uses artworks to lure poor, exhausted, and sick human beings to the side of humanity's road of suffering for a short lascivious moment; one offer them a little intoxication and madness. (89)

Nietzsche suggests here that modern culture lacks the higher art exemplified by ancient Greek and Roman festivals such as the Great Dionysia in which theatrical performances were aspects of public, religious rituals and competitions. Here Nietzsche also implicitly points to a contrast between "our art of artworks" and his own art of living. Against the "art of artworks", as we observed earlier, Nietzsche defends the ideal of making the self a work of art. He conceives this art of the self as the true art out of which life is to be improved and transformed; artworks are not the principal goal but

---

[22] In *HH* 2 Nietzsche sketched a version of this criticism of Wagnerian art, focusing on his innovation of the "endless melody", whose effect, he claimed, was analogous to "going into the sea, gradually relinquishing a firm tread on the bottom and finally surrendering unconditionally to the watery element: one is supposed to *swim*" (*HH* 2 134). Wagner's endless melody expresses what he calls the "*all too feminine* nature of music", its surrender and receptivity to all stimulus, and in doing so carries the danger that it will abolish any possibility of self-possession (*HH* 2 134).

merely the secondary outcome of an excess of power that seeks discharge (*HH* 2 174). Nietzsche presents his own art of self-cultivation as the alternative to Wagner's theatrical worship of the people. In Book 4, as we shall see, against the Wagnerian art, Nietzsche develops an account of an art that aims to cultivate "even the most personal conscience" (368).

Before turning to Book 2's last section, we might briefly pause to consider where Nietzsche's critique of Wagner's musical intoxication has led him in terms of his own attempt to revalue art, especially music, after *HH*'s icy dismissal of romanticism and romantic music. In *HH* Nietzsche had rejected his earlier claims about the metaphysical significance of music. Here Nietzsche sceptically dismissed his earlier Schopenhauerian musical metaphysics and desecrated his love of music, especially Wagnerian music. "In itself", Nietzsche declares, "no music is profound or significant, it does not speak of the will or the 'thing in itself'" (*HH* 215). Nietzsche seeks to explain how we have arrived at this metaphysical error. We mistakenly believe that music is the immediate language of the will (or the thing in itself), he argues, only when musical form has become so thoroughly entirely "enmeshed in threads of feeling and concepts" that it has conquered "the entire compass of the inner life". Without these projections, he argues, "music is empty noise" (*HH* 216). "It was the intellect itself", he explains, "which first *introduced* this significance into sounds: just as, in the case of architecture, it likewise introduced a significance into the relations between lines and masses which is itself quite unknown to the laws of mechanics" (*HH* 215).

Nietzsche also reverses the Schopenhauerian hierarchy of the arts, which placed music at the pinnacle as source of metaphysical insight. Nietzsche now claims that music is not the universal language for all ages, but grows up in and expresses the values and sensibility of historically distinct social and political conditions. Nietzsche adds that in fact in every culture "all truly meaningful music is swansong": it expresses that late fruit of a culture in decline (*HH* 2 171). Of all the arts, as he puts it "music makes its appearance last, in the autumn and deliquescence of the culture to which is belongs" (*HH* 2 171).

Nietzsche applies this claim to the art of Wagner: it is not the music of the future, as he once proclaimed, but the ultimate reaction against "the spirit of the Enlightenment" (*HH* 171). Nietzsche conceives Wagner's art, then, as a reactionary swan song, destined for the dustbin of history.

In *GS* Book 2 Nietzsche seeks to reopen the question of the value of art and music in the aftermath of this positivist experiment in viewing and explaining it naturalistically. Is the free-spirited philosopher well disposed towards music? Nietzsche suggests that free spirits might harness music to the project of creating new values. In this context, he concedes that music has no metaphysical significance or meaning, but he acknowledges that it is one of the most powerful means of shaping and transforming the soul. In this respect, he jettisons that metaphysics of music he inherited from German Romanticism, which he 'iced' in his positivistic works, but he retains the classical view of the way music is sovereign in shaping and regulating the soul. In this qualified sense, Nietzsche admits the 'magical' force of music as a form-giving, shaping force.

Nietzsche turns to ancient Greek spiritual, therapeutic and educational practices to explore this claim. In *GS* 84 he demonstrates how the ancient Greeks bestowed great importance on letting musical rhythms penetrate their speech.[23] In doing so, he explains, they sought to take advantage of "that elemental over-powering force that humans experience in themselves when listening to music: rhythm is a compulsion; it engenders an unconquerable desire to yield, to join in; not only the stride of the feet but also the soul itself gives into the beat" (84).[24] Nietzsche examines how ancient Greek philosophers crystallised long standing cultural practices that

---

[23] In *The Republic* Plato's Socrates formulates the defining philosophical statement of this ancient trope. In Book 3 Socrates claims that music is sovereign in the education of the guardians because "rhythm and harmony most of all insinuate themselves into the inmost parts of the soul and most vigorously lay hold of it in bringing grace to with them; and they make a man graceful if he is correctly reared" (401d). Nietzsche's description of the ancient conception of educational and therapeutic effects of music clearly echoes Socrates' account of the best musical education.

[24] Nietzsche's interest in the ancient concept and phenomenon of rhythm dates back to his early philological research and his Basel lectures, where he devoted two courses to the topic of rhythm (1869 and 1870/1871). James Porter exhaustively investigates the philological and philosophical significance of Nietzsche's early studies of ancient rhythm; see Porter (2000: 127–166).

deployed the rhythmic qualities of music as a therapy of the passions: "When one had lost the proper tension and harmony of the soul, one had to *dance* to the beat of the singer – that was the prescription of the healing art" (84). Ancient Greeks, he argues, sought to use this musical power in every sphere of life:

One could do everything with it: promote some work magically; compel a god to appear, to be near, to listen; mould the future according to one's own will; discharge some excess (of fear, of mania, of pity, of vengefulness) from one's soul but not only one's own soul, but also that of the most evil demon. Without verse one was nothing; through verse one almost became a god. (84)

In Book 1, as we have seen, Nietzsche stresses that all of ancient humanity continues within him to fabulate, to love, to hate, to infer, and *GS* 84 he includes the basic feeling of musical compulsion among these tendencies. In a lengthy disquisition on the sound of contemporary German language, for example, Nietzsche argues that the use of particular sounds in speaking, in this case a military tone, has "a profound effect on character – one soon has the words and phrases, and finally also the thoughts that fit this sound!" (104). Above all else, music or tone shapes our character.

Despite millennia of working against the ancient superstition about the 'divine' power of music, he claims, even today "the wisest of us occasionally becomes a fool for rhythm" when they "*feel*" a thought to be "*truer*" if it has "a metric form and presents itself with a divine hop, skip and jump" (84). Philosophers, so he claims, should not overlook the fact that we are slaves to the rhythm, since "such a basic feeling cannot be completely eradicated", yet they can, he implies, deploy this music to their own ends (84).

In Book 2's penultimate section, Nietzsche sketches the idea of a philosopher who seeks to harness music's direct, non-rational suasive power as the only possible means of promoting his philosophy:

Music as an advocate. – 'I am thirsting for a composer', said an innovator to his disciple, 'who would learn my ideas from me and transpose them into his language; that way I should reach men's ears and hearts far better. With music one can seduce men to every error and every truth: who could *refute* a tone?' – 'Then you would like to be considered irrefutable?' said his disciple. The innovator replied: 'I wish for the seedling to become a tree. For a doctrine to become a tree, it has to be believed for a good while; for it to be believed it has to be considered irrefutable. The tree needs storms, doubts, worms, and nastiness to reveal the nature and strength of the seedling; let it break if it is not strong enough. But a seedling can only be destroyed – not refuted'.

Nietzsche's musical philosopher assumes that music itself has no independent claim to truth or cognitive content; one could, after all, he claims, use it to seduce others to every *error* and every *truth*. Music, on this view, is epistemically neutral; it is only contingently connected to truth and error. It is, however, he implies, far more effective as philosophical advocate than spoken or written philosophical discourse. If, as he argues, conventional philosophical means of expression cannot prevent new doctrines or values from being easily swept aside before they have time to fully develop, then philosophers must draw on music to "reach men's ears and hearts". Nietzsche's musical philosopher implies that music has far more powerful connection to our inner lives, our drives and passions, than those philosophy commands. Music, he assumes, resonates with and transforms our values in ways are relatively immune to destructive criticism: "who could *refute* a tone?" "In Nietzsche's view", as Ridley expresses it, "music is a uniquely potent medium for the transmission of values" (Ridley 2014: 226). If philosophers aim to transform values, then they must, on this view, synthesise music and philosophy. For this reason, Nietzsche sometimes suggests that he aims to compose a 'musical' philosophy that directly shapes its readers' value feelings. It is this notion of his work as musical philosophy that partly explains why in *GS* final sections he hopes that readers will "dance to his pipe" and he appends to this book the 'Songs of Prince Vogelfrei' (383).[25]

In the final section of *GS* Book 2 Nietzsche directly addresses the reasons he thinks we should have ultimate gratitude to the arts in general:

[25] See Gillespie (1998) and Ellis (2007). Michael Allen Gillespie (1988) argues that in *TI* Nietzsche attempts to realise a musical philosophy; in particular that he models the work on the structure of a classical sonata. For a trenchant criticism of this interpretation of *TI*, see Small (2017). We do not have to read Nietzsche's texts tendentiously to see that he sought to become a musical philosopher. Nietzsche does this in an obvious and explicit way: he composes his own 'Songs of Prince Vogelfrei', and introduces these as the alternative to Wagner, the "Musician of the Future" (383).

Had we not approved of the arts and invented this type of the cult of the untrue, the insight into the general untruth and mendacity that is now given to us by science – the insight into delusion and error as a condition of cognitive and sensate existence – would be utterly unbearable. *Honesty* would lead to nausea and suicide. (107)

Why does Nietzsche claim that scientific honesty might cause individuals to suffer despair? How exactly do scientific insights contribute to making life unbearable? Nietzsche implies that science threatens to make life unbearable because it reveals that the metaphysical beliefs that have hitherto sustained our ability to value life are errors and delusions. Nietzsche fears that nihilism, as he later calls it, might follow from the scientific insight that we are dependent on metaphysical errors to sustain our belief in the value of existence. Scientific insight discredits all moral, religious and aesthetic justifications of the world that rely on a metaphysical conception of a world of reason, purpose or beauty lying above or below the world of appearances. We want to discover reason, purpose or morality behind natural phenomena to in order to value existence, but science, he implies, shows these are metaphysical delusions. The upshot, Nietzsche claims, is the pessimistic or nihilistic judgement that life is not worth the candle.

In *GS* 107 Nietzsche returns then to the central problem he set out to resolve in *BT* and that he restates in *GS* 1: how can we justify or even endure a world that 'lacks' rational purpose and moral significance? How did the Greeks derive consolation from tragedies that depicted heroes suffering a pitiless fate, subject to the amoral, purposeless forces of nature? In *BT*, as we have seen, Nietzsche argues that tragedy gave the Greeks an insight into a world beyond appearances that justifies existence: viz. the world of an eternally creative artist-god. "The Dionysiac phenomenon", as he explains, "over and over again shows us that spirit that playfully builds and destroys the world of individuals as the product of primal pleasure; dark Heraclitus compares the force that builds worlds to a child placing stones here and there, and building sandcastles and knocking them down again" (*BT* 24). Nietzsche's early view is that Greek tragedy grants us metaphysical consolation by allowing us to delight in momentarily experiencing our oneness with the eternal, artistic creator of the world rather than suffering as mere individual, mortal phenomenon subject to its creative and destructive urges.[26] Nietzsche later describes *BT* as founded on one artistic meaning behind all events viz. "an amoral artist god, who in both creating and destroying, in doing both good and ill, wishes to experience the same joy and glory; who in creating worlds, rids himself of suffering of abundance and superabundance" (*BT* ASC 5). In *BT* Nietzsche maintains that in order to enjoy this artistic metaphysical consolation we must deny our empirical individuality and see ourselves only from the point of view of this artist-god. In other words, Nietzsche's artist's metaphysics does not allow us to affirm our individual empirical existence, only the eternal world beyond it. In Dionysiac art, as he explained, "we are to seek ... [eternal delight in existence] not in phenomena themselves but behind phenomena" (*BT* 17). Nietzsche's earlier metaphysics is not a good will to transient appearances, but a good will to an eternal metaphysical world.

By the time of *GS*, however, Nietzsche has rejected all such metaphysical notions of an eternal world beyond appearances that might justify existence. Yet he still defends an aesthetic perspective as essential to overcoming nihilistic despair:

But now our honesty has a counterforce that helps us avoid such consequences: art as the *good* will to appearance. (107)

How should we understand Nietzsche's revised account of his claim that the art can counter pessimistic despair about the value of existence? How does art rescue us from nihilism? Nietzsche marks his attempt to move away from his early notion of metaphysical consolation by revising *BT*'s famous motto:

As an aesthetic phenomenon existence is still *bearable* to us, and art furnishes us with the eye and the hand and above all the good conscience to be *able* to make such a phenomenon of ourselves. (107)

[26] On the failures of Nietzsche's early artist's metaphysics see Young (1992) and Geuss (1999). Raymond Geuss explains the limits of Nietzsche's early notion of metaphysical consolation: "What looks just fine from the point of view of the Child – Raymond dying painfully in a highly interesting and dramatic way – won't be nearly so satisfactory to me as the empirical person I am. The function of art is to give me a proper glimpse of one side of the relation between the Child and me – the side of our 'identity', while at the same time hiding the other side from me, deceiving me about the non-identity that exists between myself and the Child, and the possible implications that has for my ability to see my life as worthwhile" (Geuss 1999: 107–108).

Nietzsche shifts from *BT*'s claim that "it is only as an aesthetic phenomenon that existence and the world are eternally justified" to the view that it is only by turning ourselves into aesthetic phenomenon that existence is bearable to us. Our affirmation of life no longer turns on *seeing* the world as an aesthetic phenomenon, but on *making* ourselves such phenomenon. He moves from *BT*'s aestheticisation of the world as it in itself to *GS*' aestheticisation of the individual (Came 2004: 66). In place of *BT*'s artist's metaphysics, and *HH*'s scientific optimism, he turns to a psychology of art to reconceive the possibility of affirming existence. On his revised view of the aesthetic affirmation of life, Nietzsche rejects the claim that existence is eternally justified as the phenomenon of an artist-god and therefore that we can experience this by looking above or beyond our empirical existence as mortal individuals to an eternal artistic will. In place of this metaphysical justification he endorses the view that we can make existence bearable by fashioning ourselves into artworks. Nietzsche brings art down from the skies.

In doing so, however, he does not abandon the concept of 'eternal life' as simply a metaphysical error. Instead, he conceives the art of the self as a means of transfiguring a transient, mortal self into a divine or 'eternal' phenomenon. Eternity is now a product of art. We can clarify this point by examining his description of the art of the self. How does Nietzsche mark out the self as an artwork? Nietzsche gives some sense of his answer to this question in the allusion to his famous thought of recurrence in the line immediately prior to his claim that we can bear existence by making ourselves artworks:

We do not *always* keep from rounding off, from finishing off the poem: and then it is no longer eternal imperfection that we carry across the river of becoming – we then feel that we are carrying a *goddess*, and are proud and childish in performing this service. (107)[27]

---

[27] Nietzsche emphasises that as aesthetic phenomenon existence is still bearable to us. Nietzsche revises his earlier view that we can 'justify' existence; he now asserts that we can still 'bear' it as an aesthetic phenomenon. As we shall see in Chapter 5, he argues that bearing existence is a *necessary* condition of learning how to love it. Without first bearing existence, he claims, we cannot learn to love it.

Here Nietzsche highlights the artistic metaphor of the self: to make oneself an aesthetic phenomenon is analogous to completing a poem. Importantly, he suggests that as poets of our own lives we can make sure we carry across the river of becoming – a classical metaphor of impermanence or transience – not eternal imperfection, but eternal perfection. To make our lives aesthetic phenomenon, in other words, we must make our transient lives eternally perfect. If we practice this art we are able to see our transient lives as beautiful, or to feel, as he puts it, that we are carrying a 'goddess' across the river of becoming. Nietzsche conceives the idea of the self as artwork as a way of reconciling our desire for eternity with the fact of our transience, or of synthesising being and becoming. It is an art that aims to make our transient lives worthy of eternal repetition; or to transform the finitude of becoming into the infinity of being.[28]

Nietzsche stresses that art also furnishes us with the good conscience to achieve this new ideal of the self as an artwork. By contrast, he implies, morality gives us a bad conscience for the project of turning ourselves into a work of art: it slanders a whole range of drives as immoral rather than as material of aesthetic elaboration. By furnishing us with this good conscience, art affirms our drives and experiences as elements that we might take up and shape into an artwork. So for Nietzsche, "the *good* will to appearance" entails seeing ourselves through an aesthetic lens rather than a moral perspective that severely limits the possibility of self-fashioning.

However, Nietzsche's claim that art supplies us with the good conscience to make ourselves artwork does not by itself explain why he believes that realising this project makes existence *bearable*. In what sense does Nietzsche believe turning ourselves into artworks can act as a counterforce to the nihilism that he suggests must otherwise flow from the insight into purposeless suffering or dissonance? In making our lives aesthetic phenomenon, how are we to

---

[28] As Georg Simmel suggests, Nietzsche's thought of recurrence is a way of reconciling being and becoming: "The infinite repetition of a being that is limited by finitude, and the causality through which phenomena that surge up and then disappear like waves in a continuous river win a durability and an eternity of being – which was stolen from them by their temporal destiny – make the eternal recurrence into a synthesis, or as Nietzsche would say, into an 'approximation' of being and becoming" (Simmel 1986: 177).

endure, or even love, the terrifying and questionable aspects of existence that tragedy vividly represents in the hero's fate?

Nietzsche implies that the art of the self requires the strength to see our existence through one specific artistic lens: that of the *tragic* poet. As we have seen, in Book 2 he suggests that ancient tragedy appealed to the "pride" the Greeks felt in themselves through its representation of heroes "radiant" before the abyss (80). Tragedy glorified the hero's clarity and lucidity in the face of terror. In ancient tragedy, he implies, the Greeks saw a mirror of their own highest state. Against Aristotle, therefore, Nietzsche maintains that tragic art did not overwhelm the Greeks with fear and pity, but gave them pleasure in seeing their own highest or most desirable condition mirrored in the radiance of the tragic hero.

Here Nietzsche plants the seed of his later claim that tragic or Dionysian pessimism expresses the highest state of the affirmation of existence. Nietzsche will later suggest that it is "pride" that stands behind and differentiates his own notion of the Dionysian pessimism of strength, or will to the tragic, as opposed to the romantic pessimism of weakness (*HH* 2 P 7). "With this will [to the tragic] in one's heart", he writes, "one has no fear of the fearful and questionable that characterises all existence: one even seeks it out" (*HH* 2 P 7). Nietzsche explains this delight in tragedy as the expression of pride or an excess of strength and life. Tragedians, he claims, *see* or *create* as beautiful what the weak deplore as hateful and ugly. If artists draw into the realm of art what gives us joy, as Nietzsche maintains, then *tragic* art must appeal to those with sufficient pride or strength to delight in "the *terrifying*, the *evil*, the *questionable*" (*WP* 852). For the ancient Greeks, as he later puts it, "tragedy is a tonic" or "the great stimulant to life" (*KSA* 15[10]). "Pleasure in tragedy", he asserts, "characterises strong ages and natures: their *non plus ultra* is perhaps the *divina commedia*" (*WP* 852). Put simply, Nietzsche's art of the self requires we become akin to tragic poets who delight in rather than conceal the tragic conditions of existence.

In effect, in *GS* Nietzsche brings *BT*'s artist-god down from the metaphysical realm to the psychological realm.[29] Nietzsche's amoral

---

[29] Reginster (2014: 24) plausibly observes that the metaphysical comfort Nietzsche claimed the Greeks derived from tragedy, which required that they identify with the eternal artist-god

artist-god becomes his model of highest self to the extent that he will later conflate the two:

> He who is richest in the fullness of life, the Dionysian *god and man* can allow himself not only the sight of what is terrible and questionable but also the terrible deed and every luxury of destruction, decomposition and negation. (370, emphasis added)

We will elaborate Nietzsche's model of the self as an artwork when we turn to Books 4 and 5. For the moment, however we should observe that Nietzsche's revised aesthetic model of affirmation creates a new problem for his evaluation of science. If, as he holds, scientific insight threatens us with despair, and art as the good will to appearance rescues us from this malady, then what exactly is the value of science for the highest, affirmative life? In the closing Book 2 Nietzsche recognises that the value of science, or the unconditional pursuit of truth, has become a question mark. For this reason he suggests that free spirits must comically mock their own "passion for knowledge" in order to free themselves from the "overly severe demands" they make on themselves in matters of knowledge. Their "irritable honesty", he suggests, threatens to entangle free spirits in a morality that can turn them into virtuous "scarecrows" – it threatens to scare away their "bird-like freedom" and "bird-like exuberance" necessary to their free-spirited experimentation (*HH* 2 P 4).

As we shall see, in Book 5 Nietzsche revisits the problem of the value of science or truth, arguing that it serves an *ascetic* morality. Nietzsche will suggest that science has been founded on and motivated by a metaphysical desire to look beyond and escape from the world of appearance. In sharp contrast with his aesthetic affirmation, which expresses an overabundant strength that sees beauty in appearance, this ascetic morality aims to flee from all appearances or values. Nietzsche will conceive the scientific commitment to truth at any price as the ultimate symptom of a metaphysical faith that the truth is 'divine' or that it must lie above or beyond appearance. In this sense, he will conceive the scientific assault on value creation as the expression of

---

who creates and destroys all phenomena out of its own superabundance, presupposed that they *admired* the activity of this creative god. In GS Nietzsche wants us to become akin to this creative god.

a metaphysical faith in another world that devalues this world. "Nietzsche's recognition that the scientific quest for knowledge is itself implicated in morality, that it is the last expression of the faith in morality, of the ascetic ideal, of religious piety", as Paul Franco rightly notes, "suggests a significant modification of the ideal of the free spirit that has hitherto informed the middle works. It suggests a standpoint beyond the quest for knowledge insofar as this quest remains mired in morality and asceticism. Art is indispensable to achieving this standpoint, which, insofar as it floats above morality, can be understood as the quintessence of gay science" (Franco 2011: 127).

In *GS* 107 then Nietzsche revises his earlier aesthetic affirmation of life. Nietzsche now suggests that we can bear existence if we turn ourselves into aesthetic phenomenon. Free spirits must conceive their lives as tragic works of art. In Book 3 he aims to dispel the 'shadows of God' that stand in the way of this rebirth of tragedy. In Book 4 he will then elaborate his new art of the self. Nietzsche will argue that we can see our lives as beautiful tragedies, and therefore will their eternal recurrence, if our lives satisfy the demand of our 'ownmost' conscience, which decrees: 'You should become who you are' (270).

CHAPTER 4

Shadows of God: Book 3

In the opening section of Book 3 Nietzsche first announces one of the central motifs of *GS*, indeed of his whole philosophy: "God is dead" (108). Nietzsche's motto subverts Christianity by means of the self-contradictory concept of God as transient, mortal, perishable. Modern Europeans live in the age of God's decomposition. Significantly, Nietzsche makes his famous statement under the title "*New battles.*" Book 3 opens then with a declaration of a *new* war that he encourages free spirits to wage. In a signature move Nietzsche adopts the first-person plural to directly address free spirits and identify what he thinks ought to be their response to the death of God: "And we – we must still defeat his shadow as well!" (108). By closing 108 abruptly with this exclamation mark Nietzsche underscores the significance he places on free spirits waging war against the shadow of God. *GS* 108 is a call to arms. Nietzsche later explicitly joins his philosophy to what he later calls a "war of spirits" (*EH* 'Destiny' 1). What are their new struggles and what battles have they already fought and won? Who are they fighting and under what banner?

Nietzsche engages in three related contests in Book 3. First, Nietzsche deploys his extraordinary literary skills, borrowing liberally from classical and Christian rhetorical styles, to dramatise the significance of the death of God and to dispel the so-called shadows of God. Nietzsche suggests that in the context of the history of the species, the death of God is a watershed whose consequences may take millennia to unfold. It is a pivotal event because for two millennia modern Europeans have conducted their lives within what he calls the Christian "horizon" (124). Nietzsche uses the term 'God' metonymically: it refers to a whole range of beliefs, evaluations and ways of life that he identifies as secular expressions of

Christianity. The death of God, he claims, signals the demise of a "horizon" that has made it possible for Europeans to give value or meaning to their lives and to orient their actions. Even the lives of those who now reject the Christian God, he claims, act within the limits of this Christian horizon. Nietzsche conceives this Christian horizon as a variation of the basic endowment of many millennia of the species' evolution.

One of Nietzsche's guiding task in Book 3, then, is to overcome the incomprehension of the meaning of this event and to defeat the as yet unrecognised 'shadows' of God. In his famous section 'The Madman' (125) Nietzsche imparts extraordinary urgency to this battle because he believes its outcome will determine whether our species stagnates. In waging this fight he opens up a new set of questions: How should free spirits orient themselves in this radically new period? Are there alternative horizons? Can they *create* new horizons (cf. Pippin 2010)?

Second, Nietzsche broaches one of the central questions of his philosophy: 'What is the value of the will to truth for life?' The significance of this question looms large in this context because by adopting the drive to truth our species has made itself responsible for God's demise. Nietzsche addresses this question by speculating about the emergence of the drive to truth as a new condition of life. He aims to explain the origins and development of the will to truth. He conceives the drive to truth as a relatively new phenomenon in our species' evolutionary history. Nietzsche claims that we have evolved as organisms geared towards error, not truth or its pursuit. Nietzsche maintains that our species' fundamental judgements and evaluations have been errors mechanically selected because they have turned out to be species preserving. These basic epistemic errors, he claims, have become incorporated into the species' life since time immemorial (110). To the extent that the new phenomenon of the drive to truth undermines these basic errors, which, he claims, have determined what counts as true and untrue, it constitutes a radical challenge to the basic endowment of the species (110).

In Book 3 Nietzsche formulates what will turn out to be his *preliminary* assessment of the value of truth for life. In the first edition of *GS*, Nietzsche enters the lists as a defender of the unconditional drive to truth, or at least of the project of experimenting with the possibility of incorporating the drive to truth. In doing so, however, he confronts a conundrum. According to Nietzsche, errors have been a fundamental condition of our species' life, yet the drive to truth undermines life-preserving errors, including most significantly the metaphysical errors of Judaeo-Christianity. In Books 3 and 4 Nietzsche argues we can nonetheless defend the value of the unconditional will to truth as a heroic way of life. In his preliminary account Nietzsche's 'gay science' signifies a heroically experimental way of life: viz. the attempt to pursue and incorporate the truth into life. At this point, Nietzsche values the drive to truth because it expresses the heroic virtue of courage. Among other things, it requires the courage to reject the errors that have become part of our basic endowment and to do so while acknowledging the absence of any metaphysical or eternal horizon. Drawing on one of his favourite analogies in *GS*, Nietzsche envisages free spirits as adventurous seafarers setting sail into '*the horizon of the infinite*' (124). Nietzsche conceives 'the gay science' as an endless odyssey: with the end of metaphysics free spirits have no prospect of returning to Ithaca or 'land': "Woe, when homesickness for the land overcomes you, as if there had been more *freedom* there – and there is no more 'land'!" (124)

Yet, between 1882 and 1887 he significantly revises both his genealogy of the drive to truth and his assessment of its value for life. In preparing the ground for our survey of Nietzsche's 1887 addition of a fifth book to *GS*, we will briefly sketch his emerging scepticism in the mid 1880s about "the heroism of the truthful" (*BGE* 230). Nietzsche comes to see his preliminary assessment of the value of the will to truth as an overblown moralistic *mis*interpretation of this phenomenon (*BGE* 230). By the time he adds the new fifth book to *GS*, as we shall see in Chapters 5 and 6, Nietzsche recasts the unconditional will to truth as a continuation of metaphysical idealism or the ascetic ideal, which, so he claims, diminishes rather than enhances life.[1] In the final version of *GS* (1887) Nietzsche conceives 'truth at any price' as yet another shadow of God that free spirits must vanquish. Over the lifespan of *GS* (1882–1887) Nietzsche's

---

[1] Nietzsche will later elaborate in detail the connections between the ascetic ideal and the will to truth in *GM* Book 3.

response to the problem of the value of truth thus comes the full circle.

Third, Nietzsche considers and evaluates the moral errors that have shaped the evolution of the human species. Nietzsche indirectly addresses the question: 'What is the value of these moral errors for life?' As with the species' epistemic errors, Nietzsche maintain that these moral errors are long standing evolutionary outcomes that have become part our species' basic endowment. He construes these moral errors as a particular type of epistemic error: they are judgements and evaluations that orient and structure relationships among individuals to ensure the security of the group or collective. Nietzsche brings these errors under the rubric of 'the morality of custom' or 'herd' morality. This morality, as he conceives it, ranks drives and actions in ways that most benefit the herd. Herd morality creates a moral conscience and its concomitant sensations, the "pang of conscience", which ensure each individual becomes a functional, adaptable element of the collective (117).[2] Nietzsche claims that herd morality continues to cast a very long shadow over humanity. He identifies Christian moral conscience and Kant's metaphysics of morals as highly spiritualised or sublimated variations of herd morality. Nietzsche aims to defeat the shadows of this morality.

Despite the death of God, he maintains, modern European sensibilities remain deeply wedded to Judaeo-Christian variations of herd morality. Against this morality, he aims to cultivate a new sensibility and value horizon. He identifies this as the project of 'naturalising' humanity (109). In Book 3 he takes his lead from the ancient Greeks to conceptualise this project. Specifically, Nietzsche turns to ancient Greek religion and art: Olympian polytheism and tragedy. He draws a sharp opposition between the Judaeo-Christian culture that modern Europeans have incorporated and the ancient Greek pre-philosophical culture that remains alien to their "sensibility" despite the best efforts of many generations to incorporate this world (135). Nietzsche identifies Greek polytheism as a preliminary exercise in giving form to "the free-spiritedness and many-spiritedness of humanity" (143).

---

[2] Nietzsche later elaborates the origins and development of moral conscience in *GM* Book 2.

Let us first examine one of the central motifs of Nietzsche's philosophy: the death of God. In Book 3 Nietzsche argues that modern Europeans have failed to comprehend of the radical significance of this event for the scope and possibilities of how they conduct their lives. Nietzsche aims to dispel this incomprehension so that free spirits can envisage a radically new ethos. In the opening section (108) he clearly assumes that on the theoretical plane atheism must be victorious. Even if there are still pious Christians, in other words, he assumes that "in the long run" this faith is unsustainable given the emergence of scientific scepticism about religious and metaphysical beliefs, though he concedes this victory may take a hundred thousand years (133). In this sense, Nietzsche believes that 'God is dead' is simply a statement of historical inevitability. He does not bother therefore to engage in theoretical disputes about God's existence. For Nietzsche, such debates are philosophically jejune. "What decides against Christianity now", as he explains, "is our taste, not our reasons" (132).

In broader terms, Nietzsche's famous declaration of God's demise is symptomatic of the collision of a religious worldview with an emergent nineteenth-century scientific naturalism and its project of naturalising humanity. At this pivotal moment in European culture, Nietzsche acknowledges the turn to explaining and interpreting humanity in purely naturalistic terms.[3] Against Christian metaphysics, which misinterprets humanity as distinct from and above nature, Nietzsche treats humanity as a species among other species within nature.

Nietzsche aims to shift the ground of this dispute between religion and scientific naturalism from the epistemological to the practical plane. Or to put it another way, his central concern is that we, or at least "we free spirits", have not yet understood the necessity of

---

[3] Cf. Heidegger (1991: 39–47) who attempts to purge Nietzsche of what he describes as this "alleged biologism". Recent scholarship rejects Heidegger's anti-naturalistic interpretation of Nietzsche and firmly identifies him as a 'naturalist'. However, exactly what kind of 'naturalism' he subscribes to is a matter of dispute (see e.g. Leiter 2002; Janaway 2007; Janaway and Robertson 2012; Clark and Dudrick 2012; Lemm 2016). One point, however, seems clear: Nietzsche's methods are discontinuous with those of empirical scientific enquiry. In particular Nietzsche challenges science's impersonal, affect-free search for truth (see Janaway 2007: 39–53).

conceiving a new way of life or perspective that lies beyond the Christian horizon. What is at stake for Nietzsche is how we ought to live after the death of God. Even those who intellectually assent to the proposition 'God is dead', he argues, are very far from having comprehended its radical significance for how they live. Instead of acknowledging the meaning of this event, he suggests, most will conduct themselves according to a moral perspective whose intellectual foundations they have consciously rejected.

Nietzsche is not therefore merely identifying an intellectual lag in their understanding of this event. Rather he suggests that many will unconsciously resist acknowledging its significance because they fear it may be unbearable. Nietzsche implies that this resistance is symptomatic of a fear of the emptiness that might ensue from comprehending the death of God. In section 151 he explains how under the "rule of religious ideas, one has got used to the idea of 'another world (behind, below, above)' and feels an unpleasant emptiness and deprivation at the annihilation of religious delusions and from this feeling grows now 'another world', but this time only a metaphysical world and not a religious one" (151). Nietzsche suggests that a desire to banish the feeling of emptiness motivated the invention of metaphysical worlds. It is this same fear of emptiness, he implies, that will unconsciously motivate resistance to dispelling the shadows of god. In order to stave off this distressing sense of emptiness or weakness, as he later claims, modern Europeans cling to the shadows of God, or to one or another faith, including the "impetuous *demand for certainty* that today discharges itself in scientific-positivist form" (347). Nietzsche, by contrast, "conceives of a delight and power of self-determination, a *freedom* of the will, in which the spirit takes leave of all faith and every wish for certainty, practiced as it is in maintaining itself on light ropes and possibilities and dancing even beside abysses. Such a spirit would be the *free spirit* par excellence" (347).

Nietzsche both clarifies and challenges this resistance to comprehending the magnitude of the death of God in his most famous and memorable section *GS* 125, 'The madman' [*Der toller Mensch*]. In 125 Nietzsche reports a madman who proclaims in the marketplace that 'God is dead' and who violently accuses a mocking, uncomprehending crowd of murdering god and bearing terrible guilt as the "murderers of all murderers" whose crime has had catastrophic consequences for humanity. By murdering god, the madman proclaims, they have condemned themselves to perpetual night. There is no little irony in the fact Nietzsche's personification of the madman has become one of the modern philosophy's most seminal, frequently recollected passages. Nietzsche places a madman's hyperbole at the heart of philosophy. We cannot make headway in understanding this passage, and why it has achieved philosophical fame, if not notoriety, without paying careful attention to its literary and rhetorical style. Why does Nietzsche choose a madman and his mocking audience as the *dramatis personae* to explore the significance of the death of God? It also demands that we consider other vexing interpretive questions. In what sense is this madman insane? Is the madman the mouthpiece of 'truth'? Does Nietzsche mean to endorse the madman's diagnosis of the death of God?

We can begin our survey of 125 by examining Nietzsche's figure of the madman. Through this trope of the madman Nietzsche draws on ancient rhetorical resources and conventions. In 152 he observes that for ancient humanity, "'truth' was . . . experienced differently because the lunatic could be considered its mouthpiece which makes *us* shudder and laugh" (152). Nietzsche observes in *Daybreak* that in antiquity madness played an important role in the history of morality as the instrument of new 'truths' or values. Ancient cultures, he observes, held that "a grain of the spice of madness is joined to genius" (*D* 14). In antiquity, Nietzsche claims, the creation of "new and deviate ideas, evaluations, drives" (*D* 14) was possible only if innovators adopted the mask or persona of madness. In the context of a deeply entrenched morality of custom, they called upon 'madness', understood as a "speaking trumpet of a divinity", to allay their guilt at breaking with this morality and to awaken reverence and dread of themselves. In order to break with custom, individuals had to give themselves a "voice and bearing as uncanny and incalculable as the demonic moods of the weather and the sea and therefore as worthy of a similar awe and observation" (*D* 14).

Drawing on Diogenes Laertius and Plutarch's doxographies, Nietzsche recalls Solon, one of Greek antiquity's seven sages, to illustrate this ancient convention. According to the ancient reports, Solon feigned madness to flout an Athenian law banning calls to renew war against Salamis. As Diogenes Laertius recalls: "Solon, feigning madness, rushed into the marketplace with a garland on his head; there he had his poem on Salamis read to the Athenians by the herald and roused them to fury" (*DL* 1.46). Nietzsche infers from these ancient sources that madness figured as the apology of moral innovation. "All superior men", he observes, "who were irresistibly drawn to throw off the yoke of any kind of morality and to frame new laws had, *if they were not actually mad*, no alternative but to make themselves or pretend to be mad" (*D* 14). Nietzsche reiterates this point in *GS* Book 3 where he suggests that in antiquity the "idolatry" of making individual value judgements, of positing one's own ideal, required an apology: "Not I, not I! But a *god* through me!" (143).

In antiquity, Nietzsche claims, madness constituted an apology of moral innovation, a rhetorical persona or mask that gave power and legitimacy to the overthrow of law or custom, and the means by which the innovator himself could overcome the dread of breaking with hallowed convention. Nietzsche illustrates this latter point by apostrophising an ancient prophet speaking to himself: "'I am consumed with doubt, I have killed the law, the law anguishes me as a corpse does a living man: if I am not *more* than the law, I am the vilest of all men. The new spirit which is in me, whence is it if it is not from you? Prove to me that I am yours; madness alone can prove it'" (*D* 14).

In making the madman the mouthpiece of the death of God, Nietzsche draws on the rhetorical power of this ancient custom. Nietzsche's madman, as we shall see, elicits the ambivalent mix of derision and disturbance he (Nietzsche) surmises modern audience should have when confronted with ancient figure of a moral prophet (152). They are taken aback by his mad, hyperbolic speech. However, Nietzsche's use of this ancient convention has had a far greater impact on his modern readers: they have identified the madman's apocalyptic speech as central to Nietzsche's philosophical legacy. Whether he intended it or not, by using the ancient figure of the madman Nietzsche effectively generated intense philosophical concern about the significance of the loss of the Christian moral horizon.

Nietzsche embeds his personification of the mad prophet in another ancient rhetorical practice. That this section has become part our philosophical heritage is perhaps also partly due to the fact that it deploys an ancient philosophical style closely associated with the Cynics, especially Diogenes the Dog, whose moral radicalism

compelled Plato to describe him as "Socrates gone mad" (*DL* 6.54).[4]
Nietzsche's section combines the ancient philosophical style of the
anecdote (*chreia*) and longer stories or reminisces (*apomnemoneu-
mata*) relating whole episodes of a philosopher's life. In reviving the
ancient chreia, Nietzsche draws on one of the one of the most
popular of philosophical and rhetorical forms in later antiquity
(Desmond 2006:). "Though thoroughly popular in form", as Mack
observes, "the chreia was cultivated at the highest levels of intellectual
life and became in fact a major means for characterizing [ancient]
philosophers" (Mack 2003: 38).

Unlike systematic ancient philosophies like Platonism and
Aristotelianism, the Cynics were not concerned with teaching doctrine, but with passing on models of living. Cynic teaching passed on
their exemplary style of living through anecdotes, which reported in
a few words a Cynic gesture, retort or an attitude. One learnt the
Cynic way of life not through systematic treatises, but through the
anecdotes recording their style of living. As we noted in
the Introduction, Nietzsche's early philological studies were devoted
to Diogenes Laertius' *Lives of Famous Philosophers*, the primary
ancient source of these cynic anecdotes. Through his shameless
actions, which shockingly flouted convention (*nomos*), Diogenes
aimed to scandalise his fellow Athenians into seeing the 'error' of
their conventional behaviours and desires in light of his own practice
of a living according to nature (*physis*). Ancient cynics aim to live
according to nature (*physis*), rejecting the corruptions of convention
(*nomos*). Diogenes plays the role of the madman or buffoon to shock
his contemporaries into seeing that what they think of "as human or
humane is not worthy of the name" (Shea 2010: 17). It is through his
shameless actions that Diogenes becomes a truth teller who scanda-
lised contemporary Athenians in a bid to make them acknowledge
their failure to live according to nature. In *GS* 125 Nietzsche reworks
one of the famous anecdotes about Diogenes the Dog: "He lit a lamp
in broad daylight and said as he went about 'I am looking for
a human being'" (*DL* 6.41). Diogenes' mocking action assumes, of
course, that he will not find one (Desmond 2006: 21).

---

[4] Classical scholarship suggests there are over one thousand anecdotes (*chreiai*) that involve
Diogenes, more than for any other philosopher (Desmond 2006: 21)

Nietzsche's choice to revive the form of the Cynic *chreia* is philosophically significant. Ancient Cynics not only relentlessly mocked conventional Greek laws and norms, they also poured scorn on Platonic metaphysical idealists' goal of living to according to a non-existent world of Ideas or Forms rather than nature, which Platonists conceived as a mere shadow world. Nietzsche's madman reworks the figure of the scandalous Cynic truth teller as the nemesis of metaphysical idealism (see Bambach 2010). Nietzsche extends this critique of metaphysical idealism to Christianity. Nietzsche, we might recall, holds that "Christianity is Platonism for 'the people'" (*BGE* P). In this one respect, we might call Nietzsche a neo-Cynic: he too reviles the metaphysical error "of the pure spirit and the good in itself" as "the most dangerous error of all" (*BGE* P).[5] In William Desmond's words, Nietzsche saw himself as continuing Diogenes' tradition of comic wisdom "with his own anti-Platonic, *fröhliche Wissenschaft*" (Desmond 2006: 192). However, while Nietzsche shares the ancient Cynics anti-metaphysical animus and their anti-metaphysical project of living according to nature, his project of returning to nature or naturalising humanity rests on a radically different notion of nature or life. Earlier Nietzsche acknowledged that ancient Cynics attain happiness by living like animals, entirely absorbed in the present and forgetful of the past, and by this means they overcome the pessimistic desire to escape (Plato) or radically turn against life (Schopenhauer) (see *HL* 1). Ancient Cynicism, as he conceives it, is a philosophical exercise or *askesis* aimed at reclaiming healthy animal understanding. As we shall see, however, Nietzsche only uses the Cynics' ideal of animal happiness to show the possibility of alternatives to the various pessimistic flights from life or nature, not to encompass his own ideal. It is part of Nietzsche's 'gay science' only insofar as it mocks and satirises metaphysical pessimism.

Section 125 begins with an apocryphal recollection of "that madman who in the bright morning lit a lantern and ran around the marketplace crying incessantly, 'I'm looking for God! I'm looking for

---

[5] On Nietzsche as a neo-Cynic, see Niehues-Pröbsting and Desmond (2006: 229–234); on Nietzsche's relationship to the ancient Cynicism and modern cynicism, see Bracht Branham (2004) and Jensen (2004).

God!'" (125). As with Diogenes, the madman's act of lighting
a lantern in daylight is ironic: it brings into sharp focus the fact
that something important is missing, in this case God. However,
unlike Diogenes, who aims to encourage Athenians to rediscover or
return to what they have lost, life according to nature, Nietzsche's
madman aims not to revive God but to reveal the radical significance
of God's death and the necessity of creating a new value horizon.

Nietzsche's madman is immediately mocked and jeered by
a crowd of atheists:

As many of those who did not believe in God were standing around just
then, he provoked much laughter. Has he got lost? asked one. Did he lose
his way like a child? asked another. Or is he hiding? Is he afraid of us? Has he
gone on a voyage? emigrated? – Thus they yelled and laughed. (125)

Ancient philosophical anecdotes also regularly recall cynics being
mocked or reproached for their 'mad' unconventionality. Many anecdotes report cynics turning the tables on and mocking their conventional critics who had sought to find fault with or inconsistency in the
behaviour.[6] The Cynic", as Mack observes, "reveled in these encoun-
ters, taking them as opportunities to expose the normal expectations as
ridiculous. The chreia was a perfect medium for distilling the nature of
such exchanges. In order to win, the Cynic had to put an altogether
different construction upon things. Strategies ranged from playful put
downs, through erudite observations and insights, and biting sarcasms,
to devastating self-deprecations, but always with a sense of humor to
ease the blow" (Mack 2003: 48).

Nietzsche's madman also aims to expose the limits of his own
audiences' conventional expectations, but without the cynic's dash of
humour. His hyperbolic outburst aims to unmask atheists' complete
failure to comprehend the radical meaning of their own rejection of
God:

The madman jumped into their midst and pierced them with his eyes.
"Whither is God?" he cried; "I will tell you. *We have killed him* – you and
I. All of us are his murderers. But how did we do this? How could we drink up
the sea? Who gave us the sponge to wipe away the entire horizon? What were

---

[6] E.g. "When someone reproached him for frequenting unclean places, Diogenes replied that
the sun also enters the privies without becoming defiled" (DL VI 63). Cf. *GS* P 4.

we doing when we unchained this earth from its sun? Whither is it moving now? Whither are we moving? Away from all suns? Are we not plunging continually? Backward, sideward, forward, in all directions? Is there still any up or down? Are we not straying, as through an infinite nothing? Do we not feel the breath of empty space? Has it not become colder? Is not night continually closing in on us? Do we not need to light lanterns in the morning? Do we hear nothing as yet of the noise of the gravediggers who are burying God? Do we smell nothing as yet of the divine decomposition? Gods, too, decompose. God is dead. God remains dead. And we have killed him".

Nietzsche's madman upbraids his mocking audience by piling question upon question, seventeen consecutive, rapid-fire thrusts in all, each of which exposes their blindness to their own condition. The central point the madman hammers home through this inter-rogative barrage is that the loss of an "entire horizon" should have vertigo inducing effect. If complacent atheists were to properly experience the consequences of their actions, the madman insists, they must suffer a profound disorientation. Nietzsche's madman attempts to compel them to experience "the magnitude of their deed" or to fully incorporate it into their lives rather than dismiss it as a trifling matter, an event without any significance or repercus-sions. He turns their conventional wisdom on its head: the murder of God, he declares, is not an inconsequential matter, but the greatest deed they have committed. Nietzsche's madman does not succeed in compelling his mocking audience to suffer the terrible, uncanny disorientation he thinks must follow from wiping away their entire horizon, but he does silence their laughter and force them to experi-ence his strangeness. As we noted above, however, the madman's delirious speech has had much greater sway over Nietzsche's readers' fears about the nihilistic consequences of the death of God.

We should not, however, conflate the madman's melancholic obsession with the loss of God with Nietzsche's own judgement. In particular, Nietzsche clearly does not share the madman's morbid obsession with the guilt and atonement for the murder of god (Pippin 2010: 50–51; Franco 2011: 135). One of Nietzsche's central ambitions in *GS* is to effectively criticise the irrationality or madness of guilt and sin. Yet Nietzsche shares the view the madman's diag-nosis of the radical significance of the event and his claim that this will escape the comprehension of most modern Europeans.

Nietzsche's madman identifies it as radical break in history: "Do we not ourselves have to become gods merely to become worthy of it? There never was a greater deed and whoever is born after us will on account of this deed belong to a higher history that all history up to now!" (125).[7] Nietzsche himself will later identify his own critique of morality as a catastrophic break in history: "The *unmasking* of Christianity is an event without equal, a real catastrophe. He who exposes it is force majeure, a destiny – he breaks the history of mankind in two parts. One lives *before* him, one lives *after* him" (*EH* 'Why I am a Destiny' 8). Nietzsche also shares the madman's view that the meaning of this event will not reach humanity for millennia. It is an event, as he later puts,

> that is far too great, distant and out of the way for even for its tidings to be thought of as having arrived yet. Even less may one suppose many to know at all what this event really means – and, now that this faith has been undermined, how much must collapse because it was built on this faith . . . for example, our entire European morality. This long, dense succession of demolition, destruction, downfall, upheaval that now stand ahead: who would guess enough of it today to play the teacher and herald of this monstrous logic of horror, the prophet of deep darkness and an eclipse of the sun the like of which has probably never before existed on earth? (343)

However, unlike the madman, Nietzsche does not lament the death of God, but the failure of atheists to recognise that the meaning of the event lies in the loss or collapse of an entire horizon that, he claims, even their secular form of life continues to presuppose. What these complacent atheists fail to comprehend is that with the death of God their whole moral horizon must eventually collapse. Nietzsche employs the madman's extreme, apocalyptic rhetoric of this distant loss, this unfolding 'monstrous logic of horror', in order to underscore the necessity of creating new horizons that can re-orient human action. Nietzsche does not share the madman's self-lacerating guilt about the murder of god, but he does suggest that without the creation of new horizons we must enter into a new dark age of nihilism, or a complete lack of value orientation. Nietzsche's anxiety is that without the creation of a new horizon the death of the

---

[7] Franco (2011: 247) observes that in an earlier draft of this passage Nietzsche writes that we must become the "mightiest and holiest of poet[s]" instead of gods (KSA 9:12 [77])

Christian form of moral life, which, he claims, idealises or ennobles self-sacrificing, ascetic modes of life, can only lead to a new 'dark' age of nihilism (131). "The greatest recent event – that God is dead; that the belief in the Christian God has become unbelievable", as he later glosses *GS* 125, "is already starting to cast is first shadows over Europe" (343).

Nietzsche's central task in Book 3 is to show that once we have fully incorporated the death of God we must forgo not simply metaphysical beliefs and judgements, but also *all* the forms of life that they express and shape. "Nietzsche", as Nicholas More puts it, "took no hypocritical succour from a now baseless Christian morality (as David Strauss and countless others did), failed to see inevitable historical progress of the spirit (as Hegel), gave up as untenable any aesthetic metaphysics and will denial (of Schopenhauer), scoffed at the mass-equality dream of a political utopia (Marx), and would not reconfigure nature as divine (Spinoza)" (More 2014: 73–74). If, as Nietzsche's madman obsessively insists, after the death of God we have wiped the "entire horizon" within which we once lived, are we condemned to stray "as though through an infinite nothing" or can we create new horizons? If we must now accept that we have set sail into "*the horizon of the infinite*", is it possible to orient ourselves, to give meaning, direction or purpose to our lives (124)?

After *GS* 125 Nietzsche briefly examines alternatives to Christian morality and nihilism. Nietzsche identifies his alternative, counter-nihilistic proposal as a new project of naturalising humanity. Playing on religious tropes, he describes this project as the 'redemption' of nature from the shadows of god, or, as he later puts it, redemption from the curse the ascetic ideal has placed on it (*GM* II.24). In fact, Nietzsche looks to ancient Greek religions to sketch a new kind of deification or affirmation of nature. Nietzsche turns to polytheistic religions to identify a value horizon that might provide clues about how we can realise just the godlike self-sufficiency the madman suggests will make us worthy of the new post-Christian age.

Yet, as we shall see, his account of this naturalising project is deeply ambivalent. As Christopher Janaway observes, Nietzsche's *GS* is pulled in opposite directions by the competing ideals of truthfulness and artistic invention. "The concepts of art and truth", as he puts it, "dance around one another repeatedly in *The Gay Science*, indeed from the title onwards" (Janaway 2013: 266). Pierre Klossowksi argues in his 1957 lecture at the Collegie de Philosophie that Nietzsche saw in art and religion simulacra of an affirmation of existence that repeats itself eternally and held that this mode of apprehension was perpetually denied by scientific activity. Nietzsche, he claims, "felt a solidarity with both these attitudes towards existence: that of simulacra, as well as that of science, which declares '*fiat veritas pereat vita*'" (2004: 84).[8] Nietzsche's ambivalence surfaces in as attempts to explore his naturalising project.

On the one hand, in Book 3 Nietzsche investigates the new phenomenon of the drive to truth, which clashes with life-preserving errors, and endorses the experiment of incorporating the truth. Does Nietzsche's 'gay science' signify a life devoted to the pursuit of truth at any price? Is Nietzsche's post-Christian ethos the heroism of truthfulness? Does he intend to follow Spinoza in making "knowledge the most *powerful passion*" (Middleton 1996: 177)?[9] Does art figure in Nietzsche's ethics merely as consoling illusion?

On the other hand, Nietzsche also distinguishes the human species in terms of its power to create new values and in doing so invent new modes of living that express the "free-spiritedness and many-spiritedness of humanity" (143). In this context, Nietzsche identifies the project of naturalisation with reviving this artistic power of value creation and he singles out Greek polytheism and tragic art as preliminary exemplars of this project. Here Nietzsche conceives art not as mere illusion, but as the creation of value perspectives that shape the very scope and possibility of human flourishing. Nietzsche will later distinguish between "mediocre spirits" like Darwin, John Stuart Mill and Herbert Spencer, empirical scientists, in short, who are committed to "identifying, assembling and making deductions from a host of common little facts", and higher spirits "who have more to do than merely know something new – namely to *be*

---

[8] Let there be truth and let life perish.
[9] During the writing of *GS* Nietzsche claims to have 'discovered' Spinoza as his "precursor" who shared his overall tendency of making knowledge the most power passion (Middleton 1996: 177). On Nietzsche's reception and interpretation of Spinoza, see Yovel (1989), Stambaugh (1994), Schacht (1995), Della Rocca (2008), Sommer (2012), Armstrong (2013) and Wollenberg (2013).

something new, to *signify* something new, to *represent* new values! The gulf between knowing and being is perhaps wider, also more uncanny, than one thinks: the man who is able in the grand style, the creator, might possibly have to be ignorant" (*BGE* 253). Is Nietzsche's post-Christian ethos a revitalisation of his version of ancient Greek polytheism and the values of tragic pessimism and tragic heroism? We can consider Nietzsche's response to the death of God in light of this tension between the ascetic commitment to scientific truth at any price and the poetic art of value creation.

After opening Book 3 with a declaration of war on the shadows of God Nietzsche immediately proceeds to explain what it is that free spirits must vanquish. Ironically, Nietzsche imitates a Christian rhetorical style to caution against the secularised refractions of Christian metaphysics. Drawing on the rhetorical device of anaphora, which has its roots in the biblical psalms, in *GS* 109 Nietzsche solemnly (or mockingly?) intones the opening phrase "let us beware" no less than seven times to caution against the shadows of god.

Surprisingly perhaps, Nietzsche's first target is not religious and moral beliefs or practices, but a whole range of so-called anthropomorphic projections that shape scientific, moral and aesthetic perspectives on nature (Higgins 2000: 104–105). To eliminate the shadows of God, or to 'de-deify' nature, as Nietzsche understands it, requires removing anthropomorphic projections from our account of nature. Our scientific, moral and aesthetic perspectives on nature, he suggests, are nothing more than shadows or refractions of theistic beliefs. What are these projections? As Loeb explains, they include "the needs of humans (for novelty, for permanence), the properties of humans (rational, aesthetic, and moral qualities), the properties of human communities (laws), the properties of human machines (functions, purposes), the properties of organic creatures (life, nutrition, growth, self-preservation), and the properties of our astral system (cyclical movement)" (Loeb 2013: 656). Nietzsche claims, for example, that we must beware not to think of the universe as a living being or a machine, to assume that it follows an "elegant" cyclical movement; that it follows laws of nature or purposes; to think that there are radically distinct types of phenomena, living and dead; or that the world is eternally fixed or eternally creative.

If it is possible to remove our projections, or to vanquish the shadows of God, how does nature appear? Against the idea of nature as a living being or a machine, Nietzsche asserts

The total character of the world . . . is for all eternity chaos, not in the sense of a lack of necessity but a lack of order, organization, form, beauty, wisdom and whatever else our aesthetic anthropomorphisms are called . . . and the whole musical mechanism [*Spielwerk*] repeats eternally its tune, which must never be called a melody. (109)[10]

On this view, once we remove the shadows of God the character of the world is revealed as a non-moral, non-purposive system of necessity. In a note from this period for a projected work on "new ways of living" Nietzsche identified the theme of the first book as "*Chaos sive natura*: 'of the dehumanization of nature'" (*KSA* 9:11[197])."[11] Nietzsche sees himself as recasting and purifying Spinoza's naturalism (Rosen 1995: 18; Franco 2011: 129–130). Spinoza naturalism formulates a non-teleological, amoral account of nature conceived as an intelligible system of necessity. "All beings in Nature – and there is nothing that is not a part of Nature –" Spinoza asserts, "follow with an absolute, indeed *geometrical necessity from Nature*".[12] In an oft-quoted postcard, which he sent to Overbeck at the time he was composing of *GS*, Nietzsche recognised himself in five points of Spinoza's doctrine: "he denies the freedom of the will, teleology, the moral world order, the unegoistic, and evil" (Middleton 1996: 177).

---

[10] Shortly before claiming that every man would choose non-existence over the repetition of his own life (*WWR* I: 324), Schopenhauer uses a similar image of eternal recurrence: "Every time a man is begotten and born the clock of human life is wound up anew, to repeat once more its same old tune [*Leierstuck*, lyre piece] has already been played innumerable times, movement by movement and measure by measure, with insignificant variations" (*WWR* I: 322). Nietzsche will later use this image of the *Leier* in 'The Sleepwalker's Song', where Zarathustra transforms the thought of eternal recurrence, which Schopenhauer and German pessimists conceived as the strongest symbol of nihilism, into an affirmation of existence, a "sweet lyre" (see D'Iorio 2016: 118–119)

[11] Franco (2011: 246) argues that Rosen (1995) mistakenly identifies this note from 26 August 1881 as a sketch for *Z* rather than as directly relevant to *GS*.

[12] See Spinoza: "I think I have shown clearly enough that from God's supreme power, or infinite nature, infinitely many things in infinitely many modes, i.e. all things, have necessarily flowed, or always follow, by the same necessity and in the same way as from the nature of a triangle it follows, from eternity and to eternity, that its three angles are equal to two right angles" (*E*, IP17s).

However, Nietzsche rewrites Spinoza's slogan *"Deus sive Natura"* (God *or* Nature), substituting 'chaos' for 'Deus'.[13] In doing so, he implicitly rejects Spinoza on the grounds that he is a pantheist who identifies the whole of reality with God.[14] Nietzsche contests not only Spinoza naturalistic credentials, but also the ethics his draws from the doctrine of necessity. For Spinoza a proper understanding of the necessity of events therapeutically transforms the soul, purifying it of the turmoil of the passions. Philosophy as Spinoza puts it "teaches us how we must bear ourselves concerning matters of fortune, or things which are not in our power . . . that we must expect and bear calmly both good fortune and bad. For all things follow from God's eternal decree with the same necessity as from the essence of a triangle it follows that its three angles are equal to two right angles" (*Ethics* II P 49, Sch.). For Spinoza, the doctrine of necessity is the basis of equanimity. Because the good or bad fortune we experience occurs with geometrical necessity we have no rational grounds for joy or sorrow whatever befalls us: things could not have been otherwise. Philosophical knowledge leads to tranquillity and self-control. As we shall see, Nietzsche's project of naturalisation diverges sharply from Spinoza's neo-Stoic ethical naturalism.[15] As Nietzsche later remarks, Spinoza's ethic, his "no-more-laughing and no-more-weeping . . . that destruction of the emotions through analysis and vivisection which he advocated so naively", is not "'science' not to speak of "'wisdom'" but "prudence, prudence, prudence mixed with stupidity, stupidity, stupidity" (*BGE* 198).[16]

In *GS* 109 Nietzsche complicates his own account of natural necessity with his image of these necessities as eternally repeating themselves. Nietzsche uses this musical synecdoche of the world as an eternally repeating musical box (*Spielwerk*) in a parenthetical remark that claims the "exceptions", by which he means the exception of "the development of the organic", are not the "secret aim" of our universe and that unsuccessful attempts to develop organic life are

---

[13] Nietzsche specifically recasts Spinoza's phrase 'God or Nature' from *Ethics* IV Preface: "We see, therefore, that men are accustomed to call natural things perfect or imperfect more from prejudice than from true knowledge of those things. For we have shown . . . that Nature does nothing on account of an end. The eternal and infinite being we call God, *or* Nature acts from the same necessity from which he exists . . . As he exists for the sake of no end, he also acts for the sake of no end."

[14] Cf. Nadler (2016), who argues that Spinoza is not a pantheist, properly speaking.

[15] Cf. Armstrong (2013: 6–24)   [16] Cf. Della Rocca (2008: 292–303)

the rule (109). Since Nietzsche makes the doctrine of eternal recurrence the culminating point of the first edition of *GS*, we need to briefly consider the significance of this passing allusion.

While some commentators see in this image of the eternally repeating music box the premise of a doctrine of cosmological recurrence, in *GS* 109 Nietzsche appears to use it primarily to deflate this metaphysical notion of purpose.[17] Nietzsche's goal here is to expose and reject one of the shadows of God, viz. any tacit or unrecognised assumption that the universe has a secret, concealed metaphysical purpose that lies "behind, below or above" phenomena. We cannot rationally distinguish between successful and unsuccessful attempts to develop organic life, he argues, since this implies that nature has a metaphysical purpose. The total character of the world is rather a chaotic, meaningless natural or physical reality that he conceives through the synecdoche of a "musical mechanism repeats eternally its tune, which must never be called a melody" (109). Why does Nietzsche add the qualifier that we must not describe the eternally repeating music as a melody? In the context of warning against the use of aesthetic anthropomorphisms, it seems highly unlikely that Nietzsche uses this aesthetic image to stake a claim for a cosmological doctrine.

We can grasp the significance of Nietzsche's claim that we should never call the universe a melody by briefly examining Schopenhauer's philosophy of music. For Nietzsche, "melody" is a metaphysically charged concept: it recalls Schopenhauer's metaphysics of music. Schopenhauer famously argues that music is the metaphysical art *par excellence*: it "expresses the metaphysical to everything physical in the world ... Accordingly, we could just as well call the world embodied music as embodied will".[18] Schopenhauer assigns melody a special

---

[17] Paul Loeb argues that in *GS* 109 Nietzsche provides "ample basis for a cosmological interpretation of recurrence" (Loeb 2013: 657). In this passing representation of the world as a *Spielwerk*, he claims, Nietzsche "characterizes eternal recurrence as both true and cosmological, and even offers a kind of *via negativa* argument on its behalf that is allied to what he regards as the naturalistic project of de-deifying the cosmos" (Loeb 2013: 656). It is also true, as Paolo D'Iorio shows, that GS' preparatory notes Nietzsche formulated the doctrine of recurrence in implicit polemics with contemporary scientists, notably von Hartmann, Dühring and Caspari (see D'Iorio 1995; Brobjer 2008: 77, 155; Dahlkvist 2007: 264).

[18] In *BT* 16 Nietzsche quotes a long section of *WWR* 1: 262–263 to explain and justify his (Nietzsche's) metaphysical conception of music as the expression of the world in itself, the radical difference between music and other arts, and his own corresponding distinction

significance. First, he claims that melody expresses our distinctly human capacity to conceive of our lives as having a "significant and intentional connection from beginning to end" (*WWR* 1: 259). Second, he argues that melody expresses the alternation of dissatisfaction and satisfaction that constitutes the will to life, but it does so in a way that "flatters" the will to life. Melody, Schopenhauer explains, "consists in an alternating discord and reconciliation . . . the copy of the origination of new desires, and then of their satisfaction . . . in this way music penetrates our hearts by flattery, so that it always holds out to us the complete satisfaction of our desires . . . the meeting of our desires with favourable external circumstances independent of them, and this is a picture of happiness" (*WWR* 2: 454–455). When Nietzsche cautions that we should never call the world a "melody", he is suggesting that we must reject the metaphysical notion that it is geared towards or aims at the satisfaction of human desires or happiness.

After cautioning against these shadows of God, Nietzsche gestures towards the positive outcomes of this exercise:

> But when will we be done with our caution and care? When will all these shadows of god no longer darken us? When will we have completely de-deified nature? When may we begin to *naturalise* humanity with a pure, newly discovered, newly redeemed [*erlösen*] nature?

Nietzsche's formulation here is deliberately paradoxical. How can we speak of *redeeming* nature in the process de-deifying it? What can redemption mean in the absence of God? If, in Nietzsche's judgement, other philosophies have sought redemption *from* nature, what is required for the redemption *of* nature? Is it sufficient simply to eliminate the shadows of god to reclaim a "pure, newly discovered, newly redeemed nature"? As we shall see, Nietzsche's answer is self-evidently 'no'.

Nietzsche then turns to an explanation of the origin of the drive to truth that threatens to overthrow errors that have proven "useful and species-preserving" (110). Whence the drive to truth if we have been bred for error? Our species, he suggests, has incorporated only those errors of judgement that proved useful. Nietzsche claims that basic

---

between Apollonian and Dionysian drives and arts. I quote from this same section of *WWR* 1.

cognitive errors have become "incorporated" into life; we *live* these errors. Errors have become "the principle[s] of life" (110). It follows then that to the extent that the will to truth pays no heed to utility it threatens consoling and life-preserving errors and thereby undermines the conditions of life. Through the mechanism of natural selection, he implies, we have built up and incorporated an erroneous interpretation of nature that ensures our survival. Either through random variation (Darwin) or inherited traits (Lamarck), he argues, some individuals and groups found themselves in possession of errors that gave them an edge in the struggle for survival and reproduction (110). It is the errors that have served the species in the struggle for existence that it has incorporated into itself and have become part of its "basic endowment of the species": viz. "that there are enduring things, that there are identical things, that there are things, kinds of material, bodies; that our will is free; that what is good for me is also good in and for itself" (110). Even in the remotest areas of pure logic, he claims, these norms have determined what counts as true or untrue.

Nietzsche argues that our species' theoretical or cognitive apparatus has evolved through the mechanism of natural selection and has bred in us "an extraordinarily strong" disposition "to affirm rather than suspend judgments, to err and make things up rather than wait, to agree rather than deny, to pass judgement rather than be just" (111). In other words, in Darwinian fashion, Nietzsche maintains that hecatombs of our species have perished because they had the disposition to suspend judgement, to wait or to deny. A member of our species who exercised caution or delay in subsuming cases, as Nietzsche explains, "had a slighter probability of survival than he who in all cases of similarity immediately guessed that they were identical" (111). Our species preservation hinges on natural selection gradually eliminating or minimising the opposite dispositions or drives that endanger it. "Every great degree of caution in inferring, every sceptical disposition", as Nietzsche puts it, "is a great danger to life" (111). Truth, or a commitment to truth, is maladaptive. It is a random variation that puts individuals or species at a disadvantage in the struggle for existence. Error proved species' preserving, where 'error' meant, for example, making false judgements of identity and substance (111). Nietzsche extends this argument about the necessity of false judgements to the concept of cause and effect: "there is probably never such a duality; in truth a continuum faces us, from which we isolate a few pieces, just as we always see a movement only in isolated points, i.e. do not really see, but infer" (112; *BGE* 21; Small 1994).[19]

For this reason, Nietzsche feels compelled to explain the emergence of a drive that runs counter to the species' basic endowment, its naturally evolved need for errors. How could the drive for truth have emerged if we have evolved as creatures whose organism is geared for error?

In *GS* Nietzsche identifies as the origin of the drive to truth as arising originally from the random appearance of two different propositions both compatible with the basic errors necessary to life. The appearance of such conflicting propositions, he suggests, made it possible to argue which one was more useful to life. While this made it possible for the intellect to develop as a tool for assessing relative utilities, it did not yet separate it from the commitment to the basic 'errors' – the question under examination was only which proposition best served life. The shift to a drive for truth unharnessed from utility did not emerge, he suggests, until among these new propositions some appeared as *neutral* propositions (not useful or harmful) of an "intellectual play impulse", which he describes as "innocent and happy like all play" (110).

Nietzsche's suggestion is that with the emergence of 'neutral' propositions it became possible to conceive the possibility that truth might not necessarily be connected to utility or happiness. Nietzsche moves then from conceiving the intellect as tool that produces (a) nothing but errors necessary to life; (b) an array of propositions with varying degrees of utility for life; (c) an array of neutral propositions that express a play impulse; to the view that it is (d) a drive with its own 'end': namely, a drive that does not

---

[19] Nietzsche's position on the epistemic status of science in *GS* Book 3 has provoked controversy among commentators. Nietzsche is variously held to believe that science necessarily falsifies the world *in itself*, which he conceives as chaos, flux or becoming (Young 1992; Rosen 1995); that he inconsistently insists that science falsifies the world as it is in itself despite the fact that in *GS* he adopts an anti-metaphysical perspective, a mistake he rectifies in *BGE* by endorsing science's epistemic claims (Clark 1990; Clark and Dudrick 2004); or that science is in fact the only legitimate source of truth, but that it cannot support a post-Christian regeneration of culture (Ridley 2007).

support faith or conviction (or truths compatible with life) but a drive to "scrutiny, denial, suspicion and contradiction" of basic errors. Nietzsche suggests that after (a) and (b), after the intellect had served utility and delight (the play impulse), and in doing so generated a whole cluster of propositions not strictly tied to use or pleasure, these propositions became the object of "every kind of drive" (110), each of which want to claim them for their own ends. Once these 'truths' became the object of a fight among the drives, he claims, the pursuit of truth became a distinct and independent way of life: "an occupation, attraction, profession, duty, dignity – knowledge and the striving for the true finally took their place as a need among other needs" (110). That is to say, the striving for the true became a distinctive way of life not strictly tied exclusively to the prior concerns that had shaped the intellect: viz. utility and delight. "Thus knowledge", Nietzsche suggests, "became a part of life, and as life, a continually growing power, until finally knowledge and the ancient basic errors struck against each other, both as life, both as power, both in the same person" (110).

Nietzsche then distinguishes the modern age as the scene of a new struggle (*Kampf*) between this drive to truth and the life-preserving errors that hitherto have been a fundamental condition of life. "It is something new in history", he remarks, "that knowledge wants to be more than a means" (123). For classical philosophers, he suggest, knowledge was a means to virtue or happiness and for Christians a mere ornament or luxury, but for his free spirits it is a passion; that is to say, it is an "unconditional urge and tendency" (123). Nietzsche's conception of the war of modern age resonates with his own commitment to Spinoza's naturalism, which, as we have seen, makes "knowledge the most *powerful passion*".

Yet if, as Nietzsche maintains, our entire organism has been geared for error, if we have 'incorporated' error as a basic condition of life, and if we have been "unable to live with [truth]", it is unclear what the outcome of this new battle will be and indeed whose side we ought to support (110). Nietzsche defines the thinker as the "being in whom the drive to truth and those life-preserving errors are fighting their first battle, after the drive to truth has proven itself to be a life-preserving power too" (110). Here Nietzsche further specifies the new

battle that free spirits must wage: it is the struggle *for* the unconditional drive to truth or passion for knowledge against these life-
preserving errors:

> In relation to the significance of this battle everything else is a matter of
> indifference: the ultimate question about the condition of life is posed here,
> and the first attempt is made here to answer the question through experi-
> ment. To what extent can truth stand to be incorporated – that is the
> question; that is the experiment? (110)

Can our organism be geared towards an unconditional commitment
to truth, truth at all costs? How might our lives be transformed if we
finally live "only to *know*" (KSA 9:9 [141])? Nietzsche's analysis of the
unconditional drive to truth establishes two key problems. First, if it
undermines the errors that have become necessary conditions of our
species life then how can we explain its genesis and development?
As we have seen, Nietzsche attempts to explain the emergence of this
will to truth as the accidental development of an "intellectual play
impulse" that eventually takes on a life of its own as a distinct
vocation or way of life (110). Nietzsche must also confront a second
problem: if the unconditional will to truth effectively undermines the
errors necessary to life is it possible to incorporate the will to truth
and do we have any reason for defending of supporting it? Is it both
possible and desirable to live for truth? In other words, Nietzsche
broaches the question that looms large in his later works: what is the
value of this unconditional will to truth? "[Nietzsche's] aim", as
Bernard Williams explains, "was to see how far the values of truth
could be revalued, how they might be understood in a perspective
quite different from the Platonic and Christian metaphysic which
had provided their principal source in the West up to now"
(Williams 1993: 18). If knowledge is not a means to higher life, an
ascent to God, to self-sufficient virtue, or even simply an ornament or
luxury, then what is its meaning and value?

In *GS* Books 3 and 4, Nietzsche defends the unconditional will to
truth as the free spirit's ideal. Despite his claim that the will to truth
exposes and undermines life-preserving errors, free spirits, he maintains, are distinguished by their experiment with the value of truthfulness. On this preliminary view, Nietzsche claims that to live in the
service of knowledge is the best or most powerful life (324). How does

Nietzsche justify this valuation of truth at any price? We might call Nietzsche's 1882 perspective, heroic experimentalism. We can jump ahead briefly to Book 4 to understand the heroic experimentalism that underpins his defence of the drive to truth at any price:

I find [life] truer, more desirable and mysterious every year – ever since the great liberator overcame me: the thought that life could be an experiment for the knowledge-seeker ... And knowledge itself: let it be something else to others, like a bed to rest on or the way to one, or a diversion or a form of idleness; to me it is a world of dangers and victories in which heroic feelings also have their dance ... *'Life as a means to knowledge'* – with this principle in one's heart one can not only live bravely but also *live gaily and laugh gaily!* And who would know how to laugh and live well who did not first have a good understanding of war and victory? (324)

On the one hand, then, as we have seen, Nietzsche implies that the will to truth eliminates errors conducive to life. On the other, he argues that it is liberating to make life an experiment for the knowledge-seeker; or as he explains, the free spirit's experiment with incorporating truth makes life "truer, more desirable and mysterious every year" (324), even though it eliminates these errors. The free spirit's experiment with the will to truth seems to undermine the very conditions of life (viz. error) and yet by the same stroke make life more desirable.

Nietzsche first attempts to resolve this apparent contradiction by identifying the free spirit's drive to truth with a kind of philosophical heroism. Nietzsche resolves the contradiction by valuing the free spirit's heroic sacrificing of errors for the sake of knowledge over the preservation of the errors that function as conditions of life. Life becomes a means to knowledge rather than knowledge a means to life. Nietzsche argues that free spirits value the will to truth precisely because it entails the heroic, courageous battle against necessary, comforting or consoling errors. It requires this courage, he argues, because it must fight against basic errors that have become "incorporated" into life. If we value heroism, he implies, then we will value life as an experiment for the knowledge-seeker because it entails engaging in a war against the errors that have become part of our species' basic endowment. In short, in this first version of the gay science, Nietzsche celebrates their drive to truth because by making life a means to knowledge free spirits enter "a world of dangers and victories in which heroic feelings ... have their dance- and play-grounds" (324)

Yet we should note that Nietzsche revises his history of the emergence of truth between 1882 and 1887 and in doing so also recasts the ideal of the free spirit's 'gay science'. Nietzsche articulates his new genealogy of the will to truth in *BGE* (1886) and then again more clearly in *GS* Book 5 (1887) and *GM* III (1887). We will examine Nietzsche's revised account of the gay science when we address the 1887 additions to *GS*, Book 5 and the Preface. For the moment we can sketch Nietzsche's growing concerns about the value of the unconditional will to truth in *BGE* (1886), which bridges *GS* 1882 and *GS* Book 5 1887.

In *BGE* Nietzsche formulates a radically revised genealogy of the emergence of the drive to truth. Nietzsche's amended genealogy deflates the claim that free spirit's commitment to truth expresses "honesty, love of truth, love of wisdom, sacrifice for the sake of knowledge, heroism of the truthful" (*BGE* 230) Against his own morally and metaphysically ennobling account of the free spirit's drive to truth in *GS* Books 3 and 4, in *BGE* Nietzsche argues that in fact the drive to truth is the most refined, disciplined sublimation of ascetic cruelty, or the will to life turned against itself in order to delight in its own suffering.

Rather than conceiving the emergence of the drive to truth as a distinctive, independent vocation that developed from an intellectual play impulse (110), he now identifies it as the sublimation of the basic text of the species – its asceticism or drive to cruelty. "Finally", as he explains, "consider that even the seeker after knowledge forces his spirit to recognise things against the inclination of the spirit, and often enough against the wishes of his heart – by way of saying No where he would like to say Yes, love, adore – and thus acts as an artist and transfigurer of cruelty. Indeed, any insistence on profundity and thoroughness is a violation, a desire to hurt the basic will of the spirit which unceasingly strives for the apparent and the superficial – in all desire to know there is a drop of cruelty" (*BGE* 229). Nietzsche suggests that philosophers "hardened by the discipline of science" sacrifice all the basic errors that hitherto made life possible (*BGE* 230).

Nietzsche treats the free spirit's 'murder' of God as exemplifying their ascetic self-cruelty that has led humanity to the abyss of nihilism. Nietzsche identifies the ascetic drive to truth as the sublimation of religious cruelty. He conceives three rungs on the "great ladder of religious cruelty" (*BGE* 55). As we climb this ladder we first sacrifice human beings to god; we then sacrifice our strongest instincts to god; and finally we sacrifice God, all that "comforting holy, healing, all hope in a concealed harmony, in a future bliss" and "out of cruelty to oneself worship stone, stupidity, gravity, fate nothingness" (*BGE* 55). "To sacrifice God for nothingness", Nietzsche remarks, "– this is the paradoxical mystery of the ultimate act of cruelty was reserve for the generation which is even now arising: we all know something of it already" (*BGE* 55).

In 1886 Nietzsche identifies a seemingly irreconcilable clash between what he calls the basic will of the spirit and the unconditional drive to truth. By the "basic will of the spirit", he means what he calls the commanding element that wants to dominate itself and its surroundings and to feel its domination. Nietzsche suggests that the 'spirit' has a range of techniques or strategies familiar to all organic life that enable it to live, grow and propagate (*BGE* 230). The central power of the spirit consists in a set of techniques that maintain or preserve its life by assimilating the new to the old, the strange to the familiar, simplifying the manifold and falsifying the 'external world' to suit its own interests. All these he identifies as so-called plastic powers of incorporation that transform experience into a source of energy and motivation. Nietzsche's draws an analogy here between the work of the spirit and that of the stomach: the spirit digests experience, just as the stomach digests nutrients. Nietzsche identifies the basic will of the spirit with a range of defensive techniques that also work as conditions of life, but do so not through assimilation, but through denial or exclusion. These defensive techniques block out experiences that resist the spirit's powers of incorporation so that the greater the latter the less it has need of the former, which include ignorance and forgetfulness, the will to be deceived and to deceive others (*BGE* 230). The basic will of the spirit, the will to appearance, he claims, has just those needs and capacities which "physiologists posit for everything that lives, grows and multiplies" (*BGE* 230).

Nietzsche argues that the drive to know counters or resists this basic will of the spirit, the will to mere appearance. If the basic will of the spirit is the will to appearance, it is countered "by that sublime inclination of the knower who insists on profundity, multiplicity and thoroughness with a will which is a kind of cruelty of the intellectual conscience and taste" (BGE 230). "We free, *very* free spirits", as Nietzsche conceives them, undermine all the active and reactive techniques that the spirit has forged to make it possible to live and grow (*BGE* 230). For this reason, in Book 5 of *GS* (1887) Nietzsche will explicitly canvasses the idea that "'Will to truth' – that could be a hidden will to death" (344).

In *BGE* Nietzsche unmasks the asceticism of the will to truth. It has, he suggests, developed its own verbal masks: "beautiful, glittering, jingling, festive words: honesty, love of truth, love of wisdom, sacrifice for the sake of knowledge, heroism of the truthful" (*BGE* 230). Nietzsche insists that philosophers must see through their own masquerade and recognise their own drive to truth as a continuation and sublimation of ascetic cruelty. Nietzsche identifies the philosopher's task as translating man back into nature. Just as philosophers must now confront the rest of nature hardened by the discipline of science so too they must confront human nature to gain control over "the many vain and fanciful interpretations that have been scrawled over the eternal basic text of *homo natura*" (*BGE* 230). Nietzsche identifies his very own genealogy of the unconditional will to truth as exemplifying the cruel or ascetic project of "translat[ing] man back into nature" (*BGE* 230).

After describing this cruel pursuit of knowledge as a "strange and insane task" Nietzsche immediately pauses to ask why free spirits have chosen this task, or "'why knowledge at all?'" (*BGE* 230) In posing this question he addresses the issue of the *value* of this task, not its origins. As we shall see in Book 5, Nietzsche stresses that science cannot itself justify the choice to pursue knowledge unconditionally: it is an ethical choice or orientation, ultimately a choice of a way of life.[20] What might explain or justify this ethical choice? Nietzsche admits that free spirits find justifying the value of this choice difficult and unsettling since they have asked themselves this question "a hundred times" (*BGE* 230). In other words, he admits

---

[20] See also Monod: "To place the postulate of objectivity as the condition of true knowledge constitutes an ethical choice, and not a judgement of knowledge, since according to the postulate itself, there could be no 'true' knowledge prior to this arbitral choice" (quoted in Hadot 2006: 186).

that there is no easy or satisfying answer that justifies valuing this task. Indeed, he strongly implies that they have the greatest difficulty arriving at a satisfactory answer since they obsessively return to this question. In fact, Nietzsche conceals their answer through the rhetorical device of aposiopesis (or literally, becoming silent): "we have found and can find no better answer ..." (*BGE* 230). Nietzsche's ellipsis makes it difficult, if not impossible to identify their answer, but one plausible possibility lies precisely in this silence. Nietzsche frequently uses aposiopesis to compel readers to reconstruct and complete his line of thought.[21] In this case, however, he seems to use it to signify an absence: free spirits can give no reasons for valuing their "insane task" (*BGE* 230). Nietzsche unmasks the heroic truth teller as another madman. As we shall see, Nietzsche revisits the issue of the origins and value of the unconditional drive to truth in *GS* Book 5. By 1887 he will conceive the modern scientific commitment to an unconditional will to truth as the final avatar of the metaphysical devaluation of life rather than as the highest affirmation of life.

Returning to GS Book 3, we can catch a glimpse of the reason that in 1887 edition of *GS* Nietzsche ultimately identifies free spirits as "artists" (P4) rather than heroic truth seekers or modern scientists. Scientific explanation, he implies, eliminates erroneous value or ideals (7), but it cannot do what is required to cultivate "the free-spiritedness and many-spiritedness of humanity": viz. create values. In Book 3 Nietzsche identifies the distinguishing mark of the human species precisely with its ability to create for itself new value horizons. Nietzsche claims that value horizons are not merely propositions or representations, but evaluations that we translate into "flesh and reality" (301). Our nature, we might say, is a function of our poetics. We incorporate or embody our values. On this view, our nature is inseparable from the values that shape the scope and dynamics of our drives. That is to say, Nietzsche implies that our 'nature' is a function of the values we translate into ways of life and their associated drive structures and sensations of pleasure and pain (see also *D* 38). What

---

[21] See, e.g., Allison (1994: 463–464): "Aposiopesis is an especially effective figure, since it forces the reader ... to supply additional cognitive, emotional, and semantic material to complete what was initially written or spoken ... the audience feels itself obliged to complete the utterance, to make sense out of what was only partially or incompletely expressed".

marks out our species from other animals, he claims, is precisely its unique capacity to make and remake the only world that concerns us, "the world of valuations, colours, weights, perspectives, scales, affirmations and negations", through the creation of value horizons and orientations (301).

In developing his counter-project of naturalising humanity then Nietzsche does not turn his attention to scientific explanations or descriptions of nature, but to the role of what he calls our "ideal impulse", which he sees as culturally expressed through religion, morality and art (139). Nietzsche's conceives the work of this ideal impulse by analogy with the artist's techniques of colouration. He formulates an extended sense of our artistic or idealising drive such that it encompasses the way religion, morality and arts 'colour' our experiences. Nietzsche explains in a parable, for example, how belief in the wrathful God of the Old Testament created a "Jewish landscape", a "gloomy ... perpetual day-night" that engendered a profound need for a "single sunbeam", "a ray of the most undeserved 'grace'" through the miracle of God's 'love'".[22] Only in a landscape darkened by God as judge or hangman "could Christ dream of his rainbow and his heavenly ladder on which God descended to man".[23] By contrast, he suggest, because ancient Greek polytheism made "good weather and sunshine" the rule the ancient Greeks did not need redemption from the world (137).

Nietzsche suggests then that our experiences are illuminated differently according to how different cultural forms employ their "ideal impulse" (139 see also *HH* 214). Contrasting the way ancient and modern humanity experiences life, death the future, 'truth', injustice, passion and philosophy, he observes: "We have given things a new colour; we keep painting them – but what can we nowadays accomplish in comparison to the *splendour of colour* of that old master!

---

[22] Nietzsche's interpretation of Judaism has generated significant debate. One of the central issues is whether, despite his well-documented opposition to German political anti-Semitism, especially the rabid anti-Semitism of his brother-in law Bernard Förster, he nonetheless held profoundly anti-Jewish prejudices. *GS* 135–140 suggests that Nietzsche did harbour anti-Jewish prejudices. Here he argues that that the whole world has been 'Judaised' through Christian morality, which, he claims, incorporates the Jews' moral genius, its 'evil eye' or contempt for all that is human; see Golomb (1997); Golomb and Wistrich (2002); and Holub (2016).

[23] Nietzsche incorporates and expands this analysis in *GM* II. 22.

I mean ancient humanity" (154). We may have broken with ancient masters' 'styles', he implies, but we too are artists who colour our experiences. Nietzsche's point is that our 'artistic' styles may undergo radical changes, but our nature is such that we always deploy our ideal or artistic impulse to colour our experiences and in doing so shaping the dynamics and directions of our drives. By colouring our experiences, he suggests, our ideal or artistic impulse is the means through which we are able to discharge, purify, gild, perfect and ennoble drives or annihilate, dirty, disfigure and darken them (139).

Nietzsche generalises this claim in his identification of our species as "*homo poeta*", or the human being as poet (153). Nietzsche marks out our species from other animals in terms of its poetic or idealising drive. He echoes here his opening section, which, we might recall, differentiates our species as a fantastic animal, or animal of fantasy, "that must fulfill one condition of existence more than any other animal: it must from time to time believe [it] knows why [it] exists" (1). Nietzsche suggests the human animal's transformation of itself into a fantastic animal is the source of a "tragedy of tragedies" that it has not yet resolved. Personifying humanity in the first-person singular, he writes:

I myself, who most single-handedly made this tragedy of tragedies in so far as it is finished; I, having first tied the knot of morality into existence and drawn it so tight only a god could loosen it – which is what Horace demands! – I myself have now in the fourth act slain all the gods, out of morality! What is now to become of the fifth act? From where shall I take the tragic solution! Should I begin considering a comic solution? (153)

Nietzsche's humanity conceives its history as a poetic drama of its own composition. Humanity is a poet in the sense that it composes the tragedy that it lives. Humanity creates its own drama. Nietzsche's humanity also conceives this tragedy as still incomplete or undecided: it imagines itself at the close of the fourth act and in the midst of attempting to figure out a solution to its problem in a fifth and final act. What is the "tragedy of tragedies" that humanity has created for itself?

To understand the unresolved problem Nietzsche represents humanity as confronting we need to recall how he uses the term "tragedy" in *GS*. From the beginning of *GS* Nietzsche identifies tragedy with morality, or the teaching of a "purpose" (1). In the opening section he stresses that "we still live in the age of tragedy, in the age of moralities and religions" in which the "comedy of existence has not yet 'become conscious' of it itself" (1). As we saw in our discussion of Book 1, Nietzsche argues in this section that we have become creatures with a metaphysical need for tragedies conceived as moralities that teach us that life has a purpose. The founders of moralities and religions, those he describes as the "great teachers of a purpose", he suggests, have altered human nature to such an extent that humanity has become a "fantastic animal" that requires tragedies (or moralities) that make it seem as if living is worth it (1). Without these tragedies, he argues, this fantastic animal would have no faith or trust in life. In the long run, Nietzsche claims, these tragedies are always "vanquished by laughter, reason and nature" (1). "The brief tragedy", as he puts it, "always . . . returned into the eternal comedy of existence" (1). Yet since we have become animals who need tragedies or moral teachings of purpose as *a condition of our existence* we must always invent new teachings of the purpose of existence. Humanity cannot live without morality.

Nietzsche elaborates the effects of re-inventing ourselves as fantastic animals through a playful perspectival shift. How, he asks, does this fantastic human animal look from the perspective of other animals? He answers:

I fear that the animals see man as a being like them who in a most dangerous manner has lost his healthy animal understanding – as the insane animal, the laughing animal, the weeping animal, the miserable animal. (224)

Humanity's first tragedy is that it has tied the knot of morality into existence and in doing so recreated itself as an insane animal. The fantastic animal is also a sick animal: it has made life meaningful or interesting for itself by creating ascetic moral values that burden it with a whole range of negative value judgements about nature, including its own nature. By contrast with healthy animal understanding, he implies, the fantastic animal humanity satisfies its need for meaning or purpose by turning against its own animal nature.

If the first of our tragedies is to tie the knot of morality into existence what is the tragedy of tragedies? The tragedy of tragedies is that humanity has "slain all the gods" who might have been able to cut the knot of morality and it has done so "out of morality!" Horace's instruction, in the *Ars Poetica* 189, is to the effect that in poetry a god should intervene or be introduced only if a difficulty in the plot (a knot) is unable to be unravelled at the level of human actors and action. As we have seen, Nietzsche suggests that since humanity has become a fantastic creature that require tragedies, or teachings of moral purpose, as a necessary condition of our existence, it would require a god to unravel the knot of morality. Only a god could untie the knot of morality and yet we have slain all gods. We cannot therefore unravel morality from the knot of existence. If we wish to free ourselves from morality our situation appears hopeless. Nietzsche then imagines humanity addressing to itself the following questions: "What is now to come in the fifth act? From where shall I take the tragic solution? Should I begin considering a comic solution?"

In this section Nietzsche once again frames the central issue of *GS*. It suggests that we have arrived at pivotal point in our history: we must confront the tragedy of tragedies that follows from the fact that we have created ourselves as a fantastic or metaphysical animal that has a need for morality or purpose. We cannot, so Nietzsche implies, unravel this knot from existence. In *GS* 125 Nietzsche suggests that to untie morality from existence must lead to the most extreme disorientation or nihilism. The particular Christian morality we have knotted into our interpretations and evaluations of existence, he argues, has given us a sense of purpose at the price of becoming "insane animals" who find value only in turning away from life, in their own ascetic contempt for life. Nietzsche saw this ascetic contempt for life built into Christian values gradually emerging in its purest form in modern European pessimism. The most radical atheists like Schopenhauer who argue for the ungodliness of existence condemn existence because it 'fails' to satisfy the human desire for purpose. After the death of God, modern pessimists claim, the only meaningful activity still possible is to turn against life and condemn it. In this respect, Schopenhauer represents "the prophet of deep darkness and the eclipse of the sun the like of which has probably never existed before on earth" (343). Since, according to Schopenhauer, we cannot realise our ideals in this world, our only redemption lies in turning against our existence. For those "in whom the will has turned and denied itself", as he puts in the closing line of *WWR*, "this very real world of ours with all its suns and milkways is – nothing" (*WWR* 1: 412).

For Nietzsche the central issue is not whether humanity can untie the knot of morality from existence; this, he argues, is impossible for the kind of fantastic animal we have become over millennia. It is, rather, whether, as a poet, humanity can tie the knot of a *new* morality or ideal into existence, a knot that does not grow from the ascetic contempt for life.[24] Nietzsche begins with a 'comic' solution. He identifies this as gay science that aims to liberate free spirits from the old ascetic morality by satirising it, but only as a step towards a tragic solution: the invention or reinvention of a 'Dionysian' ideal that opposes Christianity's ascetic ideal and what Nietzsche conceives as its secular democratic expressions. As we shall see, Nietzsche looks to new philosophers who in the present can reverse so-called eternal values and in doing so "knot together the constraint which compels the will of millennia on to *new* paths" (*BGE* 203). If it is impossible to untie the knot of morality from existence, can free spirits transform it or tie into existence a new life-affirming morality in place of life-denying morality?

To address this question, in GS 143, Nietzsche contrasts the polytheistic gods as supreme artists against the supreme symbol of ascetic morality, the Judaeo-Christian God. What is at stake in *GS* 153 is how free spirits should address the loss entailed by the murder of polytheism at the hands of monotheistic morality. If we interpret it this way, Nietzsche is suggesting that the tragedy of tragedies is that Christian morality has brought about the death of many gods, or polytheism. In Book 3 Nietzsche claims that polytheism was the "invaluable preliminary exercise [*Vorübung*]" that justified and enabled individuals to create for themselves their very own ideal, or to become who they are, as he will put it. It is this "preliminary form" of "the free-spiritedness and many-spiritedness", he laments, that monotheism prevented from developing through its rigid morality of a single normal type, "*the* human being" (143). As we shall see, Nietzsche will place enormous stress on the value of creating one's *own* ideal. Nietzsche's project of naturalising humanity aims to extend polytheism's preliminary exercises in enabling the individual to "to posit his *own* ideal" (143). As he observes in the next book, in a distant age "the whole of religion" might appear as "preludes and

---

[24] *BGE* 203.

preliminary exercises [*Vorübungen*]" that make it possible for a few individuals to enjoy the whole self-sufficiency of a god and all his powers of self-redemption" (300). As we shall see in the next chapter, in Book 4 Nietzsche implies that his test of eternal recurrence is just such an exercise in self-redemption.

Nietzsche suggests, then, that we can conceive ancient Greek polytheism as prelude to and preliminary exercise in the redemption of nature or the naturalisation of humanity.[25] As we have seen, Nietzsche's notion of an artistic or idealising drive encompasses morality, religion and arts insofar as all three constitute value horizons that colour or regulate our natural drives. What then is the basis of Nietzsche' complaint about the paintings of that "old master . . . ancient humanity" (152)?

Following his earlier analysis in *D*, Nietzsche claims that we have inherited a morality of custom or herd morality that typified human cultures in the many millennia prior to the beginning of the Gregorian calendar, and it is this 'social straitjacket' that has proven decisive for the fundamental character of humanity (*D* 14). Nietzsche maintain that our moral errors are long standing evolutionary outcomes that have become part our species' basic endowment. He construes these moral errors as a particular type of epistemic error: they are judgements and evaluations that orient and structure relationships among individuals to ensure the security of the group or collective. Nietzsche brings these errors under the rubric of 'the morality of custom' or 'herd' morality. Nietzsche identifies the error of this morality with the view that its table of values is eternal or good in and of itself (110, 115, 143). In other words, the fundamental error of morality resides in the notion of values as metaphysically grounded rather than as the products of natural history. Nietzsche identifies a second error in the conception of 'nature' we find in the morality of custom and its Christian avatars: viz. the erroneous assumption that our drives necessarily have a fixed value or character and that they are also tied to particular pains, sufferings or miseries (or their opposites). Rather, he argues, whether a given drive

---

[25] See Klossowski (2004:82): "If for most people Nietzsche's name is inseparable from the utterance *God is dead*, then it may seem surprising to speak of the religion of *many* gods with regard to Nietzsche".

is healthy or unhealthy depends on "the ideals and phantasms of our soul" (120) and whether we experience it as a pleasure or pain depends on how morality colours it (138, 326; *D* 38).

Herd morality, Nietzsche argues, creates a moral conscience and its concomitant sensations, the "pang of conscience", which ensure each individual becomes a functional, adaptable element of the collective.[26] This morality, as Nietzsche conceives it, ranks drives and actions in ways that most benefit the herd. Morality", as he puts it, "is herd-instinct in the individual" (116). In the context of the morality of custom, he suggests, members of the collective felt more moral to the extent that "the herd instinct not the sense of self spoke through their actions" (117). "To be a self, to estimate oneself according to one's own measure and weight", as he explains, "– that was contrary to taste in those days. The inclination to this would have been considered madness" (117). Nietzsche frames this morality as an instrument that has evolved to preserve the community or the herd at the price of individual differentiation (116/117). It did so, he argues, by ranking drives and actions in ways that most benefit the herd and in doing so creating a moral conscience and sensations that ensures each individual becomes a functional, adaptable element of the herd. This moral horizon, he argues, fundamentally shaped even our sensations of pleasure and pain: pleasure derived from conforming to the law and pain from being alone and experiencing things individually; one was, as Nietzsche puts it "sentenced 'to be an individual'" (117; see also 50). "To be *hostile* to this drive to have one's own ideal", as he puts it, "that was formerly the law of every morality" (143).

Yet, as Nietzsche later acknowledges in Book 5, to identify the erroneous interpretations that have justified morality does not address the question of the *value* of this morality (345). In Book 3 Nietzsche takes a few steps towards addressing the question of the value of this morality through the invidious contrast he draws between Christian monotheism and Greek polytheism. Nietzsche argues that polytheism has a great advantage over monotheism insofar as the former made it possible for "an individual to posit his *own* ideal and to derive his own law, joys and rights" (143). Nietzsche

---

[26] Nietzsche later elaborates the origins and development of moral conscience in *GM* Book 2.

claims that "the wonderful art and power of creating gods – polytheism – was that through which this drive [to have one's own ideal] could discharge itself, perfect and ennoble itself" (143). Nietzsche then identifies polytheism as a religion that stood outside of and opposed to the morality of custom that until recently entirely shaped our moral horizon. It gave free range to the 'madness' and self-idolatry of individuals who wished to create their own ideal and live in accord with their own measures and weights (117). Against Christianity's monochromatic morality, Nietzsche turns to Greek religion and art to sketch an alternative 'poetics' of life.

Nietzsche's makes both a general and specific point about Greek religion's use of the ideal impulse to deify or gild natural drives. Ancient Greek polytheism and tragic and epic art, he argues, made it possible to purify, perfect and ennoble the passions, where Christianity used the ideal impulse to annihilate the passions (139). The Greeks, he claims, invented tragedy to dignify or ennoble individual heroes' passions, even the most sacrilegious, where Christian religion condemned them as contraventions of supernatural or metaphysical principles (135). In *GM* Nietzsche later elaborates and clarifies this same point:

> That the conception of the gods does not, as *such*, necessarily lead to the deterioration of the imagination . . . that there are *nobler* ways of making use of the invention of the gods than man's self-crucifixion and self-abuse, ways in which Europe excelled during the last millennia – this fortunately can be deduced from any glance at the Greek *gods*, these reflections of noble and proud men in whom the *animal* in man felt deified, did *not* tear itself apart and did not rage against itself! These Greeks . . . used their gods expressly to keep at bay bad conscience so that they could carry on enjoying their freedom of the soul: therefore the very opposite of the way Christendom used its God. (*GM* II.23)

Here Nietzsche applauds Greek religion for enabling even the very 'worst' Homeric hero like the adulterer and murderer Aegisthus to avoid suffering bad conscience for their acts of 'folly' (*GM* II.24). In Book 3 Nietzsche argues just this point: in contrast to Christianity, Greek religion turned its ideal or artistic impulse "towards the passions and loved, elevated, gilded and deified them" (139). Ancient Greek individuals in the throes of the passions felt "not only happier but also purer and more divine" (139).

Nietzsche specific claim is that Greek polytheism made it possible for the Greeks to deify not simply the animal in man, but the precise drive that *distinguishes* humanity from animals. What marks out our species from other animals, he claims, is its unique capacity to make and remake the only world that concerns it through the creation of value horizons and orientations. Nietzsche claims that humanity is unique in its capacity to create new horizons and in doing so invent entirely new types of humanity, or 'over-humanity'. Nietzsche suggests that for the human species alone, "there are no eternal horizons and perspectives" (143).[27] Nietzsche's naturalism seeks to revive what we might call this uniquely human artistic power.

In *GS* Book 3 Nietzsche distinguishes humanity as the *only* animal species that has the power to create for itself new horizons (143). For Nietzsche 'perspectivism', as he later calls it, is first and foremost an anthropological rather than an epistemological category: it identifies the exclusively human capacity "to create for ourselves our own new eyes and ever again new eyes that are ever more our own eyes" (143). In Nietzsche's perspective, to live in accordance with human nature is to exercise this power to overcome or transform oneself through the creation of new value horizons. "Man", as he later puts this point, "is the animal *whose nature has not yet been fixed*" (*BGE* 62). For Nietzsche, this perspectivism opens up the possibility of individual self-overcoming as well as the "artistic refashioning" of humankind (*BGE* 62). Individual and collective refashioning is possible, he implies, because human nature is not yet finalised. Our species alone can create new values and translate these into reality. To the extent that it retains this unique power of creating new perspectives or value horizons our species cannot be fixed at a final point of evolution.

Nietzsche's free spirits fight the shadows of God in the name of reclaiming this artistic or creative power. Nietzsche uses the concept of 'art' in this sense as an expression of 'life', an excess of imaginative or artistic force that seeks to create new value perspectives and with them new forms or types of life.[28] To redeem nature, in Nietzsche's

---

[27] Cf. Lampert (1993: 8, 314). Laurence Lampert argues that Nietzsche believes in three "deadly" truths: the sovereignty of becoming, the fluidity of all concepts, types and kinds, and the lack of any cardinal distinction between human and animal.

[28] See also Lemm (2016: 71): "what we find at the heart of Nietzsche's conception of life is precisely the power to change our form of life by means of value creation".

sense, requires not simply embracing what we have become, our human animality, but also and more importantly, in Richard Schacht's words, "what we *have it in us* to become" (Schacht 1988: 75). Significantly, Nietzsche makes the worth of the "new eyes" we might create dependent on these becoming more and more our *own* eyes. It is important to recognises that Nietzsche weaves into his notion of value creation the ideal of seeing or evaluating the world through "eyes" that are exclusively our own. In key later sections he repeatedly lays great stress on variations of the adjectival modifier 'own' (*eigen*) to define this ideal (e.g. 335, 338). If, as he holds, we incorporate or drill into flesh and reality our values, then to progressively refine these values so that they become more and more our own is to make or create ourselves as distinctively ourselves. Nietzsche's emphasis on creating our own eyes implies that the free spirits' ideal is not simply to differentiate themselves from the many, but to differentiate themselves from the many in such a way that they become who they are. Nietzsche's motto 'become who you are' sums up his project of naturalising humanity.

On the other hand, Nietzsche claims the Christian horizon within which modern Europeans have lived is structured to eliminate the very possibility of creating new horizons. In this sense, Nietzsche conceives Christianity as 'anti-perspectivist' or anti-artistic. Christian monotheism has posed "the greatest danger to humanity", he argues, insofar as it attacks this uniquely human capacity (143). To seek to establish a metaphysical or eternal horizon, as Christianity does, is to turn against the 'artistic' power of human life. By this means, he suggests Christianity threatens to eliminate the species' capacity to evolve or 'overcome' itself: "The consequence of monotheism's teaching of a normal human type – that is, the belief in a normal god next to whom there are only false, pseudo-god – was perhaps the greatest danger to humanity so far: it threaten us with premature stagnation" (*GS* 143). In his later formulation Nietzsche condemns Christian morality because it

relegates art, *every* art, to the realm of lies; with its absolute standards, beginning with the truthfulness of God, it negates, judges and damns art. Behind this mode of valuation ... I never failed to sense a *hostility to life itself*: a furious, vengeful antipathy to life itself: for all life is based on semblance, art, deception, points of view, and the necessity of perspectives and error. (*BT* ASC 5)

In other words, when Nietzsche characterises Christianity as a paradoxical "life *against* life" (*GM* III.13), he means, among other things, that it turns against what he identifies as distinctive of the human species, its creative or poetic power. Nietzsche claims that the cultural expression of this threat takes the form of the morality of custom or herd morality and its sublimations, the spiritualised forms of which he identifies with Christian moral conscience and Kant's metaphysics of morals (see 193). Nietzsche claims that Christian morality threatens to both 'functionalise' individuals, such that they only value themselves to the extent that they contribute to the security of the herd, and to halt the human species' evolution by teaching one single norm as applicable to all. The rule of European Christianity, as he later expresses it, represents an "almost deliberate degeneration and stunting of man" that creates "a ludicrous species, a herd animal" (*BGE* 62). It represents the danger of translating "the morality of custom into flesh and blood" (143). Nietzsche aims to rescue or revalue art precisely because he sees it is the means through which the human species maintains its capacity for self-overcoming. Without 'art', as Nietzsche conceives, the species cannot cross the bridge from the beast to higher humanity.

Nietzsche indicts Judaeo-Christian morality on the grounds that it eliminates the species as '*polytropos*", a complicated species of 'many turns', as we might literally translate the ancient Greek word. It does so, he claims, by affirming and cultivating only those uniform traits and drives that make individuals fit for collective life. It attempts to make the species a herd animal and it therefore glorifies an ascetic life of self-sacrifice and self-denial as conditions of collective life. As we shall see, in questioning the value of the unconditional will to truth in Book 5 Nietzsche will explicitly suggest that life on the largest scale is on the side of the "*polytropos*", the word Homer famously used to describe Odysseus in the epic's first line, rather than the single-minded truth teller (344). Nietzsche's project of naturalising humanity then requires cultivating artistic powers that maintain the species as "*polytropos*".

Nietzsche's account of the human being as poet appears to be the culmination of Book 3's argument. After this section the book consists of a gallimaufry of 122 sections, many in the French moralist's style of 'cynical' maxims unmasking human, all-too-human follies and vanities. However, Nietzsche does round out Book 3 with what he later calls eight "granite sentences" (268–275) that, so he grandly asserts, "formulate a destiny for *all* ages" (*EH* 3 GS). Nietzsche writes these sentences in the style of a catechism: a single question in the informal second person, followed by a very brief one-line answer. In the final three sections Nietzsche questions the value of shame. Nietzsche's answers suggest that overcoming shame before oneself and resisting shaming others counts as "most human" (274). Nietzsche criticism of shame continues his naturalistic defence of the *polytropos*: to overcome shame is to allow oneself the luxury of all one's ownmost drives rather than banishing or concealing one's drives to meet collective moral demands. To cultivate the many-facetedness of our individuality, Nietzsche implies, requires overcoming the shame that binds us to the herd.[29] In this respect, Nietzsche closes with a nod to both the Cynic's scandalous shamelessness (*anaideia*) and the free-spiritedness and many-spiritedness of the *Provençale* troubadours whose lyric poetry and invention of love inspired *GS*.[30] "Perhaps", as Nietzsche remarks in a note from 1883, "the *Provençale* was already a high point in Europe, very rich, many-faceted human beings who nevertheless were master of themselves, were not ashamed of their drives" (*KSA* 7 ([44]).

Undoubtedly, however, the most important of Nietzsche's granite sentence quotes the ancient Greek epinician poet Pindar's second Pythian Victory Ode:

What does your conscience say? – 'You should become who you are'". (270)[31]

---

[29] We should note, however, that though Nietzsche values overcoming shame about one's drives, this does not entail that he also endorses a lack of shame at failing to *realise* one's drives in competition with others. Nietzsche's advocacy of Greek agon or competition seems to indicate that he approves of shame over competitive failure.

[30] Aristotle described the ancient Cynics as making a "cult of shamelessness [*anaideia*], not as being beneath modesty, but as superior to it". Aristotle, *Rhetoric*, "Scholium", quoted in Navia (1996: 94).

[31] For a detailed analysis of Nietzsche's use of the Pindar quotation, see Higgins (2000) and Hamilton (2004).

As we shall see in the next chapter, Nietzsche formulates and defends an alternative notion of conscience based on the principle of 'become who you are' as the naturalistic counter to the Christian moral conscience that continues to cast a long shadow over the lives of modern Europeans.

CHAPTER 5

Sanctus Januarius: *Book 4*

In *GS* Book 4 Nietzsche continues to develop his overarching project, which, as we have seen, aims to "*naturalise* humanity with a pure, newly discovered, newly redeemed nature" (109). Nietzsche aims to rediscover and redeem nature from what he later calls the ascetic ideal. His overriding hope is that he can liberate free spirits from the spell of ascetic value judgements that identify the highest life as one that limits, paralyses or denies the expression of natural drives. The ascetic ideal has been, as he later put it, "the ultimate 'for want of anything better' par excellence" (*GM* III.28).

In Book 4 Nietzsche gives one of his most sustained attempts to formulate his alternative ethics of self-cultivation by means of two of his famous 'doctrines': viz. *amor fati* and eternal recurrence. Nietzsche's goal is to explain the emergence of the ascetic denial of life and identify an alternative affirmation of life. Or more precisely, his project is to formulate an affirmation of life that enhances the prospects of the highest types of individuals. It takes the shape of seeing and selecting 'higher' ways of life and identifying interpretations or evaluations that best facilitate the emergence of higher individuals who wish for *more* life, or, as he puts it later in *GS*, who suffer from a "*superabundance*" rather than "*an impoverishment of life*" (370). Against the ascetic ideal that he believes motivates Platonic metaphysics, Stoic 'petrification', Epicurean moderation, Christian moral self-abnegation and Schopenhauer's denial of life, Nietzsche aims to formulate a new value perspective, the 'sunshine' of a new ethical doctrine that can motivate the emergence of "high spirits" (288). He holds out the enchanting possibility that such a new ideal might create human beings "of one elevated feeling, the embodiment of a single great mood" (288).

Before turning to Nietzsche's development of this ethics in Book 4, we need to understand his interpretation and criticisms of the ascetic ideal that he seeks to counter. We might recall that in *GS* 1 Nietzsche claims that though all of our ethical systems have run "contrary to nature" but nonetheless have served to satisfy a peculiarly human need to invent reasons or purpose in life (1). Humanity, he argued, has become that fantastic animal that cannot live without trust in life. Unlike other animals, we need 'reasons' for declaring that life is worth living. "If we possess our *why* of life", as he later put it, "we can put up with almost any *how*" (*TI* 'Maxims', 12). In *GS* 1, as we have seen, Nietzsche also identifies a "new law of ebb and flood", a recurring cycle of tragedy and comedy: moral teachers conceive nature in terms of a purpose or goal, creating and satisfying our need for a belief in the meaningfulness of nature, and supporting our belief that life is worth living, and yet "laughter, reason and nature" always vanquishes these interpretations (1). In this context Nietzsche conceives the "the tragic" as a faith that supports our judgement that life is worth living. He argues that "the tragic with all its sublime unreason" is a necessary condition of species' preservation (1). In *GS* Nietzsche identifies his own project with both the comic and tragic elements of this cycle: he aims to vanquish the hitherto dominant ascetic ideal and to reclaim a new conception of 'the tragic', which might instil a new trust in the value of living. In *GS* Book 3, as we have seen, Nietzsche claims that with the death of God we moderns are witnessing the culmination of the ascetic ideal, or a will directed against life. Free spirits, he suggests, are on the verge of conceiving a new horizon. As we shall see, he closes Book 4 with his new conception of a new tragic affirmation: '*Incipit tragoedia*' (342).

What is this ascetic ideal, as Nietzsche dubs it later in *GM*? Nietzsche exposes the ascetic ideal and its method of giving meaning to life in *GM*'s final section:

It is absolutely impossible for us to conceal what was actually expressed by that whole willing that derives its direction from the ascetic ideal: this hatred of the human, and even more the animalistic, even more of the material, this horror of the senses, of reason itself, this fear of happiness and beauty, this longing to get way from appearance, transience, growth, death, wishing, longing itself – all that means ... *a will to nothingness*, an aversion to life, a rebellion against the most fundamental prerequisites of life, it is and remains a *will*. (*GM* III. 28)

As we noted in the Introduction, Nietzsche identifies a terrible paradox in the ascetic ideal: it values or gives meaning to life only as the instrument of its own extinction. The ascetic ideal makes life denial the highest value or meaning. At the same time, he analyses this life-denying ideal as a means of redeeming the will: it has served to protect the species from "suicidal nihilism" by giving its suffering a meaning. "The meaninglessness of suffering, *not* the suffering", as Nietzsche puts it, "was the curse that so far blanketed mankind – and *the ascetic ideal offered man a meaning*!" (*GM* III.28). The ascetic ideal preserves life by giving it a meaning, but it does not affirm life (Hatab 2008: 170). Nietzsche recognises that to will nothingness, as the ascetic ideal demands, is to will something; or, as he famously put it, "man still prefers to will *nothingness*, than *not* will" (*GM* III 28). The ascetic ideal 'saves' the will only by willing nothingness.

Nietzsche identifies Platonism's notion of the philosophical life as a preparation for dying as the original expression of the ascetic ideal. In the *Phaedo*, Plato's Socrates conceived philosophical asceticism as preparation for the soul's separation from the body and its ascent to a transcendent world. "True philosophers", as Socrates explains, "make dying their profession and ... to them of all men death is least alarming" (*Ph.* 67 c–e). In *GS* Nietzsche identifies Stoicism and Epicureanism as variations on the ascetic ideal insofar as they extirpate or minimise the passions (respectively) to achieve tranquillity in this world. Similarly, Christianity, he claims, paradoxically preserves an attachment to life by granting the highest value to slow suicide as the means to eternal redemption (131).

As we observed in the Introduction, despite all the important differences among our philosophical and religious traditions, Nietzsche believes they all express weakness or disease in this ascetic denial of life. Nietzsche identifies Schopenhauer's "unconditional and honest atheism", his rejection of belief in otherworldly transcendence or this-worldly redemption, as a turning point (357). After the death of God, Schopenhauer argues, we must recognise that this is the worst of all possible worlds: life is nothing other than unrelieved and meaningless suffering. Schopenhauer argues that voluntary denial of the will is our only salvation from the suffering that is life.

He propose that we must, like ascetic saints, seek out and inflict suffering on ourselves in order to achieve the only salvation possible: the annihilation of the will that causes us to suffer. Schopenhauer's radical denial of life promises as its highest reward that one shall not be reborn: 'You will not again assume phenomenal existence' (*WWR* I: 356). As we shall see, Nietzsche's affirmation of life engenders the wish for rebirth. For Schopenhauer "Nirvana" or "nothingness", must suffice as our only consolation (*WWR* I: 411).

It is in this sense that Nietzsche conceives Schopenhauer's will to nothingness as the culmination of the "hitherto reigning ideal" (*GM* II.24). Schopenhauer's pessimism is the culmination of the nihilistic devaluation of life that, so Nietzsche claims, is the "secret code" to the entire Western philosophical and religious tradition (Hatab 2006: 31). European culture's deeply entrenched nihilism, he suggests, finally became explicit in Schopenhauer's judgement that ascetic self-denial itself is our only salvation. Here the ascetic will to the denial of life emerges fully fledged as unconditional nihilism, "the great nausea, the will to nothingness" (*GM* II.24). For Nietzsche, Schopenhauer's radical pessimism emblematises the nihilism that we moderns have inherited and must confront.

How does Nietzsche explain the emergence and durability of the ascetic ideal? How has our species come to give meaning to the suffering of life by turning against its own nature and in doing so inflicting upon itself even more suffering? How, in Nietzsche's rhetorically charged language, has the world become such a "madhouse" (*GM* II.22)? The ascetic ideal, Nietzsche claims, is the interpretive framework that sustains the *weakest* forms of life. It gives meaning to the suffering of individuals too ill to affirm natural life and who suffer from it as from a disease. The ascetic ideal gives meaning to their lives by granting the highest value to their desire for nothingness, or their desire to not exist. It transforms their diseased or pathological inability to affirm life into a highly valued 'ethical' project. By means of the ascetic ideal their inability to affirm life is interpreted as a virtue and revalued as a meaningful project of freeing themselves from the very conditions of natural life. Our 'highest' value systems, Nietzsche claims, have all served to justify and preserve the weakest or most incapacitated forms of life. Nietzsche diagnoses how variations of the ascetic ideal have given meaning to depressed, diseased ways of life. Platonism, Hellenism and Christianity, he suggests, share a strong family resemblance insofar as in different ways they give meaning to and ennoble this hatred of natural life. They preserve diseased life by granting the highest value to the desire not to live or the will to nothingness. They grant the highest value or meaning to life turned against itself or life as a preparation for death. They are different shadings of "affective nihilism", or the will turned against life (see Gemes 2013).

Nietzsche argues that our ascetic philosophical traditions not only prop up the majority of weak individuals by satisfying their need to give meaning to their suffering but also support them by presenting as the highest values precisely those that undermine the value conditions necessary to sustain and promote strong, healthy individuals. "One should not embellish or dress up Christianity", as he explains in *AC,* "it has waged a *war to the death* against [the] *higher type* of man, it has excommunicated all the fundamental instincts of this type . . . it has taken the side of everything weak, base, ill-constituted, it has made an ideal out of *opposition* to the preservative instincts of strong life . . . my assertion is that all the highest values in which mankind at present summarises its highest desideratum are decadence values" (*AC* 5 and 6). Nietzsche attacks ascetic philosophical and religious doctrines not simply because they are false, but also because he believes they enfeeble the life of the best individuals. In other words, Nietzsche *diagnoses* asceticism as a symptom of illness and *condemns* it as a predatory morality: it is the means by which the weak take revenge on the strong. Nietzsche's goal of creating new life-affirming values and his aristocratic politics are two sides of the one coin. If asceticism has served diseased life at the expense of healthy life, Nietzsche intends his life affirmation to serve healthy life and he is by no means afraid to draw the consequence that it must therefore be at the expense of those who suffer from life and who find meaning and security in defeating this healthy, ascending life.

Let us sum up this survey of Nietzsche's diagnosis of the ascetic ideal. Nietzsche argues that a sense of meaning or purpose is now a condition of human life. Up to this point, he claims, the ascetic ideal has satisfied this condition. Nietzsche argues that until now the ascetic ideal has supplied the *only* meaning; it embodies a fundamental aversion to life; it conceives suffering as meaningful insofar as it is a means to escape from the very conditions of life itself; and it preserve the weakest individuals by exalting their weakness and in doing so undermining values that promote higher, healthier individuals. Nietzsche's grand claim is that almost all previous philosophies fall into the former category and that the value judgements required to sustain higher and lower, stronger and weaker individuals are mutually incompatible. If until now higher individuals have suffered under the curse of an ascetic ideal that values and reinforces a hatred of life, in Book 4 Nietzsche aims to formulate an affirmation of life that will show them the possibility of a new ethics of self-cultivation.

Against the ascetic ideal, then, in Book 4 Nietzsche aims to sketch an 'affirmative' ethics that redeems nature. Naturalising humanity entails identifying evaluative perspectives or interpretations that contribute to its highest flourishing. "*Every* philosophy, indeed *every* art", he suggests, "is a cure or aid in the service of growing, struggling life" (370). Nietzsche aims to distinguish between philosophies that preserve declining life and philosophies that facilitate the flourishing of 'higher', 'healthier' individuals. If one philosophy is the expression of enervated or dying life, another might serve the needs of active, growing, flourishing life.

In Book 4 Nietzsche calls on new philosophers to create "new suns", or philosophical justifications of different "ways of living": "even the evil man, the unhappy man, and the exceptional man should have their philosophy, their good, their sunshine!" (289). Nietzsche explicitly endorses the creation of new philosophies for the sake of the higher forms of life that the ascetic ideal devalues and condemns. Nietzsche figures these free-spirited philosophers as explorers of uncharted seas, "argonauts of the ideal", as he later calls them, not only because they explore how our past ideals have glorified weakness, but because they also seek to discover new values that might instead facilitate strength or greatness (382). Nietzsche exhorts philosophers to "get on the ships" for the purpose of discovering philosophical justifications of exceptional, higher ways of life (289). There are as yet, he suggests, unknown worlds or values that might serve to enhance life. What he values in these prospective new philosophies is not their 'truth', but their capacity to cultivate 'higher' ways of life than those preserved by the ascetic ideal. The role of the new free-spirited philosopher is to create or invent philosophical justifications that establish the conditions of existence for the *antipodes* of the 'good', 'happy' and 'ordinary'. In this context Nietzsche aims to create a new sun that will serve rare individuals who suffer not from an *"impoverishment of life"*, but a *"superabundance of life"*. Nietzsche's famous ideas of '*amor fati*' and eternal recurrence are the "new suns" that he hopes will enhance the flourishing of the healthy few.

We can then unpack Nietzsche's doctrines in light of this grand project of overcoming the ascetic ideal and creating a new value horizon. We can take our initial bearings from Nietzsche's framing on Book 4. Unlike the first three books of *GS* Nietzsche gives Book 4 a title, date, location and an epigraph poem in the form of rhyming couplets:

> **St Januarius**
> You who with your lances burning
> Melt the ice sheets of my soul
> Speed it toward the ocean yearning
> For its highest hope and goal:
> Ever healthier it rises,
> Free in fate most amorous:-
> Thus your miracle it prizes
> Fairest Januarius!   Genoa in January 1882

After the madman's announcement of the death of God in Book 3 Nietzsche opens with this surprising, albeit tongue-in-cheek nod to the miracle associated with the Roman Catholic martyr and patron saint of Naples, St Januarius or Gennaro. According to Catholic legend, Gennaro, the young Bishop of Naples, was a victim of the last great series of Roman persecutions of the Christians under Emperor Diocletian. The great persecution and Gennaros' martyrdom symbolically mark the collapse of Roman paganism and the rise of the first converted Christian Emperor, Constantine. Catholics believe that a reliquary allegedly containing some of Gennaro's blood miraculously liquefies three times a year and on other important occasions. Why did Nietzsche frame his book in term of this Catholic legend of martyrdom and miracle?

First we should note that this allusion to the *miracle* of St Januarius' blood enables Nietzsche to identify the ethics of Book 4 as the expression of a radical and unexpected conversion or melting of the soul. Second, Nietzsche specifies that this conversion takes the form of a 'resurrection', a return to life of a suspended, frozen will, which is free to flow towards its "highest goal". In the rhyming couplet, the first published reference to his Book 4's famous opening New Year's wish, '*amor fati*', Nietzsche identifies it as the outcome of his own *miraculous* resurrection, the melting of his 'frozen' soul and its elevation to new heights. Nietzsche's title and epigraphic poem frames Book 4 as the expression and celebration of a miraculous recovery that results in a paradoxical sense of freedom in "fate most amorous". Third, we should note that by giving his book of ethics the title of a Catholic martyr, Nietzsche implies that his own ethics may also entail martyrdom, or at least the willingness "to rush into a lion's jaw". In a letter to his friend Overbeck written later in the summer of 1882, ten days before the book's completion (15 June), Nietzsche played on these religious overtones of his newly won love of fate: "Also I am possessed of a fatalistic 'surrender to God'– I call it *amor fati*, so much so, that I would rush into a lion's jaw, not to mention" (Middleton 1996: 184).[1]

Following the St Januarius image, one might say that his blood is quickened by anticipation of and craving for the future. Nietzsche identifies '*amor fati*' as a state of possession that transforms his orientation towards *future* action. The ice sheets of the soul that miraculously melt are those fears that inhibit anticipatory desires or passions. Far from engendering indifference or resignation, Nietzsche's fatalism inspires a passion or craving for future goods. With its ice sheets melted, Nietzsche's soul speeds towards "the ocean yearning / For its highest hope and goal". Nietzsche stresses that for one who recovers the love of fate, hope is reborn.

Nietzsche also locates Book 4 in Genoa where he had composed it in the winter of 1882. During the composition of Book 4 he writes in

---

[1] If this is a biblical allusion, then it implies that '*amor fati*' is a faith that one will be rescued from every evil by divine dispensation or grace. See 2 Timothy 4:17–18. Beatrice Han-Pile (2011) identifies this passage as a reference to the book of Daniel 6:16–23, in which Daniel is thrown by Darius into the lions' den to test the power of God.

a letter to Ida Overbeck: "I am bound to Genoa by a work that here alone can come to an end because it has a Genoese character in itself" (19 January 1882). One of the signatures of Nietzsche's texts is what Hadot calls their "emotional geography" (Hadot 2010: 60). Nietzsche incorporates places into his philosophical sensibility. His philosophical dispositions take on or borrow from the character of particular places. Nietzsche represents the Genoese, the city and buildings of Genoa, and the natural promontory of Portofino, as embodiments of the philosophical attitude towards life that he endorses in Book 4. In their architecture and landscapes, as he puts it, the Genoese demonstrate that "they were well disposed towards life" (291).

Nietzsche's suggestion that the *GS* (especially Book 4) has Genoese character indicates that he develops his ethics, his conception of how to live, not only or even primarily from philosophical texts, but from the techniques and styles of architecture, gardens, paintings and music. Nietzsche shows how in some cases these artistic practices disclose a philosophical attitude or disposition. More importantly, he argues that to realise an affirmative ethical ideal requires applying artistic techniques and learning processes. Nietzsche will suggest in Book 4, for example, that we learn to love fate in the same way we become receptive to music. If life is analogous to music, as Nietzsche holds, then we can learn to love it in the same way we become enamoured of a particular tune. Nietzsche's broader point is that realising an affirmative life is partly a matter of artistic technique.

In drawing on the arts as the source of his ethical ideal and techniques of life Nietzsche distinguishes his philosophical practice from contemporaneous German philosophy. Nietzsche does not survey the history of philosophy or formulate a speculative philosophical system in the manner of German idealism. Of the Book's sixty-six sections only two titles explicitly name philosophical figures, and these titles refer only to philosophers or philosophical school that defend the ideal of philosophy as a way of life: *viz.* the Stoics, Epicureans and Socrates (306, 340).[2] Rather, in Book 4, he compiles

---

[2] Nietzsche explicitly mentions two other philosophers in passing: Spinoza and Kant. The former, he argues, develops a mistaken conception of consciousness and the latter, he suggests, is an unwitting philosophical servant of moral dogmatism.

a series of notes sketching his personal wishes, habits and quirks and peppers the book with reflections on the value of artistic techniques for the practice of life. Indeed, Nietzsche declares in his letter to Rohde "there is an image of myself [in *GS*]" (Middleton 1996: 187). The book as whole, as Nietzsche conceives it, is a self-portrait. As Cohen observes, roughly half of the passages in *GS* Book 4 are composed in the first-person singular (2014: 50). As we observed in the Introduction, Nietzsche conceives philosophy as intrinsically biographical: not only do philosophies give an account of the self, they are ways of life as well as exercises in transforming oneself and how one lives. It is these meta-philosophical assumptions that brings Nietzsche into the orbit of the Hellenistic philosophies and explains his radical philosophical and stylistic divergence from conventional German philosophy.

In Book 4 Nietzsche shares the classical model of philosophy as a way of life, which unites Socrates and the Hellenistic schools. What was "fundamentally new in the style and goals of what we call Hellenistic philosophy", as A. A. Long argues, "was most aptly summed up in Michel Foucault's fine expression, 'technology of the self' . . . With the help of philosophy, we can work on ourselves, like a craftsman . . . The Hellenistic art of life makes the remarkable proposal that genuine happiness depends on our making the most *skilful* use of ourselves and the circumstances in which we find ourselves" (Long 2006: 27). Yet though he shares this model of philosophy, Nietzsche suggests that these schools fundamentally misconceived the highest ideal of life affirmation and he develops his analysis of artistic techniques to correct their errors. Indeed, that Nietzsche does not look to the philosophical tradition for his own ethics of the good life is hardly surprising given his diagnosis of all past philosophies as symptoms and reinforcements of illness.

Let us summarise our preliminary orientation to Book 4. Nietzsche's title and epigraph cast this book as the expression of a 'miraculous' or extraordinary transformation that expresses itself as an amorous embrace of fate. It marks a significant turn-point in his philosophical odyssey. Far from this fatalism inspiring resignation or despair, he identifies it with renewed and powerful hope in and anticipation of the future. Nietzsche's framing of the book brings it into connection with the Hellenistic, and especially Stoic ideal of loving fate, but its prizing of *passions* indicates that he intends moving well beyond the Hellenistic schools and formulating a new ethics of self-cultivation.

In Book 4 Nietzsche formulates his doctrines of *amor fati* and the eternal recurrence to elaborate a type of aesthetic education that might counter the ascetic ideal in its various classical, Christian and modern guises and open the way to a new affirmation of life. Nietzsche's aesthetic education is his alternative to the ascetic ideal. In what follows we will consider what Nietzsche means by love of fate, how he thinks we might consummate this love and its connection to the doctrine of eternal recurrence.

Let us first consider his emphatic declaration of his new love, *amor fati*:

For the new year. – I'm still alive; I still think: I must still be alive because I still have to think. *Sum, ergo cogito: cogito, ergo sum.* Today everybody permits himself the expression of his dearest wish and thoughts: so I, too, want to say what I wish from myself today and what thought to run first crossed my heart – what thought shall be for me the reason, warranty, and sweetness of my life! I want to learn more and more to see as beautiful what is necessary in things; then I shall be one of those who make things beautiful. *Amor fati*: let that be my love henceforth! (276)

Here Nietzsche addresses the question, 'How can we learn to love our fate?' Put simply, Nietzsche claims that if we are to love our fate we need to make it appear beautiful, and, I will argue, in making it beautiful we will motivate the desire for its eternal repetition. Nietzsche implies that those who learn how to love their fate will celebrate the idea of their own eternal recurrence as a divine or godlike doctrine. If we conceive Nietzsche thought of the eternal recurrence as an expression and test of self-affirmation, then the means of preparing for and passing this test is learning how to love one's fate, the notion of *amor fati*, as he calls it (276).[3] We need to consider Nietzsche's doctrine in some detail to see how he conceives

---

[3] Here I follow Elgat (2016: 186): "if we are to understand the Eternal Recurrence as a kind of test, then . . . the question arises: How is one to prepare for this test? It is here that *amor fati* enters the picture, for to practice *amor fati* 'from morning till evening' [*GS* 304] to learn to see the necessary and ugly as beautiful and say 'Yes' to it, is, I suggest, precisely the right kind of practice that can enable one to successfully affirm the idea of Eternal Recurrence".

the possibility of loving one's fate to the point of wanting its exact and eternal repetition.

In Book 4's opening section Nietzsche identifies his "dearest thought" as the New Year wish that henceforth he will love his fate (276). Nietzsche highlights the personal nature of his philosophy: he expresses it in terms of one of the most intimate types of wishful thinking. New Year's wishes identify what we might call our 'own-most' hopes for ourselves. Nietzsche identifies the particular nature of his thought by reversing the order of Descartes' famous cogito: "I'm still alive; I still think: I must still be alive because I still have to think. *Sum, ergo cogito: cogito ergo sum*". Nietzsche alludes to Descartes' famous claim in his second *Meditation* that thinking indubitably confirms my existence. Nietzsche's cogito does not identify the epistemic significance of thinking as a refutation of radical scepticism, but the importance of thinking for life.[4] Nietzsche focuses on how thinking is a necessary condition of life: I must still be alive because I still *have* to think. Nietzsche's concern is not to establish an indubitable claim to knowledge, but to identify how we might transform the quality of our personal existence. He investigates the connection between thinking and self-transformation.

Nietzsche suggests that we can learn how to radically transform or transfigure our lives by learning how to love fate. He stresses that he is not merely wishing that this love will happen of its own accord or that he will be overcome with love of fate. On the contrary, Nietzsche expressly states that he now wants to *learn* how to love fate. He does not conceive the love of fate as matter of grace, but as a matter of education.[5] Nietzsche identifies the love of fate as a skill or technique we can gradually develop and perfect so that eventually we will be only 'Yes-sayers'. Nietzsche specifies this technique as a certain art of seeing: "I want to learn more

---

[4] In the free-spirit trilogy Nietzsche conceives and praises Descartes as an advocate of philosophy as a way of life; see also D 550. As the epigraph to the 1878 edition of *Human, All Too Human* Nietzsche used a German translation of a passage from Descartes' 1644 Latin version of his *Discourse on the Method of Rightly Conducting Reason*. On the significance of Nietzsche's Descartes epigraph, see Rethy (1976: 289–297) and Wienand (2015: 49–64).

[5] Cf. Pippin (2012: 13), who argues that Nietzsche, because of his scepticism about self-reflective reason or consciousness, never presented this way of life, the life of *amor fati*, as a recommendation or injunction. However, Nietzsche in fact does present this idea in the form of an injunction, as the title of GS 334 indicates: "One must learn to love".

and more to see as beautiful what is necessary in things; then I shall be one of those who make things beautiful" (276).

Nietzsche identifies 'fate' with necessity and argues that to love what is necessary in things requires making them beautiful. Nietzsche makes the ideal of loving fate a matter of aesthetic perception and judgement. It is not the result of disinterested contemplation of what is necessary in things, he suggests, but the consequence of making them beautiful. Nietzsche wants to learn to *make* things beautiful, not discover and represent beauty as independently existing property of things. To love fate we do not hold up a mirror to nature, but we create or make the qualities of the objects we experience. Beauty, as Nietzsche conceives its, is not the impartial judgement of a disinterested spectator, as Kant and Schopenhauer maintained, but the artefact of the interested agent who wants to make things beautiful. Nor does Nietzsche think that the creation of 'beauty' calms or tranquilises spectators, as the German idealists maintained. Rather he suggests that if we make necessity appear beautiful we engender a passionate desire to experience it again and again. As Nietzsche later explains, "What does all art do? Does it not praise, does it not glorify, does it not select, does it not highlight? By doing all this it strengthens or weakens certain valuations . . . Art is the great stimulus to life" (*TI* 'Skirmishes' 24). Rather than following the German idealist tradition that analyses art in terms of the spectator's judgements and expectations, then, Nietzsche focuses on artistic techniques as the fabrication of appearances.

By learning how to see things as beautiful, he asserts, we can love our fate. The question then is 'How can one *make* things beautiful?' How does Nietzsche think it is possible to satisfy this personal wish to love our fate? Nietzsche addresses this question in the section immediately following his New Year's wish. Nietzsche's develops musical and artistic analogues to conceptualise the affirmative life. In *GS* 277 he develops his account of the artistic technique and skills one must learn to make it possible to love one's fate. To love their fate, he suggests, free spirits must become akin to accomplished musicians: the instrument they play is their own life and its events. Nietzsche specifies this as a theoretical and practical skill of interpretation and arrangement of events and he specifies no limits on the kind of events to which it applies. It consists in making "the beautiful chaos of existence" appear as if it were designed to be "full of deep meaning and use precisely *for us*" (277).[6] For an event to be meaningful for us, as Nietzsche conceives it, we must judge that if it had *failed* to happen our life would lack its proper or full meaning.

We should recall that in *GS* 109 Nietzsche describes the "chaos of existence" in terms of necessary events that lack "order, organization, form, *beauty*, wisdom" or whatever else we call these "aesthetic anthropomorphisms". In *GS* 277 Nietzsche does not reject his principle that we can describe the "total character of the world" as "necessity", but he claims that we can weave these necessities into a beautiful harmony. Nietzsche's free spirits acknowledge the de-deification of the world and therefore reject providence, or the idea that the gods arrange events to suit their wishes and needs. Yet he also maintains that this should and does not preclude them from making the world's necessities appear to them as beautiful or meaningful. Nietzsche describes this as the "dexterity of our wisdom", but unlike the Stoic affirmation of fate, it does not rest on belief in divine providence. He identifies the free spirit's 'compositional' flair as the skill of transforming necessity into a personally meaningful narrative.

In this context Nietzsche identifies "a certain high point in life" at which we perfect this skill (277). At this point, he cautions, we are in danger of losing our scepticism about providential reason and goodness. Instead of abandoning our scepticism, Nietzsche suggests that we should credit the appearance that "everything that befalls us continually *turns out for the best*" as the outcome of our own 'musical' skills of composition (277).[7] If we exercise our dexterity, Nietzsche implies, nothing in our lives could have turned out better. If we acknowledge that everything has turned out for the best then we could not imagine a better alternative life. To the extent that we agree that everything has turned out for the best we must also wish that nothing be any different to how it was. For Nietzsche wisdom is

---

[6] Cf. Danto (1988: 13–28), who argues that Nietzsche's therapeutic aim is to free us from the need to give meaning to existence, especially to our suffering: "Nietzsche sought like a cat a comfortable corner of Europe, and his preposterous exultation at discovering the alleged salubrities of Turin are an index to his discomforts. He did not suffer, however, in the way in which, on his view, the bulk of mankind suffers: from meanings that truncate the lives they are supposed to redeem" (27). Janaway develops a cogent argument against this interpretation. See Janaway (2007: 241–242).

[7] See also *EH*, 'Wise', 2. Nietzsche suggests that for the "well-turned-out" person, "everything *must* turn out for his best".

a kind of musical dexterity or technique of interpreting and arranging events of our life so that we would not want them to be any different to how they have turned out, even though we acknowledge that how they turned out was strictly a matter of impersonal, non-providential necessity.

By Nietzsche's analogy, the events of our lives are like keys or strings of an instrument that we play to create harmonies and melodies. In other words, he suggests that 'meaning' is our own artefact or creation. Whether or not we have a meaningful life is not a function of divine or rational providence, but a function of our own musical or interpretive skills. Nietzsche cautions free spirits not to fall into the danger of believing in divine providence. Nietzsche suggests that belief in providence will engender "spiritual unfreedom" (277). Presumably he thinks that if they believe that a "petty deity" serves their personal needs and wishes they must fail to practice the skill they need to make their lives beautiful (277). Nietzsche suggests that free spirits should acknowledge the value of this skill, but not think "too highly" of it insofar as occasionally "chance" does play a role in guiding our hand as we invent a harmonious life (277). That is to say, Nietzsche acknowledges that chance events can serendipitously contribute to the harmony or meaning we are constructing and do so in ways that are beyond both our skills and the "wisest providence" (277).

Nietzsche stresses that to make our lives a musical composition requires skills of improvisation: since we do not know in advance the chance events that will befall us we must spontaneously "incorporate into a thematic order the most accidental note to which a stroke of a finger . . . drives [us], breathing a beautiful meaning and a soul into an accident" (303). According to Nietzsche's musical analogy, free spirits cannot 'play' their lives by following a pre-existing score but must spontaneously compose a beautiful score from the accidents of their existence. Their "soul" is a beautiful harmony of their own composition whose notes are the events and accidents that befall them, not a transcendent, immaterial soul entombed in the body. Nietzsche's ideal of *amor fati* assumes then that events are 'necessary' (they could not have been otherwise); that in order to love these events we must see them as 'beautiful' – love is tied to or motivated by the object's beauty; and we can learn to 'see' or make beauty.

Nietzsche argues that this love of fate particularly requires over-coming Hellenistic indifference to the world and revaluing the pas-sions that imbue it with value. In Book 4 Nietzsche focuses on Hellenistic versions of the ascetic ideal, especially the Stoic and Epicurean ethical ideal of living according to nature. Nietzsche trains his critical eye on these latter philosophies because they are rival ethical naturalisms that aim at realising a blessed or happy life. Nietzsche's concern is that free spirits might be tempted to conceive ancient philosophical wisdom as the alternative model of life affirma-tion, as he had done in the previous two free spirit books. "We must", as he emphatically states, "overcome even the Greeks!" (340).

In Book 4 Nietzsche particularly focuses on the pitfalls of the Stoic version of the ascetic ideal. Stoicism, he observes, identifies external things as indifferent or valueless. Stoics, as remarked in Book 1, idealise a painless life and they realise this goal by training themselves to become insensitive or indifferent. The Stoic, he mocks, "trains himself to swallow stones and worms, glass shards and scorpions without nausea; he wants his stomach to be ultimately insensible to everything that chance pours into him" (306). In an 1881 note Nietzsche underscores his antipathy to Stoic ethics: "turning oneself into stone as a weapon against suffering [. . .] What significance can be attached to embracing a statue in wintertime if one has become entirely deadened against the cold? [. . .] I am very antipathetic to this line of thought" (*KSA* 9: 15 [55]). The Stoic trains himself to remain undisturbed by good and bad fortune alike. Even in extreme mis-fortune or fortune, Stoicism teaches individuals to remain unmoved by passions of anger or joy, which they conceive as errors of reason.

In the Preface to *GS* Nietzsche conceives the book as his attempt to 'thaw' what we described earlier as his own earlier intellectual Stoicism. We might recall here that in *HH* Nietzsche assumed that scientific knowledge would eliminate moral and aesthetic passions and replace them with evaluative neutrality. In a purely scientific culture, he suggested, we would recognise in things only causal necessities, not aesthetic qualities or moral significance. By eliminating our metaphysical beliefs in teleology or progress, science, he held, "pours mockery and contempt on the passions which reach out to the future and promise happiness in it" (*HH* 34). Nietzsche later described the outcome as a kind of "stoicism of the intellect", which "finally forbids itself a 'no' just as strictly as a 'yes'" (*GM* III. 24).

By learning how to see what is necessary in things as beautiful and in wanting only to be a 'Yea-sayer' Nietzsche sought to *unlearn* seeing things indifferently, as neither good or bad, beautiful or ugly. We can discern the beginning of this 'thaw', his rejection of indifference or evaluative neutrality in *D*:

> We have thought the matter over and finally decided that there is nothing good, nothing beautiful, nothing sublime, nothing evil in itself, but that there are states of soul in which we impose such words upon things external and within us. We have again *taken back* the predicate of things, or at least *remembered* that it was we who lent them to them; let us take care that this insight does not deprive us of the *capacity* to lend, and that we have not become at the same time *richer* and *greedier*. (*D* 210)

In *GS* Book 4 Nietzsche investigates the "states of the soul" that might undo or prevent this miserliness and enable us to learn to bestow the predicate 'beautiful'. The Stoics held that external goods have no value, and Schopenhauer maintained, "in itself, existence has no value" or "*genuine intrinsic worth*, but is kept in *motion* by want and illusion. But as soon as this comes to a standstill, the utter barrenness and emptiness of existence becomes apparent" (*PP* II: 287). Nietzsche agrees that the things of nature have no intrinsic value: "Whatever has *value* in the present world has it not in itself, according to its nature – nature is always value-less – but has rather been given, granted value, and *we* were the granters and givers!" (301).[8]

---

[8] Nietzsche's claim that we bestow values on a value-less nature has become the occasion of a contemporary philosophical debate about his meta-ethical perspective. Commentators have identified Nietzsche with a range of different meta-ethical views. Nietzsche has been identified as an 'anti-realist' about values who holds that there are no objective facts about value (Leiter 2002); a normative 'fictionalist' who engages in make believe about objective values to stave off moral disorientation (Reginster 2006); a non-cognitivist who holds that values are expressions of affective responses, but that such responses can be more or less objective depending on the extent to which one sees the world from different perspectives (Clark and Dudrick 2007); and a "response dependent" virtue ethicist who holds that values are only intelligible through emotional responses or sensibilities that can be more or less sophisticated, informed and undistorted (Swanton 2015). Clark and Dudrick add to their claim a developmental story. They argue that in *HH* Nietzsche held that moral evaluations are cognitive states of belief about moral properties, but that these beliefs are errors since science discloses that these properties do not exist in the empirical world. *GS*, they suggest, represents a major shift in Nietzsche's thinking to a non-cognitivist meta-ethics, i.e. an account of values as projections of passions and feeling, yet a non-cognitivism, so they claim,

Yet he holds that simply because we discover or recall that we bestow these predicates is not a good reason for withholding them. On his view, like artists, we can use these predicates even if we know or recall that they are not 'objective' or belong to things in themselves, but are impositions or projections. We can legitimately project these value predicates because they contribute to human flourishing. "What means", he asks, "do we have for making things beautiful, attractive and desirable when they are not? And in themselves I think they never are!" (299). Nietzsche in fact argues that we should learn (or re-learn) the artistic capacity to lend or endow value-less objects with value. Against the Stoics and Schopenhauer, Nietzsche suggests we should learn from artists to "look [at things] through coloured glass or in the light of the sunset, or to give them a skin that is not fully transparent" and that we should become the "poets of our lives, starting with the smallest and most commonplace details" (299).

Nietzsche clearly endorses the application of aesthetic techniques and categories to endow one's own life with a beauty that it would otherwise lack. The art of the beautiful, as he conceives it, sustains our love of existence or *amor fati*. To become the poets of our lives demands this artistic practice of creating values. Nietzsche does not dismiss values because they are 'errors' that identify properties such as purposes, laws, reason or beauty that correspond to nothing in the natural world. Rather, he acknowledges 'errors' as judgements that facilitate certain modes of living. Errors grow directly from the exigencies of life; they are natural processes as vital to life as any other organic function. He therefore concedes that they are necessary conditions of human survival and flourishing. All evaluations, he believes, have natural foundations in the sense that they emerge from and serve 'life', but some facilitate rather than limit the growth and enhancement of drives. On his view, human survival and flourishing are tied to the creation of values that express, facilitate and guide our natural inclinations or drives. Indeed, Nietzsche defines and endorses 'higher' individuals precisely as the often-unwitting agents of value creation who *give* value to an otherwise value-less nature. Successful value creators, he maintains, drill their values into "flesh and reality" (301).

that endorses objective moral judgements as a function of seeing the world from many different perspectives.

Nietzsche's account demands that we bracket a simple opposition between nature and values: his view is that in creating values we serve life and these values themselves become part of our nature or reality. As we shall see, it is not valuation per se that Nietzsche rejects, but valuations that prohibit the flourishing of the highest forms of life.

Nietzsche suggests *amor fati* requires a certain state of the soul or type of love that makes it possible to bestow value and then to internalise this value. Love, as he conceives it, is not learning about the object as it is 'in itself'; rather, it is learning a particular disposition towards the object that transforms our experience and valuation of it. Nietzsche illustrates this point by way of analogy: in the case of music "one needs effort and good will to bear [*ertragen*] it despite its strangeness . . . Finally comes a moment when we are *used* to it; when we expect it . . . and now it continues relentlessly to compel us and enchant us until we have become its humble and enraptured lovers who no longer want anything better from the world than it and it again . . . this happens to us not only in music: it is just in this way that we have learned to love everything we now love. We are always rewarded in the end for our good will, our patience, our fair-mindedness and gentleness with what it strange, as it gradually casts off its veil and presents itself as a new and indescribable beauty" (334). When Nietzsche later writes that greatness requires that we "not merely bear [*ertragen*] what is necessary" but that we "*love* it" (*EH* 'Clever' 10), we should recognise he does not think that bearing life is a weakness, deficit or 'failure'. On Nietzsche's view, affirming life might require more than bearing it, but the former is impossible without the latter. The reason Nietzsche assays for this view is that only by first bearing the strange and questionable is it possible to see it as beautiful. We do not bear existence by concealing it behind beautiful illusions; rather we bear it as a means of seeing otherwise veiled beauties. Love discloses this indescribable beauty and in doing so makes us prefer this object to all other possibilities and to will its eternal return.

Nietzsche gives beauty great importance in his aesthetic education because he assumes that it is closely connected with and motivates this kind of strongly 'eternalising' love. In sharp contrast to Schopenhauer who argued that beauty is an experience of contemplative detachment from will or desire (*WWR* 1: 195–200), Nietzsche argues that it incites will or desire. Nietzsche keys into the idea that the experience of beauty seems to incite or even require the act of replication or repetition (Scarry 2001: 3). Nietzsche conceives love of beauty as a kind of desire that is not immediately exhausted by the possession of its object. Beauty creates a different kind of desire to needs-based desire like thirst or hunger. These desires are exhausted by the possession of their object, whereas love of beauty conceives its object as endlessly desirable. Beautiful objects solicit the desire for their repetition. What defines the love of the beautiful is the desire for the eternal return of the object of love. Learning how to see or hear beauty in one's fate or oneself, he implies, is the key to willing the eternal recurrence. Beauty incites the desire for its perpetual duplication or eternal return. Nietzsche's New Year's wish is to become such a lover. As he makes clear love entails wanting an object (and only it) to return again and again. If lovers' wishes could be fulfilled they would wish for the eternal return of their object.

Nietzsche adds an important coda to this section: "Even he who *loves himself* will have learned it this way – there is no other way. Love, too, must be learned" (334, emphasis added). While we ordinarily conceive love as directed towards others, Nietzsche's coda draws attention to the possibility and conditions of self-love and self-affirmation. If *amor fati* requires learning how to see what is necessary in things as beautiful, Nietzsche implies, this also applies to the how we see ourselves. We can learn to love ourselves such that we become "humble and enraptured lovers who no longer want anything better from the world than it and it again" (334). Nietzsche's love of fate entails learning how to love oneself as a "new and indescribable beauty". As we shall see, Nietzsche's coda is important in this context because he conceives this self-love as the antithesis to the self-contempt that, he believes, is built into moral conscience. Nietzsche presents this practice of self-love as the alternative to the self-contempt he claims defines moral conscience.

In the middle sections of Book 4, Nietzsche develops this account of the art of self-fashioning and self-affirmation by distinguishing it from negative moralities whose essence is "self-denial" (304). Nietzsche ideal of self-fashioning underpins his critique of moral conscience, including Schopenhauerian and Kantian morality.

We can therefore clarify his ideal of self-affirmation by examining this critique of morality. As we shall see, Nietzsche's ethics rejects the validity of moral conscience and replaces it with what he calls our "ownmost conscience" that directs us to becoming who we are.

Nietzsche distinguishes between 'positive' moralities aligned with his ideal of self-affirmation and negative moralities that express the ascetic ideal, or the will turned against life. We can illuminate his distinction in terms of Foucault's historical account of morality as a code, or a set of universal and compulsory laws that prohibit certain actions and an ethics that is a supplement or luxury that proposes styles of moderation and a*skēses* or practices for the sake of forming a certain kind of ethical subject. Greco-Roman ethics, as Foucault explains "were much more oriented towards practices of the self and the question of *askesis* than towards the codification of conducts and the strict definition of what is permitted and what is forbidden" (Foucault 1985: 29–30).[9] Nietzsche revives the latter Greco-Roman ethics as voluntary mode of self-formation or self-stylisation against morality conceived as a universal, mandatory code of proscriptions. Nietzsche's ethics shares with the Greco-Roman tradition the notion of ethics as a set of methods, techniques and practices for giving style to one's life, to becoming who one is. In this ethical framework, the code one follows matters only to the extent that it enables him/her to achieve a certain kind of agency or mode of being.

In a letter to Rée, Nietzsche explained that Book 4 expressed his own morality as "the sum of the conditions of *my* existence which prescribe an *ought* only if I *want myself*" (quoted in Kaufmann 1974: 20). In other words, Nietzsche endorses a version of the Greco-Roman model of ethics. He prescribes imperatives for himself only because he wants himself or wants to affirm himself. Nietzsche's ethic follows the form: if I want myself I ought to follow these principles. Yet, even though it is broadly consistent with the form of the Greco-Roman model, Nietzsche's ethics rejects the central ethical *teloi* of the classical and Hellenistic philosophies: it does not aim at radical

---

[9] Foucault acknowledges that both Greco-Roman and Christian morality contained both codes and practices of the self, but he argues that in the former, the dynamic element is to be found in the practices of the self. In pagan ethics, he suggests, rule following was advocated and practised for the sake of giving style to one's life (Foucault 1985: 29–30).

detachment vis-à-vis the world, perfect tranquillity or total insensitivity to the agitation of the passions.[10]

Rather Nietzsche's positive ethics entails a practice of the self that is open to the drives and passions as possible instruments of self-affirmation and self-enhancement. It establishes the conditions of existence necessary for a self-affirming or noble disposition. Recalling his analysis of nobility in Book 1, Nietzsche claims that the distinguishing feature of nobility "has always been to have no fear of oneself, to expect nothing contemptible from oneself, to fly without misgivings wherever we're inclined – we free-born birds!" (294). As we saw at the close of Book 3, Nietzsche noble ideal requires permitting the expression of natural drives without shame or contempt. In defining his own morality Nietzsche declares that "he abhors every morality that says: 'Do not do this! Renounce! Overcome yourself! But I am well disposed towards those moralities that impel me to do something again and again from morning to evening and to dream of it at night, and to think of nothing else than doing this *well*, as well as *I* alone can!'" (304).

Nietzsche's ethics, then, entails both an openness to and affirmation of the many drives of the self and value judgements that cultivate an all-consuming passion to exercise and perfect those drives that lend themselves to realising personal distinction. If negative virtues slander the natural drives, Nietzsche's positive morality endows them with value as means to our self-affirmation. These positive, noble moralities therefore incite individuals to strive for their own self-affirmation, not their self-denial. Such moralities focus on affirming an ideal goal, rather than on prohibiting certain drives or passions; they are exclusively *for* something, not *against* something. Nietzsche supports positive moralities that make what we do (the all-consuming pursuit of personal distinction) determine what we forgo, and opposes negative moralities that make what we must forgo determine what we can do. In the former case we forgo things not because we 'must' or out of moral contempt for or shame about some of our natural drives, but merely because these particular drives are superfluous to our self-affirmation. If some drives fall away from our lives in this case they do so because they are superfluous to our craving to

---

[10] This paraphrases Foucault's thumbnail sketch of the main classical ethical teloi (Foucault 1985: 28).

repeat and relive the cherished ideal, not because they are hated or proscribed. "When one lives that way", as Nietzsche explains, "one thing after another drops off: without hate or reluctance one sees this take its leave today and that tomorrow, like the yellow leaves that every faint wisp of wind carries off a tree" (304).[11]

On the other hand, Nietzsche personally condemns morality as a proscriptive code as a symptom and cause of disease: "I do not want to strive for my own impoverishment with open eyes; I do not like negative virtues – virtues whose very essence is ... self-denial" (304). According to Nietzsche, if we suffer from our natural drives this is by no means a consequence of exercising them, but of the slanderous judgement that they are "evil" (294). It is this moral judgement, he argues, that is the "cause our great injustice towards our nature, towards *all* nature!" (294). If we become sick from exercising natural drives this sickness stems from moral judgements that compel us to interpret and experience them as contemptible or shameful. As Nietzsche sees it, the drives themselves are 'innocent' and cause no suffering or illness unless they are morally slandered. Moral judgements, he claims, disfigure the drives. Nietzsche diagnoses moral codes or negative moralities as afflicting us with the disease of self-denial, "a constant irritability at all natural stirrings and inclinations and as it were a kind of itch" (305).

Nietzsche implicitly identifies Stoicism as the archetype of moralities that afflict us with this disease. The Stoic suffers from the disease of self-denial:

Whatever may henceforth push, pull, beckon, impel from within or without" he explains "will always strike this irritable one as endangering his self-control: no longer may he entrust himself to any instinct or free wing-beat; instead he stand there rigidly with a defensive posture, armed against himself, with sharp and suspicious eyes, the eternal guardian of his fortress, since he has turned himself into a fortress. (305)

It is the ancient Stoics who are best known for conceiving the inner citadel as the analogue of philosophical freedom.[12] Through this Stoic

---

[11] Nietzsche famously develops this in his distinction between noble and slave moralities; see *GM* I.10.

[12] Isaiah Berlin captures the Stoic idea of freedom: "I must *liberate* myself from desires that I know I cannot realize. I wish to be master of my kingdom, but my frontiers are long and vulnerable, therefore I contract them ... to ... *eliminate the vulnerable area* ... The tyrant threatens me with imprisonment ... But if I no longer feel attached to property, no longer

moral disease, Nietzsche claims, we risk becoming "impoverished and cut off from the most beautiful fortuities of the soul! And indeed from all further *instruction*! For one must be able to lose oneself if one wants to learn something from things that we ourselves are not" (305).

In Book 4 Nietzsche extends his critique of the morality as self-denial by applying it to the idea of conscience that informs modern European moral philosophy. In doing so, he aims to show that the very concept of moral conscience that shapes these philosophies is symptomatic of the ascetic denial of life. Nietzsche suggests that his alternative ethics of self-fashioning and self-affirmation ultimately take its directions from what he call our "own most conscience" rather than from moral conscience (338). As we have seen, in Book 3 Nietzsche foreshadows the meaning of our 'ownmost conscience': "*What does your conscience say?* – 'You should become who you are'" (GS 270). Our "ownmost conscience", as he conceives it, impels us to follow our own "*path*", a trajectory we follow independently of, and oblivious to anything other than the realisation and perfection of our own unique set of possibilities (338).

We can clarify Nietzsche's ethics by examining how he defends this "ownmost conscience" against the force of moral conscience. Nietzsche's central objection to Kantian and Schopenhauerian morality is that they both entail "losing myself *from my path*" by compelling us to follow generalisable rules or to live for others (338). If moral conscience makes us cowards, as he will implicitly suggest, our ownmost conscience makes us heroically singular individuals. It censures us for betraying our own unique individuality. We can see how Nietzsche builds this case by examining in some detail the lengthy and important section 335.

Nietzsche's opens his critique by applying what in Book 1 he calls our "intellectual conscience" (2) to examine the validity of our moral conscience. Our intellectual conscience, as he conceives it, takes the form of questioning the veracity of our moral principles and judgements. It liberates us from moral conscience and in doing so makes it possible to pursue the project of becoming who we are. Applying this intellectual conscience in *GS* 335 Nietzsche argues that in the case of

care whether or not I am in prison . . . then he cannot bend me to his will . . . It is as if I had performed a strategic retreat into the inner citadel" (Berlin 1969: 129).

moral judgements and action we have been terrible at self-observation, despite our claims that in the case of morality we are experts. We have claimed knowledge of morality, he contends, that in fact we spectacularly lack. In this respect at least, Nietzsche follows Socrates: he too aims to showing that we do not know what virtue is despite our claims to expertise. Nietzsche, however, radicalises Socrates' moral questioning: he questions our moral errors not to have us seek better moral foundations, but to reveal the impossibility and undesirability of universal moral judgement. Nietzsche aims to show how proper self-observation demonstrates that we do not have legitimate grounds to believe our moral judgements are true or infallible and that we are also ignorant of why we listen to or heed our moral judgements.

In *GS* 335 Nietzsche argues first that we cannot legitimately hold our moral judgements as true because they "have a prehistory in our drives, inclinations, aversions, experiences" and what we have "failed to experience".[13] Nietzsche's tracing of the pre-history of our drives is contingent on his naturalistic account of the emergence of consciousness as a mechanism that derives from a multiplicity of largely "unconscious and unfelt" drives or instincts. In *GS* 333 Nietzsche claims that consciousness is merely the tip of the iceberg beneath which operates a much greater mass of unconscious drives. Our conscious thought, he claims, is merely the after-effect of unconscious conflicts among competing drives. Nietzsche argues that the judgements or perspectives that we become conscious of are the outcome of a dynamic, unceasing conflict among the drives that operate beneath the level of our consciousness. It is therefore mistaken to identify all thought with consciousness since the greater part of our mental activity never surfaces in consciousness. Our intellectual conscience must therefore seek means to access unconscious drives and inclinations and to decipher the internal struggle among the drives that results in moral conscience.

---

[13] Whether or not Nietzsche's genealogical explanations of moral conscience and moral beliefs, or more broadly naturalistic explanations of the evolutionary origins of morality legitimately debunk moral beliefs is a matter of controversy. See e.g. Risse (2007), Prinz (2007) and Handfield (2016).

In tracing the pre-history or genealogy of our moral beliefs Nietzsche's perspective rejects the idea of a metaphysical or intelligible moral self. As he says in his discussion of Spinoza (333), there is in our 'intelligere' "nothing divine, eternally resting in itself", only a 'self' that is contingent outcome of unconscious conflicts. Nietzsche argues that the Kantian moral conscience that divinises the moral self, or the "holy will", which Kant conceives as unconditioned by nature or drives and as identical in us all, is as far from divinity as one could possibly imagine (see Kant *GMM* IV: 413). Rather the moral self, Nietzsche claims, is the symptom of a conflict among unconscious drives. We are therefore mistaken, he argues, if we think of ourselves as impersonal, unconditioned selves who must bring our particular actions under general principles, the sublime demand 'thou shalt'. Our moral conscience does not have metaphysical 'grounds', Nietzsche maintains, only the shifting sands of contingent inclinations and aversions.

Foreshadowing his later genealogical method of criticism, he argues that our insight into how our moral conscience emerges is sufficient to undermine our faith in the validity of any notion of unconditional, universal duty. Nietzsche's genealogical method, as Foucault aptly put it "is not made not for understanding ... but for cutting" (Foucault 1984: 88).[14] Its task is to cut the self free from all universalist pictures of moral consciousness. In Nietzsche's view this is a knowledge that liberates us from "'duty'" and "'conscience'", or, as he puts it, that "spoils these emotional words" in the same way that metaphysical scepticism spoils words like "sin" and "salvation of the soul" (335). One might concede to Nietzsche that our moral conscience and judgements are historically contingent products, but his main critical charge is "that morality causes us to be ill, self-conflicted, self-hating and deluded in ways that are ugly and unnecessary for us" (Janaway 2007: 247). As Nietzsche intimates in *D* and argues in detail later in *GM,* we misinterpret our moral conscience as pure, practical reason when it is a symptom of an unconscious drive

---

[14] See also Janaway (2007: 250): "[Nietzsche's] critique of morality produces not so much a body of doctrine ... as a sharp and versatile working tool that can detach us from accustomed attitudes, enabling us to grasp the psychology and history that underlies them, and to assess their potential worth to us in the present and future".

to aggression that we have directed back on ourselves. As he puts it in
D, Kant's categorical imperative conceals "a remnant of ascetic
cruelty", and in *GM* "it smells of cruelty" (*D* 339 and *GM* II.6).[15]
Nietzsche's genealogy aims to show how philosophical rhetoric that
conceives moral conscience as 'divine', as the voice of God in man,
hides the fact that it derives from instincts of cruelty that we turn
against ourselves (*WS* 52). Nietzsche argues then that not only is
morality merely one contingent structuring of our unconscious
drives, but that it is, as he later puts it, "*mortally dangerous*" (*AC*
11). Nietzsche suggests that this moral structuring of our drives is
tantamount to a living death. It makes us automatons of duty.

Second, and most importantly, in *GS* 335 he argues that following
moral or categorical imperatives is symptomatic of a lack of self-
affirmation, of a petty rather than what he described in Book 1 (21) as
our grand "*Selbstsucht*". In Book 1 and 2 Nietzsche took aim at the
metaphysicians of morality, identifying himself as physician concerned with individual rather than universal conditions of health:

Deciding what is health even for your *body* depends on your goal, your
horizons, your powers, your impulses, your mistakes and above all ideals
and phantasms of the soul. Thus there are innumerable healths of body;
and the more one allows the particular and incomparable to rear its head
again, the more one unlearns the dogma of the 'equality of men', the
more the concept of a normal health ... must be abandoned by our
medical men. (120)

In *GS* 335 Nietzsche develops this argument against universal
prescriptions. He argues that to maintain that "here everyone must
judge as I do" is a form of selfishness insofar as one generalises and
imposes these law on others, but it is only a *petty, blind* selfishness
insofar in doing so one looks to legislate laws that apply to all rather
than laws that apply specifically to oneself (see also Risse 2007: 59).
Morality, Nietzsche claims, marks a dramatic failure of self-
cultivation. Nietzsche argues that to follow the Kantian principle of
acting according to a law that we believe should apply to all is
necessarily to lose sight of what specifically and uniquely might

---

[15] Nietzsche establishes here the groundwork of Freud's psychoanalytic theory of repression as
the introversion of the drives and his theory of civilisation as dependent on the development
of bad conscience or a superego morality.

enable us to become ourselves; or to put the point another way, to observe a generalised principle is to commit ourselves to becoming impersonal, generalised, collective entities. The Kantian notion of moral judgement, which, as Nietzsche construes it, claims that "here everyone must judge as I do", shows, so he claims, that "you haven't yet discovered yourself or created for yourself an ideal of your very own – for that could never be someone else's, let alone everyone's, everyone's!" By this means we 'condemn' ourselves to becoming undifferentiated, 'herd' animals rather than singular, self-created individuals. If we follow allegedly universal prescriptions, he implies, we treat ourselves as anonymous, collective units, not as a unique and yet to be realised creations or artworks.

Nietzsche later spells out this criticism of Kantian morality more explicitly and stridently:

A word against Kant as moralist. A virtue has to be *our* virtue, *our* most personal defence and necessity: in any other sense it is merely a danger. What does not condition our life *harms* it: a virtue merely from a feeling of respect for the concept 'virtue' as Kant desired it, is harmful. 'Virtue', 'duty', good in itself, impersonal and universal – phantoms, expressions of decline, of the final exhaustion of life . . . The profoundest laws of preservation and growth demand the reverses of this: that each one of us should devise *his own* virtue, *his own* categorical imperative. (*AC* 11)

By means of Kantian morality, he argues, we systematically misrecognise ourselves as 'herd animals' and in doing so annihilate our individuality; it is, as he conceives it, a thoughtless "morality of unselfing" (*EH* 'Destiny' 7). Nietzsche challenges this morality not simply because it is erroneous, but because it is 'anti-natural': "It is not error as error which horrifies me at the sight [of moral decadence]", as he later explained, ". . . it is the lack of nature, it is the ghastly fact that *anti-nature* itself has received the highest honours as morality and has hung over mankind as law, as categorical imperative!" (*EH* 'Destiny' 7). For Nietzsche the moral self is the stage upon which a veiled or unconscious civil war is waged against the possibility of creating a unique, incomparable self. If, as Nietzsche maintains, each person is the scene of an unconscious war among their drives, the emergence of moral conscience spells the victory of one set

of drives: viz. those drives that compel us to conform to the
needs of the majority (333).[16] Our moral conscience, he implies,
is the symptom and symbol of this victory. Moral conscience
breeds a herd animal. The illness Nietzsche diagnoses, as
Janaway explains, "lies in the fact that, in the process of self-
interpretation of which morality is symptomatic, we disown the
vast bulk of what truly composes the self" (Janaway 2007: 251).
"Nothing", as Nietzsche later declares, "works more profound
ruin that any impersonal duty, any sacrifice to the Moloch of
abstraction – Kant's categorical imperative should have been felt
as *mortally dangerous*! ... What destroys more quickly than to
work, to think, to feel without inner necessity, without a deep
personal choice, without *joy*? as an automaton of 'duty'?" (*AC*
11).

In GS 335 Nietzsche claims then that self-observation demonstrates that our moral conscience emerges from historically contingent and ignoble sources, specifically from aggression turned against
ourselves. Moral conscience, on his view, is the agency that executes
and enforces the ascetic ideal, the will turned against life. Second, he
argues that if we continue to conceive our moral judgements as
universally binding in the Kantian manner we prevent ourselves
from formulating an ideal that enables us to differentiate ourselves

---

[16] In *GS* 333 Nietzsche quotes Spinoza critique of moralists like the Stoics who he (Spinoza)
claims prefer to laugh at, lament or curse the affects rather than understand them (*Ethics*
III pref). Spinoza makes the same claim against the Stoics at *Politics* 1.4: "And in order to
enquire into matters relevant to this branch of knowledge [Politics] in the same unfettered
spirit as is habitually shown in mathematical studies, I have taken great care not to deride,
bewail, or execrate human actions, but to understand them. So I have regarded human
emotions such as love, hatred, anger, envy, pride, pity, and other agitations of the mind
not as vices of human nature but as properties pertaining to it in the same way as heat,
cold, storm, thunder, and such pertain to the nature of the atmosphere. These things,
though troublesome, are inevitable, and have definite causes through which we try to
understand their nature. And the mind derives as much enjoyment in contemplating them
aright as from the knowledge of things that are pleasing to the senses". Like Spinoza,
Nietzsche does not conceive the passions as vices. However, in 333 Nietzsche argues against
Spinoza that (a) consciousness is not distinct from, or opposed to the drives; (b) the
greatest part of the mind's activity is unconscious and unfelt; and (c) these drives compete
against one another for supremacy rather than seek the agent's self-preservation. Michael
Della Rocca (2008) argues that Nietzsche's misinterprets Spinoza and that in fact
"Spinoza's view of reason as joyful and affective mirrors Nietzsche's own view of the
right kind of understanding" (296).

from others and create ourselves as unique individuals. Moral judgements are epistemically flawed and existentially damaging.

Nietzsche argues that if we free ourselves from moral conscience we can turn our attention to the "*creation of tables of what is good that are new and all our own*" (335). In sharp contrast to the "great majority" who simply repeat past ideals, Nietzsche free spirits "envisage new ideals" (335). And the free spirits' newly created ideals are those that serve them in becoming the exceptional individuals they are: "We . . . want to *become who we are* – human being who are new, unique, incomparable, who gives themselves laws, who create themselves!" (335). Nietzsche's account of the unique and incomparable dimensions of the self echoes his earlier claim in *SE*:

> In his heart every man knows quite well that being unique, he will be in the world only once and that no imaginable chance will for a second time gather together into a unity so strangely variegated an assortment as he is: he knows it but hides it like a bad conscience – . . . let him follow his conscience, which calls him: Be yourself! All you are now doing, thinking, desiring, is not you yourself. (*SE* 1)

As we shall see, the notion of our ownmost conscience, which he develops in GS, remains true to his view in *SE* that we all have a "secret bad conscience" (*SE* 1). Our secret bad conscience, he maintains, is our recognition of "the law that every man is a unique miracle", a law that implores us to fashion ourselves into a unique unity (SE 1). We shall return to the significance of the next chapter. In *GS* 335 Nietzsche explains the failure of self-cultivation as largely a product of a moral conscience, grounded in unconscious drives, inclinations and aversions, that legislates what is in the interests of the collective. Kant's picture of the self as a dutiful fulfiller of universal obligations is psychological structure that evolved as that best suited to the requirements of, as Nietzsche puts, 'herd' society. Nietzsche's emerging genealogy of morality shows that the obstacles that stand in the way of self-creation lie not merely in the personal 'vice' of laziness, as he had thought in *SE*, but in a highly evolved moral conscience that functions to integrate individuals into the collective and that blinds them to their own existence as distinct, unique individuals. Nietzsche's genealogy of the self attempts to liberate us from the conceptual and practical grip of moral philosophy's picture of this unconditioned, universal moral consciousness.

Nietzsche alternative to the automaton of 'duty' is the ideal of self-fashioning individuals.[17] Nietzsche's self-fashioning individuals formulate their *own* virtue, which in *GS* he identifies with individual excellence (304) and more fully later in terms of a Renaissance styled notion of *virtù* defined in terms of the expansion of one's power, proficiency and excellence. He maintains that the selection of one's own virtue requires, "a deep personal choice" based on a knowledge of one's own unique array of drives and inclinations and their 'pre-history' (*AC* 2) Nietzsche later suggests that the right choice of action is confirmed by the feeling of joy in action, and joy is felt when one feels that his power or proficiency increases (*AC* 11). Nietzsche's ethics affirms rather than denies this feeling of joy in self-affirmation and self-enhancement.

We have seen in this chapter then that Nietzsche values artistic self-fashioning. Against self-denying moralities like Stoicism and Kantianism, he values the ethical project of reweaving the web of our drives in such a way that that the life we lead and our actions all bear the impress of our uniqueness or originality. Nietzsche's aesthetic education aims to create a higher type of human being, a type that can integrate its unique array of natural drives into a singular, incomparable whole. It is in the context of this ethical project that Nietzsche introduces his famous doctrine of the eternal recurrence of the same. What is the relationship between Nietzsche's ethics of self-cultivation and self-fashioning and the doctrine of recurrence? We will address this question in the next chapter.

---

[17] See also Bittner (2012: 262): "Nietzsche's individuals do not undertake to legislate for all rational beings. Yet they do legislate, for themselves, and thus do not act erratically but according to their own self-given form".

CHAPTER 6

Eternal Recurrence: Personal Infinity

One of Nietzsche's great laments about modern philosophy is that it has forgotten or rejected the ethics of self-cultivation: "Woe to the thinker who is not the gardener but only the soil of the plants that grow in him!" (*D* 382). Among his favourite analogues of self-cultivation was the art of horticulture: "We have the ability to cultivate our temperament as a gardener" (*KSA* 9:7 [211]).[1] "One can dispose of one's drives", as he explains, "like a gardener and, though few know it, cultivate the shoots of anger, pity, curiosity, vanity as productively and profitably as a beautiful fruit tree on a trellis" (*D* 560). Nietzsche maintains that we are at liberty to cultivate our 'temperament', or the order and dynamics of our drives, yet modern philosophers have neglected this art. By failing to become the gardener of our drives, he warns, they risk falling into philosophical pessimism (*D* 382). He conceives pessimism as the result of a lack of self-cultivation (*D* 382). Our "morose and grey" pessimistic "*conclusions*", he maintains, derive from failing to cultivate our drives, not from the exercise of pure, disembodied reason.

As we observed in the Introduction, Nietzsche feared that the modern professionalisation of philosophy had swept aside this ethics of self-cultivation. Modern philosophy, he complained, had become a purely theoretical discipline detached from and oblivious to the ancient model of philosophy as a way of life. Professional philosophers aimed at 'systematic' theoretical knowledge or the critique of such systems, not at the realisation of a way of life. Nietzsche saw it as his task to reclaim self-cultivation as central to philosophy conceived as an art of living. "The only critique of philosophy that is possible

---

[1] Parkes (1994) brilliantly elaborates Nietzsche's horticultural analogies for self-cultivation.

and that proves something, namely trying to see whether one can live in accordance with it", he asserted, "has never been taught at universities: all that has been taught is a critique of words by means of other words" (*SE* 8).

It is in the context of Nietzsche's untimely project of reviving the ethics of self-cultivation that we need to understand his famous doctrine of eternal recurrence of the same. Eternity plays a key role in his ethics of self-cultivation. In fact in one of his characteristically grandiose moments he conceived it as "the great cultivating thought" in the sense that it might weed out those too weak to bear the thought of living again (*WP* 1053). In a more tempered fashion, however, he framed the thought of recurrence as part of an ethics of self-cultivation and self-transformation. "If you incorporate this thought within you, amongst your other thoughts", he maintains, "it will transform you. If for everything you wish to do you begin by asking yourself: 'Am I certain I want to do this an infinite number of times?' this will become for you the greatest weight" (*KSA* 9:11 [143]).

Nietzsche links together the thought of eternity and self-transformation in the famous penultimate section of *GS*:

The heaviest weight. – What if some day or night a demon [*Dämon*] were to steal into your loneliest loneliness and say to you: 'This life as you now live it and have lived it you will have to live once again and innumerable times again; and there will be nothing new in it, but every pain and every joy and every thought and sigh and everything unspeakably small or great in your life must return to you, all in the same succession and sequence – even this spider and this moonlight between the trees, and even this moment and I myself. The eternal hourglass of existence is turned over again and again, and you with it, speck of dust!' Would you not throw yourself down and gnash your teeth and curse the demon who spoke thus? Or have you once experienced a tremendous moment when you would have answered him: 'You are a god, and never have I heard anything more divine'. If this thought gained power over you, as you are it would transform and possibly crush you; the question in each and every thing, 'Do you want this again and innumerable times again?' would lie on your actions as the heaviest weight! Or how well disposed would you have to become to yourself and to life to long for nothing more fervently than for this ultimate eternal confirmation and seal? (341)

What role does the thought of recurrence play in Nietzsche's ethics of self-cultivation? To answer this question we first need to understand the overall telos of Nietzschean self-cultivation. What kind of self does he wish to cultivate? As we have intimated, Nietzsche's ethics values above all else the cultivation of the self as a unique, immortal artwork. The great work of art is his model of the affirmative life. Nietzsche suggests that those who artistically fashion their own unique, unrepeatable life wish for its eternal repetition. Nietzsche's ethics of self-cultivation idealises creating a life for ourselves that we would wish to live again and again such that we also wish that eternal recurrence were *literally* true. Eternal recurrence is, as it were, the wish fulfilment of those who have created their own lives.

However, Nietzsche implies the thought of eternal recurrence not only expresses, but also cultivates the self as an artwork. Nietzsche dramatises this doctrine as a motivational force for transforming our lives. Nietzsche conceives the idea of eternal recurrence as the voice of what we he calls, as we noted above, our "ownmost conscience, " which decrees, "You should become who you are" (338, 270). Nietzsche's *Dämon* figures the thought of eternal recurrence as the expression of this ownmost conscience. By means of this framing, Nietzsche attempts to give recurrence a motivational force that compels us to cultivate ourselves in light of the imperative 'become who you are'. It follows that Nietzsche conceives the thought of recurrence not as a theoretical doctrine that we simply need to understand, but as what we might call a 'spiritual exercise'. Nietzsche conceives the thought of recurrence as a particular spiritual exercise: viz. a meditation on the idea of our recurrence that incorporates this prospect into the way we conduct our lives. Nietzsche's assumption that this spiritual exercise compels us to cultivate ourselves specifically as singular works of art hinges on his claim that individuals do in fact have the potential to become unique and incomparable selves and the romantic belief that the realisation of this end is the highest desideratum. We will consider each of these claims about the significance of eternal recurrence in turn.

If Nietzsche endorses an ethics of self-cultivation, then what kind of self does it aim to cultivate? Nietzsche values above all else the cultivation of the self as a singular and immortal artwork. We noted in the previous chapter that his celebration of artistic self-fashioning stretches back to *Schopenhauer as Educator* (1873). The artist of life, as he put it, does not masquerade in borrowed fashions, but is "uniquely himself to every last movement of his muscles" and in being "strictly consistent in uniqueness he is beautiful" (*SE* 1). To become who one is, in Nietzsche's sense, requires that in the self we construct, each 'movement' or part expresses what is unique to oneself, rather than what characterises the neighbour. Nietzsche suggests that giving style to oneself requires that we survey all the strengths and weaknesses of our own nature and then by means of "long practice and daily work" fit all of its parts into an artistic plan (290). For each of us, Nietzsche implies, what makes our lives worthy of eternity is living "according to our own laws and standards" and in doing so shaping our nature so that it bears the "monogram of our most essential individual essence, a work, a deed, an uncommon inspiration, a creation" (*HL* 3).

We can see how in Book 4 Nietzsche celebrates cultivating the self as a singular, unrepeatable artwork in his reflections on death and immortality. In *GS* 278 he applauds the people who thirst for life rather than meditate on death. Nietzsche recalls here a line from Spinoza that he had recorded in his 1876 Sorrento notebooks: "The free man thinks of nothing less than death, and his wisdom is a meditation on life, not on death".[2] "It gives me a melancholy happiness", he writes in this postcard-like section, "to live in the midst of this jumble of lanes, needs and voices: how much enjoyment, impatience, desire; how much thirsty life and drunkenness of life comes to light every moment of the day!" (278).[3] Nietzsche takes this intoxicated Dionysian life as a measure of higher or healthier life against which he implicitly measures and condemns Platonism's ascetic desire for a transcendent world, the Epicurean and Stoic desire for tranquillity, and Schopenhauer's explicit morality of life denial. In sharp contrast to philosophers these intoxicated people do not seek to purify their souls of embodied desires and passions, they do not make dying their profession, but rather intensely pursue these desires.

Nietzsche suggests that in general these "life thirsty ones" live with such intensity that they rarely give any thought to their imminent

---

[2] Nietzsche quotes Spinoza's Latin sentence: "*Homo liber de nulla re minus, quam de morte cogitat, et ejus sapientia non mortis, sed vitae meditatio est*" (*Ethics* IV P. 67); (*KSA* 8: 19[68]).

[3] Nietzsche's allusion to the Dionysian is evident if we recall that in *BT* he explains it as "most immediately understandable to us in the analogy of intoxication" (*BT* 1).

death (278). "It makes me happy", he exclaims, "to see that [they] do not at all want to think the thought of death!" (278). Nietzsche applauds their refusal to meditate on death because to do so is to become aware of their shared fate as mortals, of the fact that "death and deathly silence are the only things common to all in this future!" (278). If we think about death, Nietzsche maintains, we recognise that we are united in a "brotherhood of death" (278). In Nietzsche's judgement, when we contemplate death we become aware of our commonality or equality as mortal creatures. "Ashes", as Seneca remarked, "level all men" (*Ep.* 91.16).

Yet Nietzsche is happy because these passionate people "are *farthest* removed from feeling like a brotherhood of death" and their "commonality barely makes an impression on them" (278). By applauding this popular refusal to meditate on death as the great leveller, Nietzsche lends his support to the focus on the individual pursuits and drives that separate or distinguish them from one another and a corresponding resistance to conceiving themselves in terms of a common humanity. Nietzsche writes that for those life thirsty people who are intoxicated by their own desires and goals he want to make the thought of life "even a hundred times more *worth being thought*" (278). If the thought of death demands acknowledgement of our common mortality, then its antithesis, what he calls the "the thought of life", must concern what distinguishes us from one another. The "beautiful meaning" we breathe into our life must be one that distinguishes us from all others (303). For Nietzsche to think the thought of life must be to think about our distinctiveness and singularity. Nietzsche identifies the doctrine of eternal recurrence as this thought of life. It is, he claims, "the sunshine of this doctrine" that enables a life devoted to self-fashioning to "*flourish* a hundred times more strongly" (*KSA* 11 [165]).

Nietzsche emphasises that we can immortalise ourselves through the creation of lives that we shape into singular, unrepeatable artworks. In his famous account of the doctrine of eternal recurrence Nietzsche observes that to celebrate our own recurrence we must become "well disposed" towards our lives and ourselves (341). For Nietzsche to become well disposed towards oneself requires creating ourselves as singular, unique individuals and giving this singularity a posthumous existence. Nietzsche identifies being well disposed towards oneself and life as a condition of wishing to repeat our lives.

Nietzsche illustrates what he means by this life-affirming disposition in a brief portrait of aristocratic Genoese individuals. It is his allegory of the affirmative, self-fashioning life. For Nietzsche how these individuals transformed their environment so that it bore their unique stamp is a model for how those who cultivate themselves must transform themselves into singular works of art. Contemplating the magnificent villas and pleasure-gardens overlooking the bay of Portofino Nietzsche reports that he sees in these a region dotted with "images of bold and autocratic human beings" (291). Nietzsche metaphorically describes these villas as "*faces*" to underscore his view that they express architecturally their unique, personal, unrepeatable essence. They have built, as he puts it, to express their "superiority" and to place their "personal infinity" between themselves and their neighbour (291).

Nietzsche admires in great Genoese individuals their "magnificent lust for possessions and spoils" that took shape through the incorporation and refashioning of their world so that it reflected their own "personal infinity" (291). Nietzsche stresses that their architectural styles expressed their singular individuality and their envious desire to destroy the old and impose on the world an image that reflected back to them nothing but their own unique identity. These life-loving individuals are only "sated", as he explains, when they have put their own meaning into everything old and established and they see "only what is their own and nothing alien appears to [their] eye" (291). "Each conquered his homeland again for himself", he observes, "by overwhelming it with his architectural ideas and refashioning it . . . into a house that was a feast for his eyes" (291). Their affirmative life took shape as the desire to express their 'ownmost' self in immortal works of art. These bold individuals, Nietzsche remarks, "have *lived* and wish to live on – this is what they are telling me with their houses, built and adorned to last for centuries and not for the fleeting hour: they were well disposed towards life however badly disposed they often may have been towards themselves" (291). While the Genoese became well disposed towards life by refashioning their world into an immortal expression of their singularity, Nietzsche suggests that self-cultivators must extend this to their own self.

"We should learn from artists", as he explains, "while otherwise being wiser than they. For usually in their case this delicate power stops where are ends and life begins; *we* however want to be poets of our lives" (299). Nietzsche's ideal of self-cultivation requires then making of *oneself* a unique and immortal work of art.

In this way Nietzsche's ethics of self-cultivation echoes pre-Socratic notions of immortality. For the pre-Socratic Greeks, as Hannah Arendt observed, the distinctiveness of men among mortal creatures lies in the fact that "individual life, with a recognisable life-story from birth to death, rises out of biological life" (Arendt 1958: 19). If nature guarantees members of a species eternity through cyclical recurrence, it cannot guarantee this to individuals qua individuals. "This individual life", as she put it, "is distinguished from all other things by the rectilinear course of its movement, which, so to speak, cuts through the circular movement of biological life" (Arendt 1958: 19). On the pre-Socratic view, individuals can defy their mortal condition through the attainment of immortal greatness. As she explains it:

> The task and the potential greatness of mortals lies in their ability to produce things . . . which would deserve to be . . . at home in everlastingness, so that through them mortals could find their place in a cosmos where everything is immortal except themselves. By their capacity for the immortal deed, by their ability to leave non-perishable traces behind, men, their individual mortality notwithstanding, attain an immortality of their own and prove themselves to be of a 'divine' nature. (Arendt 1958: 19)

Against the Platonic philosophical notion of eternity (and the Christian notion of eternal salvation), and its condemnation of the vanity and vainglory of transient appearances, Nietzsche strove to resuscitate the pre-Socratic striving for immortality through the creation of a unique self worthy of eternity. Nietzsche's affirmative life defies mortality, not by means of the Platonic and Christian flight from the 'vanity' of transient appearances, but through this task of creating the self as a singular and immortal work of art.

We can illuminate this point by contrasting Plato's Socrates and Nietzsche. On the one hand, Socrates conceives philosophy as a preparation for dying cheerfully, an exercise of purifying the soul of the burdens of the body so that at death it can escape the wheel of recurrence. The philosopher looks forward to death as liberation from eternally repeated embodied life. Socrates maintains that death separates the philosophically purified soul from the body and its cycle of rebirth. He greets death cheerfully as the liberation from the eternal repetition of embodied life. If death does not liberate the philosophically purified soul from the eternal recurrence of the body, he argues, the philosopher's soul would be condemned "once more to bondage, thus taking upon itself an endless task, like Penelope when she undid her own weaving" (*Ph.* 83b).

On the other hand, Nietzsche conceives his ethics of self-cultivation as teaching individuals to harmonise all the accidents of existence so that they become essential or necessary parts of a beautiful and singular whole. Following Nehamas, Rorty captured this aspect of Nietzsche's counter-Platonic ideal: "[Nietzsche] hoped that once we realised that Plato's 'true world' was just a fable, we would seek consolation ... not in having transcended the animal condition, but in being that peculiar sort of dying animal who, by describing himself in his own terms, had created himself" (Rorty 1989: 27). As Nietzsche explained in a note from this period:

Let us etch the image of eternity upon *our* life. This thought contains far more than all those religions, which hold our present lives in contempt as being ephemeral, and which have taught us to raise our sights towards some dubious *other* life. (*KSA* 9:503)

Nietzsche believes that to compose an artistic or 'musical' life makes it possible to will its eternal repetition. Nietzsche assumes that the harmoniously composed soul will want to repeat its life, including every last accident into which it has breathed a beautiful meaning. Plato's philosophy prepares the soul's liberation *from* eternally repeated life; Nietzsche's art of living prepares one to create an individual life that bears the image of this singular self and that one wants to live again and again. Platonic philosophy liberates the soul so that it can be free of this repetition. Nietzsche argues that through his art of living free spirits can weave together a beautiful life that they will want to live repeatedly. Free spirits do not seek liberation from their desires, as Platonists do, but to make of their thirst for life a beautiful composition worthy of eternal recycling. Nietzsche aims to replace the Platonic ideal of transcendent redemption *from* life with his own aesthetic model of redemption *within* life.

Granted Nietzsche defends an ethics of self-cultivation that values the creation of the self as a singular, immortal artwork, why does he introduce the strange and untimely idea of eternal recurrence? In Nietzsche's view the Genoese nobles he celebrated lived an affirmative life without any need to reflectively affirm its real or imagined recurrence (Gemes 2008: 462). If an affirmative life is realisable without any need to will its eternal recurrence, why does Nietzsche introduce the ancient idea of cyclical cosmology? What is its significance in his ethics of self-cultivation? Nietzsche's critics argue against his assumption that the thought of eternity is integral to the ethics of self-cultivation. Properly understood, they claim recurrence is strictly a matter of indifference.

Many commentators argue that the thought of eternal recurrence is psychologically incoherent and/or insignificant. Even if we believe it is literally true as a cosmological thesis, they argue, rather than gnashing our teeth at the thought of our own recurrence or proclaiming the demon's declaration of recurrence as divine we ought to greet it with profound "*indifference*" (Reginster 2006: 211; Soll 1973). On this view, the doctrine of eternal recurrence has no weight, it cannot compel us to take our choices more seriously, because the recurring lives cannot be *my* experiences in any relevant sense; these future selves are simply not me. We should remain unmoved by the doctrine of the eternal recurrence of identical lives since it necessarily rules out any psychological continuity between the reiterated selves.[4] Soll argues, for example, that it is

impossible for there to be among different recurrences of a person the kind of identity that seems to exist among the different states of consciousness of the same person within a particular recurrence . . . Only by inappropriately construing the suffering of some future recurrence on the model of suffering later in this life does the question of eternal recurrence of one's pain weigh upon one with 'the greatest stress'. (Soll 1973: 343)

---

[4] Cf. Kain (2007: 54) and Loeb (2010: 14–16), who challenge the view that complete qualitative identity of recurrence logically precludes any awareness of recurrence.

The Roman Epicurean Lucretius first expressed this objection to the practical and psychological significance of the doctrine of recurrence. Lucretius did so in the context of formulating a therapeutic argument designed to alleviate the fear we might have about repeating our life (see Ure and Ryan 2019). Lucretius argues that even if the atoms that compose us now have been assembled in exactly the same way in the past or they reassemble in the future, we should have no concern about that past or future self. He claims that since we have no psychological continuity with these hypothetical past or future selves "the suffering of these selves do not touch us" (*Lucr. De Re. Nat.* III. 854–855). Death, as he puts it, snaps the chain of our identity (III. 854–855).

Commentators illuminate this Epicurean-inspired argument by means of a spatial analogy: just as the possible existence of an infinite number of identical selves in other locations cannot add or subtract to our experience so too the temporal recurrence of identical selves is irrelevant to us since they lack any connection to our present self (Magnus 1978: 191; Clark 1990: 268). "It seems reasonable for me", as Reginster explains this point, "to worry about myself in some future cycle only if there is some sort of continuity . . . between my current self and the self re-experiencing the same pains and failures" (Reginster 2006: 211). If there is no psychological continuity between me and my future identical selves, then we cannot view their suffering as tantamount to my experiencing further pain. If we accept this claim, then Lucretius' therapeutic argument seems to succeed: a proper understanding of recurrence means we have no reason for alarm that we will suffer again since we will not have any psychological connection to future duplicate selves. Far from adding infinitely to the suffering and joy of our own lives, so this argument runs, these duplicates add nothing to it (Magnus 1978: 191).

If we conceive Nietzsche's thought of eternal recurrence as a thought experiment rather than as a theory concerning the nature of the universe a similar problem concerning its psychological insignificance arises.[5] As Williams reflects,

[5] Nietzsche himself considers the potential significance of recurrence as a thought experiment: "Even if the circular repetition is only a probability or possibility, even the thought of a possibility can shatter and transform us – not only experiences or definite expectations! How the (mere) possibility of eternal damnation has worked" (*KSA* 9:11 [203]). Cf. Loeb (2010: 18n13). Nietzsche's analogy between eternal damnation and eternal recurrence is

it is a good question what this model [eternal return] could possibly achieve. The affirmation is supposed to be immensely costly, an achievement commensurate with the dreadfulness of what it wills. Yet . . . the affirmation . . . occurs in the gravity-free space of the imagination. Can the "greatest weight", as Nietzsche calls it, really weigh anything, when it consists in willing an entirely contrary-to-fact recurrence? Can it be more than a Styrofoam rock on a film set of cosmic heroism? (Williams 2006: 53–54)

Williams reasons that since by affirming the eternal recurrence of our lives we merely affirm a purely imaginative or contrary-to-fact recurrence it can have no great weight or significance. "If it is a mere fantasy", he asks rhetorically, "then how can 'willing' the Eternal Recurrence cost one anything at all?" (Williams 2001: xvi). On both the literal and imaginative interpretations of the thought of recurrence then it is difficult to see how it could have any psychological significance.

Yet arguably these criticisms fail to comprehend the nature of Nietzsche's thought experiment. We can see how Nietzsche gave significance or 'weight' to the thought of recurrence by examining how he dramatises the demon's challenge. In the first place, he stages this thought in a way that precludes you from thinking that there can be any psychological break between you and your replica. If Nietzsche's demon were to remain strictly true to the Epicurean claim that there is psychological discontinuity among the exact replicas then it would have to say: "This life as you now live and have lived it *another, yet identical person* would have to live once again". But Nietzsche's demon insists that life you have led will "return to *you*" not merely to an exact replica (341, emphasis added). Nietzsche's demon challenges you to face the prospect that *you*, your present self, will live the same life again, not the prospect that *another* person will lead the same life you have led. It is not a question of another person living the same life as you now lead it, but of your present self living it again.

Against Williams' view, Clark shows how Nietzsche's thought experiment has psychological significance. As she argues, Nietzsche asks us to imagine the eternal recurrence "unrealistically, on the

---

questionable. For Christians eternal damnation is not a thought experiment. Christians experienced the death-bed as a bed of torture because they believed in the reality of eternal damnation, not because they conceived it merely as a remote possibility (*D* 77).

model of a later occurrence in one's present life" (Clark 1990: 269). "To use eternal recurrence as a test of affirmation", as she explains, "one must ... imagine the recurrences of one's life as continuous with and therefore as adding suffering and joy to one's present life" (Clark, 1990: 270). We must then imagine the recurrence of our future selves as continuous with our present self. We must imagine, in other words, that our present self will re-experience again and again all of the joys and sorrow of our present life. If we conduct the thought experiment of imagining that we will relive the same life again and again then, as she suggests, "the extreme reactions Nietzsche describes ... make sense and complete indifference would seem psychologically impossible" (Clark, 1990: 270). The purpose of the demon's challenge is to test your evaluation of your present life by ascertaining whether *you* want to live it all over again. "The question" as Kain puts it "is whether I love my life, my present life – love it so completely that I would live it again. I am being asked if I would live my life again to see if I love my present life" (Kain 2007: 55). To say that you do not identify with that future person is merely to avoid undertaking the test of whether you value your life sufficiently to want to repeat it *ad infinitum.*

Indeed, even if you insisted on the Epicurean-inspired notion that there is no psychological continuity between yourself and your past and future *doppelgängers* this merely displaces the demon's question. Psychological discontinuity does not justify the further claim that we should be indifferent to future selves. We can see why this is so when we consider the conclusions one commentator draws from these same Lucretian arguments about the alleged practical insignificance of recurrence: "So I live and die, and eons later someone is born whose life has exactly the same characteristics as mine, including temporal/spatial relation to everything in its cycle. No connection exists between the two lives, nothing carries over from my death to the birth of my double in the later cycle. A clear conception of this lack of *connection* should reduce a person's concern for her double in the next cycle to the level of concern one would have for any human being" (Clark 1990: 267–268). We should note that at most, if true, the Epicurean-inspired argument only justifies 'reducing' our concern for our future self to the same level of concern we have for any other human being. "If I insist on viewing the liver of my next life as an other", as Kain puts it, "the least I should do is ask myself whether I love my present life enough that I could wish it on another" (Kain 2007: 55). In other words, the standard objection to the psychological significance of Nietzsche's doctrine only serves to displace the question from "Are you willing to live the exact same life again and again?" to "Would you wish the exact same life on another?" And your concern for another person leading the same life as you have might turn out to be greater than your concern for yourself.

If then Nietzsche's thought of recurrence can engender concern about how one lives by imagining one must confront and evaluate the prospect of its eternal repetition we might ask how this lends itself to the cultivation of oneself as a singular, immortal artwork. Part of the answer lies in the way Nietzsche dramatises this thought as the expression of our ownmost conscience. Nietzsche frames the thought of recurrence not only such that you must suppose that your present self will re-experience the same life again and again, but also that you must assess this prospect in light of what he calls your "ownmost conscience" (338). Nietzsche's dramatisation gives the thought the force of this conscience. In an earlier figuration of this concept, as we observed in the previous chapter, Nietzsche suggested that we all have a "secret bad conscience:" "the law that every man is a unique miracle", that implores us to fashion ourselves into a unique unity (*SE* 1).

Nietzsche's demon's challenges you to assess your present life and actions in light of your "ownmost" or "secret bad conscience".[6] That Nietzsche wants us to assess the thought of our recurrence in light of our ownmost conscience follows from the mise-en-scène: the demon confronts you in a moment of the profoundest loneliness when all that matters to you is your own singular fate independent of or standing apart from all others. Nietzsche suggests that our evaluation of our own recurrence, the weight it has for us, must ultimately derives from what he call our "ownmost conscience" (338). He identifies the law or principle of this conscience in the imperative: 'You should become who you are' (270). Our "ownmost conscience", as he explains it,

---

[6] Nietzsche, as Loeb observes, alludes to Socrates' *daimonion* (Loeb 1998: 131–143; 2010: 35–38). However, Nietzsche conceives his *Dämon* as playing the exact opposite role to Socrates' *daimonion*. Socrates' *daimonion* only dissuades him from acting, and never urges him on (*Ap.* 31 c–d). In sharp contrast, Nietzsche's *Dämon* challenges us to affirm life and to do so by becoming who we are.

impels us to follow our own "*path*", a trajectory we follow independently of, and oblivious to anything other than the realisation and
perfection of our own unique set of possibilities (338).

As we saw in the previous chapter, Nietzsche defends this "ownmost
conscience" against the force of moral conscience. One of his key
objections to Kantian and Schopenhauerian morality is that they both
entail "losing myself *from my path*" by compelling us to follow generalisable rules or to live for others (338). Nietzsche's ownmost conscience
censures us for betraying our own unique individuality. Nietzsche
observes that this morality says, "Live in seclusion so that you *are able*
to live for yourself!" (338). Nietzsche's *Dämon* creates this moment of
seclusion and separation by stealing into your loneliest loneliness to
announce the doctrine of recurrence. He stages the demon's challenge in
such a way that we cannot take "refuge in the conscience of the others"
and we must therefore consider the prospect of recurrence strictly in
terms of whether or present lives realise our personal infinity (338).

The thought of eternal repetition is crucial to Nietzsche's ethics of
self-cultivation because answering the question 'do you want it again
and again?' is the means by which we can disclose our ownmost
conscience. We disclose our ownmost conscience by testing whether
or not each and every action can bear the weight of eternity.
By compelling us to imagine we have one and only one identical
life and that we will repeat it to all eternity Nietzsche's *Dämon*
compels us to determine how we must live to abide by the imperative:
become who you are. Eternity compels us to consider what we believe
makes our transient lives worthy of this repetition. Nietzsche assumes
that when we examine our lives through the lens of eternity (or
eternal repetition) we will judge that only a life that bears the
monogram of our own existence, of what is singular or unique to
ourselves is worthy of repetition. Eternity makes us hone in on our
singularity. Or to put the point another way, Nietzsche supposes that
if we take the view from recurrence we must despair if we discover
that our lives are merely replications or minor variations on
a common theme. For Nietzsche what evokes a despairing response
to the thought of our own recurrence is not the return of our
suffering, but the return of a life that is not our *own* or that does
not bear the monogram our existence. The thought of recurrence
evokes the dread of not living a life according to our own laws and

standards and in doing so failing to become the unique individuals we are. It is the dread of failing to become who you are. Nietzsche's assumes that the exercise of eternal recurrence both reveals our singularities and motivates the ideal of creating our lives as immortal artworks.

Nietzsche also stresses that for the thought of recurrence to function as instrument of self-cultivation we must employ it as an experiment or exercise. As Magnus rightly claims, mere belief in eternal recurrence "does not cause or induce genuine affirmation . . . once the doctrine is 'understood' no automatic liberation seems to follow" (Magnus 1978: 156). Yet Nietzsche does not conceive eternal recurrence as a theoretical doctrine we simply need to understand, but as what we might call a 'spiritual exercise'. As Hadot defines this term, spiritual exercises are practices (meditation, memorisation, dialogue and so on) that share the fundamental aim of transforming our vision of the world and placing us in the perspective of the Whole (Hadot 1995: 82–109). The object of these exercises is to bring about such a transformation in the way we live.

Nietzsche conceives the thought of recurrence as a particular spiritual exercise or practice: viz. a repeated meditation on the significance of idea of recurrence. It is an exercise through which we transform our present life such that it becomes such that we would desire its eternal repetition. Following a classical analogy we can conceive eternal recurrence as a spiritual gymnastics that makes us more adept at imposing the image of eternity on our lives. In this sense, as Hadot recognised, Nietzsche's philosophy follows in the footsteps of the ancient schools. Following the ancient model, Nietzsche rejects the idea of philosophy as the teaching of abstract theory – much less an exegesis of texts – and embrace it as an art of living (Hadot 1995: 83, 108). We therefore miss something essential about his doctrine if we conceive it as imagining or believing in recurrence as a logical or theoretical possibility. Nietzsche does not ask us to contemplate recurrence as a theoretical doctrine, but to incorporate the thought of recurrence into our lives as a practice of self-cultivation. Rather than contemplating or imagining recurrence, he asks how you might be transformed if "this thought gained power over you" (341).

In other words, the cultivating effect of the thought of recurrence hinges on it overpowering us, which is an entirely distinct proposition to idly contemplating it as a theoretical doctrine. Nietzsche stresses that thought of recurrence must exercise the force of conscience: that is it must exercise mastery over our lives. As Nietzsche conceives it, the thought of recurrence transforms or crushes us only if it exercises this mastery over our judgement and does so in the sense that "the question in each and every thing: 'Do you want this again and again and innumerable times again?' Would lie on [our] actions as the heaviest weight!" (341). Nietzsche implies that thought of repetition is only cultivating insofar as it is overpowering, applies to all of our actions and becomes incorporated into our lives as a repeated practice. Nietzsche's thought of recurrence demonstrates how he adopted the ancient model of philosophy as a way of life. As he conceives it, the ethics of self-cultivation entails trying to see whether we can live in accordance with the thought of recurrence.

Yet even as Nietzsche models eternal recurrence on the ancient conception of philosophy as a technique of self-cultivation, he believes it achieves the opposite of the ancient exercises. According to Hadot the goal of the ancient exercises is to enable individuals to transcend their individual, passionate subjectivity and ascend to an impersonal, universal perspective (Hadot 1995: 97). "Seneca", as he explains, "finds joy not in Seneca, but in the Seneca identified with universal Reason. One rises from one level of the self to another, transcendent level" (Hadot 2009: 136). The goal of Nietzsche's exercise, on the other hand, is to rise from the level of a common, collective self to a higher, singular level. If Stoics are necessarily uniform and unvaried, Nietzscheans must be irregular and varied. The Hellenistic schools more generally maintained that the ideal life is the realisation of a universal human nature. In order to realise this ideal they argued that philosophy must liberate us from false conventional values that encourage us to neglect a life in agreement with our universal nature. The Hellenistic idea, as Long puts it "is that an understanding of this nature can and should serve as the technologist of the self, shaping our innate potentialities in more life-enhancing ways than cultural norms themselves offer to us. This is not a project of making one's life into an artwork" (Long 2006: 27–28).

By contrast Nietzsche maintains that the ideal life requires constructing ourselves as unique artworks, not agreeing with universal nature. In order to realise this ideal he argues philosophy must liberate us from the structures of consciousness that compels us to neglect the cultivation of our singularity. We have, as he put in *GS* 8, "unknown or badly known" qualities, which have "lines and subtleties and sculptures that might give pleasure to a god with a divine microscope" (8). Nietzsche's thought of recurrence is a technique of self-cultivation that aims to counter-act the limits of consciousness. Nietzsche explains the origins and evolution of consciousness as an instrument of social integration that belongs to our existence not as individuals but rather as what he disparagingly calls herd animals. What we 'know' of ourselves through consciousness, he argues, is only that aspect of ourselves that is dependent upon the community. The limits on self-knowledge, he argues in Book 5, are built into the evolutionary history of consciousness: it has been shaped by evolutionary pressure to allow us to know and communicate only "that in ourselves which is 'non-individual' or 'average'", i.e. those frailties and vulnerabilities that we share with all the members of our community (354). Nietzsche explains this limitation through a political analogue: consciousness is the tyranny of the majority extended into our 'depths'. When we 'translate' our unconscious thoughts into consciousness all that becomes visible is the typical, general or herd-like. And yet, Nietzsche claims, "at bottom all our actions are incomparably and utterly personal, unique and boundlessly individual, there is no doubt; but as soon as we translate them into consciousness, *they no longer seem to be*" (354). Our personal infinity is lost in translation.

Nietzsche assumes then that thought of recurrence is a technique or exercise that can help us to identify and cultivate this unrealised, yet potential singularity. The view from recurrence compels us to identify, value and cultivate our singularity or personal infinity, he suggests, because we suffer despair at the thought of the eternal repetition of commonality and joy at the thought of our eternal singularity. Nietzsche's exercise motivates the desire to create an uncommon life because it implicitly draws on one of the most powerful modern ethical ideals. "Artistic creation", as Taylor observes, has become "the paradigm mode in which people can come to self-definition. The artist becomes in some way the paradigm case of the human being, as agent of original self-definition"

(Taylor 1991: 62). Nietzsche's belief that this exercise will cultivate our singularity is contingent on it mobilising background values, specifically the romantic value of the self as artwork.

We can say then that by means of the thought of eternal recurrence Nietzsche formulates a coherent and psychologically significant exercise of whether or not you affirm or love your present life: the exercise is whether or not you are willing to live it again and again as the measure of your ownmost conscience. Nietzsche conceives our 'ownmost' or secret conscience as setting us the task of weaving a unique, integrated self such that we want our life and ourselves again and again. The success of Nietzsche's art of the self-fashioning lies in creating a life that we wish to repeat eternally.

CHAPTER 7

Dionysian Pessimism: *Book 5*

Nietzsche's begins Book 5 with his ominous account of the eclipse of the old Christian God and closes with a flashing glimpse of the return of the pagan god Dionysus. In his extraordinary, hyperbolic autobiography, *Ecce Homo*, he later describes the significance of these two 'events': "The *unmasking* of Christian morality is an event without unequal, a real catastrophe. He who exposes it is a force majeure, a destiny – he breaks the history of mankind into two parts. One lives *before* him, one lives *after* him" (*EH* IV 8). Nietzsche believes that his birth year 1844 will eventually mark the first year of a new era. This new era will live under the sign of the pagan god Dionysus. "Have I been understood? – *Dionysus against the Crucified*" (*EH* IV 9).

In Book 5, as we shall see, Nietzsche moves beyond the brand of ethical perfectionism that characterised Book 4 to what we might call a type of political perfectionism. What is at stake in Book 5 is Nietzsche's grandiose vision of the recreation of European culture on new foundations. Nietzsche conjures up 'free spirits' as the earliest advocates of the rebirth of European culture. He celebrates them as the first to dimly recognise that the demise of belief in the Christian god must signal the inevitable collapse of the foundations of European culture. Nietzsche depicts this as a menacing prophecy:

And now that this faith has been undermined, how much must collapse because it was built on this faith, leaned on it, grown into it – for example, the entire European morality. This long, dense succession of demolition, destruction, downfall, upheaval that now stands ahead: who would guess enough of it today to play the prophet of deep darkness and the eclipse of the sun the like of which has probably never existed on earth? (343)

Yet Nietzsche sees in this eclipse the promise of a new dawn and a new cheerfulness. After the death of God, he hopes for the emergence of free spirits who have the strength to counter Christianity and practice an affirmative type of life and recreate a tragic culture. Nietzsche paints Christianity pitch black. From the late 1870s onwards he criticises Christianity not just as an intellectual error but also as a profoundly malignant error. Nietzsche claims that Christian culture has been in the service of extreme ascetic ideal that cultivates humans as herd animals. With his matchless rhetorical virtuosity he seeks to evoke the deepest contempt for the Christian domestication of the species. "Does it not seem", he asks, "that *one* will has dominated Europe for eighteen centuries, the will to make of man a *sublime abortion*?" (*BGE* 62). As he later mocks, Christian morality has transformed a beast of prey into a household pet (*GM* I.11).

In *BGE* and *GS* Book 5 Nietzsche revises the figure of free spirits: they are not merely sceptical Enlightenment critics of superstition and fanaticism, or ethical perfectionists. Instead they strive to articulate and embody Dionysian self-affirmation against Christian self-denial. Nietzsche claims that the realisation of this counter-ideal necessarily entails a grand aristocratic political project. "Only after me", he declares in *EH,* "will there be *grand politics* on earth" (*EH* 'Destiny' 1). Nietzsche claims that free spirits must overthrow democracy as a project that continues to create tame, herd animals. The full affirmation of life, he argues, requires free spirits to subvert Christianity's domestication of the species. Nietzsche aims to expose modern democratic egalitarianism as the secularised culmination of the Christian ideal. Free spirits must prepare the ground for future philosophers who have the will and discipline to engage in the "artistic refashioning of mankind" (*BGE* 62). These future philosophers will take charge of the cultivation of the species and create the type of aristocratic political order that Nietzsche insists is necessary to enhance the highest human types (*BGE* 61). Nietzsche's grand philosophical vision conceives free spirits as agents who promote the conditions for the birth of a pan-European, aristocratic political order dedicated to the enhancement of the highest human types.

Nietzsche adds *GS* Book 5 to take into account the radical project of ethical and political transformation he mapped out in *Z* and *BGE*. It is a manifesto of this revised free-spirit ideal and a moral exhortation to its potential agents whom he repeatedly addresses in the first-person plural as "we godless, antimetaphysicians", "we home-less ones", "we . . . *good Europeans*", "we incomprehensible ones", "we fearless ones" or "we . . . artists of contempt" (344, 377, 379).[1] Book 5 is a call to arms for free spirits; a "herald call [. . .] challenging the most courageous to *their* courage" (*BGE* 30).

Nietzsche's worst fear is that the death of God will fail to promote this radical revaluation of our moral foundations, but that Christianity's ascetic values, the values "of those who suffer from life as from an illness", will perpetuate themselves in new guises: democracy and positivistic science (*BGE* 62). Nietzsche identifies the death of God as the opportunity for free spirits to investigate the hidden meaning of European morality and discover a new world of affirmative ideals:

Indeed, at hearing the news 'the old god is dead', we philosophers and 'free spirits', feel illuminated by a new dawn: our hearts overflow with gratitude, amazement, forebodings, expectation – finally the horizon seems clear again, finally our ships may set out again, set out to face any danger; every daring of the lover of knowledge is allowed again; the sea, *our* sea, lies open again; maybe there has never been such an 'open sea'. (343)

Nietzsche's free spirits are the Christopher Columbuses of the moral world. It is their relentless questioning, he hopes, that will eventually overthrow the reign of Christian morality and culture. Nietzsche aims to show free spirits how to see their most familiar, venerable commitments to morality and truth from a new perspec-tive. He claims that because we stand so close to some things, such as truth and morality, we cannot see them properly (355/*GM* III.24). To comprehend them we need to see them from a new vantage point. Nietzsche personifies this perspectival method in the figure of the wanderer who leaves town to see it from a distant perspective (380). The task of free spirits is to become wanderers who question very familiar and enduring commitments to truth and morality from a distant vantage point. From this perspective, Nietzsche suggests,

---

[1] Robin Small notes this dramatic shift from Book 4 to Book 5: "It is jarring to go from a challenge set in the individual's "loneliest loneliness" to Nietzsche's self-assigned role as the team coach for an imagined group of 'new philosophers'" (Small 2017).

free spirits can take the measure of Christian morality and question the *value* of these hallowed values.

Nietzsche's first step then is to experimentally put into question the value of our moral and intellectual conscience. Up to this point, he claims, philosophers have singularly failed to address these questions. Rather, he suggests, they have unquestionably affirmed their value; they have not seen morality or truth as problems (345/*GM* III.24). Once free spirits acknowledge these *as* problems, however, Nietzsche believes they will be compelled to address new questions: Is there a justification for the will to truth (science) or morality? Why have we treated them as unquestionable or as metaphysically warranted? Do they warrant this high valuation? What is the value of morality and the will to truth? Why not immorality and untruth?

By asking these questions, Nietzsche's free spirits pursue a perilous path: they place in question the values that provide the foundations of their own existence. Addressing himself to future free spirits, he observes, "what meaning does *our* being have, if it were not that ... will to truth has become conscious of itself as a problem *in us*?" (*GM* III.27). In other words, it is on the basis of their own unconditional commitment to truth, itself a moral commitment, that they question the justification and value of truth and morality (*GM* III.27). They risk undermining their own commitment to truth and morality through this radical questioning of their value. From their new vantage point then, these free-spirited wanderers may discover that the town they left behind does not have the sacrosanct value they once accorded it.

Indeed, Nietzsche argues that they must discover that the commitment to Christian morality and its discipline of truth does not have metaphysical grounds, but is a historically contingent symptom of an extreme asceticism, or, as he puts it, of "life *against* life" (*GM* III.13). Taking the free spirit's distant view to its extreme, he observes in *GM*:

Read from a distant planet, the majuscule script of our earthly existence would perhaps seduce the reader to the conclusion that the earth was the ascetic planet *par excellence*, an outpost of the most discontented, arrogant and nasty creatures who harboured a deep disgust for themselves, for the world, for all of life and hurt themselves as much as possible out of pleasure in hurting – probably their only pleasure. (*GM* III.11)

Nietzsche wants free spirits to *see* that up to now our species as whole (not just European culture) has granted the highest value to life denial or self-crucifixion. From this new vantage point these lovers of knowledge can set sail again, as Nietzsche puts, investigating why this has been the case, evaluating this seemingly self-contradictory project of life denial, and exploring the possibility of a radically different, life-affirming model of existence. Nietzsche identifies this affirmative model with the god Dionysus, a figure of "overflowing energy" or "superabundance" who stands in sharp opposition to the Christian god, the symbol of the "impoverishment of life" (370).

In *GS* Book 5 then Nietzsche's realigns his ideal of the free spirit with his grand project of a total revolution. On the verge of his collapse into insanity in 1889 Nietzsche wrote in his last testament:

I know my fate. One day there will be associated with my name the recollection of something frightful – of a crisis like no other before on earth, of the profoundest collision of conscience, of a decision evoked *against* everything that until then had been believed in, demanded, sanctified. I am not a man I am dynamite. (*EH* 'Destiny' 1)

Does Nietzsche give free spirits reasons for exploding the foundations of European civilisation? In *GS* Book 5 Nietzsche develops a rhetorically charged case against European civilisation as a pathological project that has ruined humanity. It develops a highly compressed version of his critical perspective on European values, especially the value of truth and morality, and offers flashes of his 'positive' account of a higher morality and an affirmative life. We shall focus on his unmasking of the will to truth as the last avatar of an ascetic aversion to life and his attempts to think beyond this life-denying ideal and articulate a 'higher' perspective of life affirmation.

In GS Book 5 Nietzsche grapples with whether the unconditional will to truth, a fundamental presupposition of modern science, is continuous with the ascetic aversion to life that he believes defines Christianity. Nietzsche identifies science as a sublimation of the Christian commitment to truth at all costs (357). If science's unconditional commitment to truth rests on such discredited metaphysical foundations, then we are within our rights to question this commitment. "From the very moment that faith in God of the ascetic ideal is denied", he explains, "*there is a new problem*: that of the *value* of truth-" (*GM* III. 24). Why truth rather than untruth (*BGE* 1)?

Nietzsche's answer to the question of the value of truth is open to a number of interpretations. These often hinge on their understanding of his view of the relationship of art to truth. On this issue Nietzsche remained deeply ambivalent:

About the relation of art to truth I became serious at the earliest time: and even now I stand before this dichotomy with a holy terror. (*KSA* 13: 550)

It is in the context of the problem of the value of truth that Nietzsche examines the relation of art to truth. We saw that in *GS* Books 1 and 2 Nietzsche argued that science undermines our faith in reason in life (1), yet that satisfying this faith is one of our deepest needs, and that science also delivers the bitter truth that it can never satisfy our deeply entrenched need for reason or meaning in our life.

According to one popular view, in the face of this conflict between truth and the conditions of life, Nietzsche resolutely commits to the unconditional value or ideal of truthfulness. On this view, Nietzsche took it to be an "ethical necessity" to value truth and truth seeking over comforting illusions (Williams 2001: xix). According to Bernard Williams, Nietzsche retains support for an unconditional will to truth, valuing truthfulness above all else, regardless of the costs (Williams 2004: 13). "Indifference to truthfulness", as Williams puts it, "is for him merely an aspect of nihilism" (2004: 18). Nietzsche's free-spirit ideal, therefore, prioritises truth and concedes the necessity of artistic deception and simplification only if it satisfies this priority (Ridley 2007: 82–84). For Nietzsche, the value of truth trumps the pleasure of artistic illusion. That is to say, Nietzsche values art only if it serves to make it possible to possess the truth. "We possess art", as he famously put it, "lest we perish of the truth" (*WP* 822). Williams glosses Nietzsche's point to highlight his commitment to truth over illusions: "we possess art so that we can possess the truth and not perish of it" (Williams 2001: xix). "Beauty", as Michael Tanner puts it, "is both an intimation of the horror of life and a consolation for it . . . Art at its greatest, tells

the truth and makes it possible to bear it" (Tanner 1993: xxix).[2]
Art serves the truth by making it bearable.

If this view is correct, Nietzsche conceives art as analogous to a narcotic that takes the edge off otherwise unbearable truths. It does so by sweetening, falsifying, or veiling the truth so that we can possess it without perishing (*BGE* 39). Art sweetens the bitter truth. Nietzsche's ethical commitment to overriding value of truth also requires that when we resort to art, we merely round off the poem, so to speak, we do not invent it *ex nihilo* (107). On this view, Nietzsche's measure of value is the courage to bear as much truth as possible and to resort to artistic narcotics only when the truth is too much to endure and only then to sweeten the truth, not engage in wholesale invention or falsification. "The last role of truthfulness", as Ridley explains, "is truthfully to surrender to the necessity of deceiving oneself, having stood firm against one's heart's desire to capitulate sooner" (Ridley 1998: 140). Art is a capitulation to one's human, all too human frailties.

A second plausible view is that Nietzsche does not prioritise truth over artistic illusion, but makes the value of *both* truth and untruth conditional on their contribution to human flourishing. In this context, Nietzsche maintains that unconditional commitment to truth at any price is nothing more than a moral prejudice and that our flourishing may require the *sanctification* of lying and deception. Christopher Janaway argues that Nietzsche's commitment to the value of truth is contingent on its connection to other values that he deems superior. Nietzsche's alternative to the unquestioning value of truth, as he explains, "is an attempt to see the value of truth-acquisition as conditional on the values of health, strength, affirmation or the degree of viability, bearability and self-satisfaction we can sustain" (Janaway 2014:53). On this view, Nietzsche experiments with putting "life first, and sacrific[ing] truth-seeking to life if need be" (Janaway 2014: 53). Paul Franco argues that *GS* is distinct from the first two books of the free-spirit trilogy in its questioning of the unconditional will to truth and its corresponding revaluation of art. The difference between "the ascetic science" that characterises the first two works of his trilogy

---

[2] Cf. Rilke, *Duino Elegies*: "For beauty is nothing but the beginning of terror/which we are barely able to endure."

(*HH* and *D*) and "the gay science" of the third (*GS*), he argues, is that in the latter Nietzsche "abjures the unconditionality of the will to truth and thereby opens the door to a more profound appreciation of the role of art and appearance in life" (Franco 2011: 206).

In making the value of truth and untruth conditional on life, Nietzsche came to see that we must often value untruth, deception and artistic illusion rather than their opposites. In *BGE*, for example, he argues that it is not unconditionally valuable to hold true beliefs rather than false beliefs:

We do not consider the falsity of a judgment as itself an objection to a judgment; this is perhaps where our new language will sound most foreign. The question is how far the judgment promotes and preserves life, how well it preserves, and perhaps even cultivates, the type ... To acknowledge untruth as a condition of life: this clearly means resisting the usual value feelings in a dangerous manner. (*BGE* 4)

For the sake of the flourishing of life, he claims, it is often indeed better to be deceived, deceive oneself or others than the opposite. Nietzsche challenges the "blind rage" with which philosophers resist being deceived: "*Why not?* It is no more than a moral prejudice that truth is worth more than mere appearance; it is even the worse proved assumption there is in the world. Let at least this much be admitted: there would be no life at all if not on the basis of perspective estimates and appearances" (*BGE* 35). In *GS* 344 Nietzsche makes the Homeric hero Odysseus emblematic of the value of error, perspective and appearance for life. If we value flourishing, he seems to imply, we ought to model ourselves on Homer's Odysseus, not Plato's Socrates. We should not seek to establish and live according to a single, eternal truth, the good in itself, but to master the play of appearances or perspectives. Odysseus is the exemplar of the pre-philosophical Greek notion of cunning (*polymetis*), the man of many turns (*polytropos*) who succeeds through trickery, deception and lies.[3] "Life on the largest scale", Nietzsche claims, "has always shown itself to be on the side of this most unscrupulous *polytropoi*" (344). If this is the case, he reasons, then it seems to follow we ought to conceive the will to truth not merely as quixotic, but as "a principle hostile to life and

---

[3] Marcel Detienne and Jean-Pierre Vernant (1991) excavate the pre-philosophical Greek notion of 'cunning intelligence' that Nietzsche glosses in his allusions to Odysseus.

destructive" (344). "Will to truth", he concludes, "that could be a hidden will to death" (344).

Nietzsche's suggestion of a connection between the will to truth and a will to death suggests a third possible interpretation of his analysis of the value of truth and the relationship of truth to art. On this view, Nietzsche does not value truth unconditionally and look to art simply to counter our despair over the bitter truth with lies, deceptions and falsifications. Rather Nietzsche sees the unconditional will to truth as a symptom of an ascetic aversion to life and he identifies art, or at least tragic art, as the highest expression of the affirmation of the value of existence, not its falsification. We can see this line of thought emerging in GS Book 5 (344/357), and he explicitly takes up its threads in his next book *GM*.[4] Nietzsche outlines his concern about the complicity between the will to truth and an ascetic aversion to life in the famous section 344.

Here Nietzsche's argues that the unconditional will to truth has always been predicated on metaphysical faith in the divine, and that this faith expressed an ascetic contempt for this world:

> Those who are truthful in the audacious and ultimate sense which faith in science presupposes *thereby affirm another world* than that of life, nature, and history; and insofar as they affirm this 'other world', must they not by the same token deny its counterpart, this world, *our* world? . . . But you will have gathered what I am getting at, namely, that it is still a *metaphysical faith* upon which our faith in science rests – even we knowers of today we godless anti-metaphysicians, still take *our* fire too, from the flame lit by the thousand year old faith, the Christian faith which was also Plato's faith that God is truth; that truth is divine. (344)

Why have philosophers sacrificed everything to the will to truth? Put simply, Nietzsche's answer is that they have held the world in contempt and conceived the truth as divine, or as connecting us to another, metaphysical world.[5] Nietzsche believes that the symptom of suffering, impoverished life is contempt for this world and its sufferings and with it the metaphysical need for another world. The Platonic assumption that truth is divine, that we 'ascend', as it

---

[4] In *GM* Nietzsche quotes at length and elucidates *GS* 344 and 357. See *GM* III.24/27.
[5] See e.g. "The true world, attainable to the wise, the pious – he dwells in it, *he is it*" (*TI* 'World' 1).

were, to another world of perfect, eternal forms is symptomatic of an ascetic aversion to life and it is this that motivates the unconditional will to truth. Nietzsche admits, that even "we godless anti-metaphysicians" (344) or "we free, *very* free spirits" (*GM* III.24) have not yet freed themselves from the ascetic contempt for this world that originally motivated the unconditional will to truth. Nietzsche suggests that genuine free spirits must in some way release themselves from the bind of their commitment to truth since he identifies "*so-called* 'free spirits'" with a faith in truth that is "more rigid and more absolute than anyone else" (*GM* III.24).

Nietzsche argues that the contempt for the world implicit in this unconditional will to truth culminates in modern science: it sacrifices all the metaphysical dreams purely in the name of its faith in the truth. Modern science, he maintains in *GM*, is not the enemy of the ascetic contempt for life, but its "kernel": it denies the value of this life and eliminates all metaphysical illusions of another world (*GM* III.27). The victories of science over metaphysical illusions are victories, as he explains, but *not* victories over the ascetic ideal. "The ascetic ideal", he claims, "was decidedly not conquered, it was on the contrary, made stronger, I mean more elusive, more spiritual, more insidious by the fact that science constantly and unsparingly detached and broke off a wall or outwork that had attached itself to [the ascetic ideal] and *coarsened* its appearance" (*GM* III.25). Atheism is the culmination of this contempt for the world. "Unconditional honest atheism (*its* air alone is what we breathe, we more spiritual men of the age!)", he asserts, "is therefore *not* opposed to the ascetic ideal as it appears to be; instead it is only one of the ideal's . . . final forms and inherent logical conclusions" (*GM* III.27). It represents, as he puts it, "the awe inspiring *catastrophe* of two thousand years in truthfulness that finally forbids itself the lie involved in the belief in God" (*GM* III.27/357). Nietzsche identifies the metaphysical illusions that free spirits must now forbid themselves as a consequence of this rigorous commitment to the truth:

Looking at nature as if it were proof of the goodness and care of a god; interpreting history in honour of some divine reason, as a continual testimony of a moral world order and ultimate moral purposes; interpreting one's own experiences as pious people have long interpreted their, as if everything were providential, a hint, designed and ordained for the sake of the salvation of the soul – that is *over* now, that has conscience *against* it. (357)

Obviously, Nietzsche sees the catastrophe of truthfulness not in its demolition of Christian metaphysics, which he embraces "as a victory of the European conscience", but in its final destruction of all possible belief in the value of human existence (357). "As we thus reject Christian interpretation and condemn its 'meaning' as counterfeit", he observes, "*Schopenhauer's* question immediately comes at us in a terrifying way: *Does existence have any meaning at all?*" (357). Nietzsche's worry is that under the impress of the ascetic ideal that denies the value of this world, science generates a "*piercing* sensation of (our) nothingness", by demonstrating the purposelessness or valuelessness of existence (*GM* III.25). In *BGE* he identifies nihilism, the sign of a despairing, mortally weary soul, with "puritanical fanatics of conscience who would rather lie down and die on a sure nothing than an uncertain something" (*BGE* 10). Nihilists, as he later puts it, would rather will nothing, than not will at all (*GM* III.28).

At the same time that Nietzsche diagnoses science as a symptom of asceticism, he also strongly implies that art is not merely illusion, falsehood or untruth that we need as a condition of preservation or enhancement. On this view, art does not simply sweeten the bitter truth, or prove itself a useful fiction, rather it is a perspective or interpretation of the world that discloses what science cannot: viz. *values*. In *GS* Nietzsche argues that we are mistaken if we believe that science alone can apprehend all that counts as meaningful and that art merely misleads or deceives. We can see an early glimmer of this view in his recycling of one of Schopenhauer's jokes. Artistic geniuses, Schopenhauer claims, have no aptitude for mathematics, but "conversely distinguished mathematicians have little susceptibility to works of art" (*WWR* 1: 189). Nietzsche quotes the anecdote Schopenhauer used to illustrate his claim:

'What is beautiful about that?' said the surveyor after a performance of *Iphigenia*. 'Nothing is proved in it!' (81)

Nietzsche mocks the surveyor's (or mathematician's) absurd category mistake in applying quantitative calculations to judge the value of art, in this case Racine's version of Euripides' last tragedy. It is worth noting that Nietzsche believes finding beauty in, for example, the tragedy of *Iphigenia,* which tells the tragic story of Agammenon's sacrifice of his daughter, expresses what he calls Dionysian affirmation. Self-evidently we cannot discern beauty of tragedy if we interpret the world only through the lens of science, but there is, it seems, another 'artistic' perspective that allows us to see the beauty of appearances.

Nietzsche clarifies and elaborates this line of thought in GS Book 5. Nietzsche rejects the interpretation of natural historians and mechanistic scientists as symptoms of the impoverishment of life. Natural historians merely reinforce the degeneration of the species through their unconscious idealisation of the morality of the weak. Mechanistic scientists interpretation of the world contributes to depriving the world of value or significance.

Natural historians of morality, he laments, endorse European culture's moral ideals rather than unmasking them as expressing the needs of the weakest forms of life. Despite demoting morality to the realm of natural phenomenon or 'appearance', and criticising the metaphysical errors used to justify it, he claims, their moral prejudices compel them to misinterpret morality as a necessary condition of existence. Recalling his criticisms of Herbert Spencer and Paul Rée in Book 1, he claims that they merely act as shield-bearers of the morality of compassion rather than seeing it as a sinister morality of decline (345). It is their unconscious fear of overflowing life and their hope to staunch it, he argues, that explains their support for a type of altruistic, self-sacrificing morality that protects the weakest forms of life at the expense of the strongest (373). Their moral horizons are limited by their fear of superabundant life. It is this that makes them the object of Nietzsche's untrammelled ire. From the free spirit's perspective Spencer's view, Nietzsche fulminates, is a "disgusting possibility" worthy of "contempt and annihilation" (373; also *EH* 'Destiny' 4) Charles Darwin also goes astray, he claims, mistakenly identifying the will to self-preservation as the basic instinct of life rather than seeing it as a symptom of distress and weakness (349).[6] By interpreting life

---

[6] John Richardson argues that Nietzsche's criticism of Darwinism wrongly imputes to his theory a teleological conception of a drive to self-preservation. See Richardson (2002: 545; 2004: 22). On Nietzsche's debt to and dispute with Darwin and nineteenth century

through the lens of the values that preserve the weak and impoverished, Nietzsche claims, these so-called naturalists endorse moralities that systematically undermine the highest forms of life and in doing so "deprive existence of its *great* character" (EH 'Destiny' 4).

Nietzsche's profound exasperation with these natural historians of morality is that they do not treat the phenomenon of morality as a *problem*: that is to say, they do not go beyond justifying a particular morality or identifying "the weeds of errors that may have overgrown it" to examine it 'medically' (345). For Nietzsche to treat morality as a problem is to pose the question: 'Does it contribute to cultivating the highest, as yet unexhausted possibilities of the species', or does it 'contribute to what he describes as the "*collective degeneration of man*"' (*BGE* 203)? Nietzsche defines this problem later in *GM* P 3: "Under what conditions did man invent the value judgements good and evil? *And what value do they themselves have?* Have they up to now obstructed or promoted human flourishing? Are they signs of distress, poverty and the degeneration of life? Or, on the contrary, do they reveal the fullness, strength and will of life, its courage, its confidence, its future?" (*GM* P 3). As we shall see, it is Nietzsche's Dionysian pessimism, his purely artistic and anti-Christian doctrine that underpin these questions.

In GS 373 Nietzsche turns his attention to mechanistic science, arguing that it is a sign of naiveté or illness for science to decree that a mechanistic interpretation of the world, which "permits counting, calculating, weighing, seeing, grasping, and nothing else", is the only permissible interpretation of the world (373). The "'scientific' interpretation of the world", he suggests, "might be the *stupidest* of all possible interpretations of the world; i.e. the one most lacking in significance" (373). In other words, Nietzsche claims that the stupidity or irrationality of this mechanistic account of the world lies in the fact that it discloses "an essentially *meaningless* world!" (373). If, then, Nietzsche argues that this mechanistic interpretation of the world is the stupidest interpretation of the world, and its idiocy resides in its failure to disclose meaning or significance, it follows that he is

Darwinians more generally, see also Gayon (1999), Moore (2002a, 2002b), Richardson (2004), Small (2005) and Johnson (2010).

committed to the view that there is an alternative interpretation that does reveal a *meaningful* world. He insists that something does lie beyond the horizon of the scientist and that "good taste" requires "reverence", which we might also translate as awe or deep respect, for "everything that lies beyond [this] horizon!" (373). Nietzsche does not rule out a perspective that properly apprehends a meaningful world that inspires awe.

As we have seen, Nietzsche argues that the collapse of Platonic and Christian metaphysics does not necessarily entails a nihilistic devaluation of this world. Contra Schopenhauerian and romantic pessimists, Nietzsche's free spirits do not judge the world is worth less because it 'fails' to measure up to metaphysical standards. In *GS* 373 Nietzsche adds that free sprits should also reject the prejudice that the scientific dismissal of or blindness to value is the only legitimate interpretation of the world. After the collapse of metaphysical interpretations, he implies, we are not condemned to accept the scientific view of the meaninglessness of the world. Nietzsche suggests that there is another interpretation of the world that in some sense legitimately comprehends the value of existence. This alternative, he implies, is a perspective analogous to aesthetic, especially musical, interpretation. It is a style of interpretation that conceives life itself as analogous to aesthetic phenomenon. In Book 4, as we have seen, Nietzsche used this analogy in his description of the higher human being as one who mistakenly thinks of himself as a spectator and listener "before *the great visual and acoustic play that is life*" when he is in fact "the actual poet and author of life" (301).

In his critique of philosophical idealism Nietzsche makes direct use of this analogy between life and art: it has been and remains a common mistake of all philosophers, he claims, to fail to "listen to life *insofar as life is music*; [they] *denied* the music of life" (372).[7] Nietzsche diagnoses this philosophical denial of "the music of life" as an "illness" that in the case of past philosophers has sprung from fear of the senses and in the case of contemporaries from atrophy of the senses. For philosophers, he suggests, idealism is away of stopping

---

[7] See Seneca *Ep.* 31.2: "You will be a wise man, if you stop up your ears; nor is it enough to close them with wax; you need a denser stopple than that which they say Ulysses used for his comrades". Stoic philosophy is the instrument for closing one's ears to the siren song.

themselves hearing the music of life. Alluding once again to Odyssean trickery or cunning, which, as we have seen, he insists is on the side of life, Nietzsche suggests: "'Wax in the ear' was virtually a condition of philosophizing" (372).

Odysseus, we might recall, famously outwits the Sirens who lure sailors to their death with their enchanting singing. Odysseus manages to listen to the Sirens' song by getting his crew to tie him to the mast of his ship and plug their own ears with wax so that they remain deaf to the music and can row undisturbed past the island (*Odyssey* XII). Nietzsche's Odyssean allusion poses a challenge for philosophers: is it possible to listen to the music of life, that which fills us with "awe", without suffering shipwreck? Or alternatively, as Nietzsche suggests, does the problem arise from "the philosopher's superstition that all music is siren-music" (372)? It is only the philosopher's fear of the senses and passions that make them appear dangerous. Nietzsche will suggest that it is a question of health or strength that determines whether philosophers flee the music of life or not.

Nietzsche claims that modern philosophers have also stopped their ears to the siren songs, not through idealism, but through their mechanistic interpretation of the world. Like the ancient philosophical idealists, he argues, scientists "who nowadays like to pass as philosophers" fail to listen to the music of life (373). If philosophical idealists fled the music of life by inventing a metaphysical world beyond the senses, scientific materialists, he suggests, deny it by limiting their interpretation of the world to mathematical computation. "Do we really", he mockingly asks, "want to demote existence in this way to an exercise in arithmetic and an indoor diversion for mathematicians?" (373). In doing so, he asserts, scientific materialism commits an absurd category mistake:

Suppose one judged the *value* of a piece of music according to how much of it could be counted, calculated, and expressed in a formula – how absurd such a 'scientific' evaluation of music would be! What would one have comprehended, understood, recognized? Nothing, really nothing of what is 'music' in it! (373)

Nietzsche is *not* claiming the scientific method falsifies the world, or that science does not grasp something of the world. Rather his claim is that it singularly fails to comprehend "the world *that concerns human beings*", namely "the world of valuations, colours, weights, perspectives, scales, affirmations, and negations" (301).[8] That is to say, he stresses that from the mechanistic perspective there simply are no siren songs – no beauty or ugliness, good or bad, nobility or ignobility. Nietzsche taunts Mr Mechanic that he comprehends exactly "nothing".[9]

Nietzsche claims then that science cannot comprehend "*value*" – or, in terms of Nietzsche's Odyssean allusion, the siren's song that lure sailors to their doom. The world Mr Mechanic comprehends is valueless. For this reason, Nietzsche stresses science cannot oppose the ascetic ideal, "it is not nearly independent enough for that, in every respect it first needs a value-ideal, a value-creating power, in whose *service* it *can believe* in itself – science never creates values" (*GM* III. 25). To this point, he claims, science has been in the service of the ascetic ideal in stripping the world of value. Nietzsche highlights the fact that the scientist's denial of value is not a claim that is subject to scientific demonstration: it is, rather, a faith or prejudice that the world is valueless. Mr Mechanic's value anti-realism is a prejudice based on naivety or illness. Nietzsche's first point is then that the scientific perspective errs insofar as it decrees that there are no other rightful interpretations of the world.[10] "I think", Nietzsche says in the next section, "that we are at least as far away from the ridiculous immodesty of decreeing from our angle that perspectives *permitted* only from this angle" (374).[11] Second, Nietzsche diagnoses the scientific faith that there is nothing beyond

---

[8] Patti Smith illustrates this point in recalling a compass she found as a child: "The compass was old and rusted but it still worked, connecting the earth and the stars. It told me where I was standing and which way was west but not where I was going and nothing of my worth" (Smith 2015: 82).

[9] Franz Kafka's revision of the Odyssean story captures the unwitting fate Nietzsche attributes to modern scientists: "Now the Sirens have a still more fatal weapon than their song, namely their silence. And though admittedly such a thing never happened, it is still conceivable that someone might possibly have escaped from their singing; but from their silence certainly never" (Kafka 1983: 431).

[10] In a much quoted note from this period Nietzsche expresses his critique of positivism: "Against the positivism which halts at the phenomena – 'There are only facts' – I would say: no, facts are just what there are not, only interpretations" (*KSA* 12:7 [60]).

[11] P. F. Strawson makes a similar point in defending a relaxed pluralism against the hard-line naturalistic skeptic view that values are illusions. There is no basis for the judgement that the scientific view is correct and the value based one incorrect, he argues, because it wrongly presupposes a metaphysically absolute standpoint from which we can judge between the two standpoints. Or in his words, "I want to say that the appearance of contradiction arises only

its own horizon: it is, he insists, an illness. Third, since Nietzsche believes that science is not the only "rightful interpretation of the world" (373) he implies that there is another perspective that expresses the "taste of reverence" or *awe* for *everything* that lies beyond the horizons of the mechanistic account of the world. This alternative, as we shall see, is Nietzsche's so-called Dionysian pessimism.

Nietzsche suggests that the unconditional or exclusive commitment to scientific truth is predicated on the ascetic ideal or life denial, the denial of the music of life. From scientific perspective "Mr Mechanic" sees no values in the world and declares therefore that there are none (cf. Clark and Dudrick 2012: 123). But for Nietzsche this latter claim is an expression of an ascetic illness: a will to nothingness, or a will to deny the value of life. Or to put the point another way, the naturalistic, mechanistic perspective is not just an intellectual error but also a symptom of the weakness or illness. "Science", he suggests, "rests on the same base as the ascetic ideal: the precondition of both one and the other is a certain '*impoverishment of life*' . . . gone are the overflowing energy, the certainty of life, the certainty as to the *future*" (*GM* III.25). We should note that in suggesting science lacks 'overflowing energy' Nietzsche explicitly references his "fundamentally opposite doctrine and valuation of life – purely artistic and *anti-Christian*", which he calls "Dionysian" (*BT* ASC 5). In Nietzsche's lexicon, 'Dionysian' stands precisely for an overflowing, superabundant energy that wants a tragic outlook and insight into life (370). On the issue of the value of science for life he directs his readers to consult the 1886 Preface to *BT*:

And science itself, our science – indeed, what is the significance of all science, viewed as a symptom of life? Is the resolve to be so scientific about everything perhaps a kind of fear, a flight from pessimism? A subtle form of self-defence against – *the truth*? And, morally speaking, a sort of cowardice and falseness? Amorally speaking, a ruse. (*BT* ASC 1)

if we assume the existence of some metaphysically absolute standpoint from which we can judge between the two standpoints I have been contrasting. But there is no such superior standpoint" (Strawson 2008: 30).

From *HH* to the *GS* Book 5 Nietzsche's reflections on the value of truth and art for life come full circle. He shifts from *HH*'s (ambivalent) endorsement of science as a means of liberation from metaphysical idealism and Christianity to his late diagnosis of science as a flight from pessimism that is continuous with, indeed, a subtle version of the ascetic aversion to life that has its origins in Platonic and Christian metaphysics. On this late view, science is no longer the key to liberation from the metaphysical aversion to life, but is its last and most subtle avatar, not a healthy embrace of truth, but a pathological self-defence against "*the truth*" (*BT* ASC 1). Accompanying this shift in his diagnosis of science, Nietzsche also moves from endorsing art as a "cult of the untrue" (107) that our weakness and frailty requires to anaesthetise our suffering, to celebrating tragic art as a deeper truth that only a few demand as a consequence of their overflowing strength. Arguably, then, Nietzsche's Dionysian pessimism, which, as we have seen, involves a 'musical' conception of life as a beautiful chaos that can become meaningful through art, entails in a broad sense of the term a 'metaphysical' view of the world. That is to say, he implies that in tragic art we can perceive a higher truth about our lives and the world that cannot be found *in* the world but which is nonetheless true *of* it.[12]

Nietzsche conceives *GS* Book 5 as part of his account of grand project of revaluing the highest values of European culture. He diagnoses the highest values of European culture as preserving the most impoverished and harmful forms of life. Nietzsche wants to offers free spirits the hope that Europe might one day cultivate the highest forms of life. As we have seen, Nietzsche rules out science as the source of this cultural revolution. Under the aegis of the ascetic ideal, he argues, science only serves to strip existence of meaning and value and it cannot create new values or ideals. Nietzsche claims that science either interprets the world as lacking in significance or it supports the very moral ideals that impoverish life. Scientists are deaf to the siren's song or seduced by the Circe of morality (*D* P 3; *EH* 'Clever' 5).

---

[12] I owe the phrasing of this point to Michael Janover (personal communication). See also Lawrence Hatab, who argues that Nietzsche "understood tragedy as expressive of certain truths about existence" (2008: 177).

Rather than turning to science to formulate his revaluation of values Nietzsche develops a "purely artistic and *anti-Christian*" doctrine and valuation of life, which he calls "Dionysian" (*BT* ASC 5). In *GS* Book 5 Nietzsche suggests that the rebirth of a tragic values is the only possible redemption from the life denial or romantic pessimism that he believes characterises modern European culture. Nietzsche identifies in tragedy redemption *from* morality. In other words, he returns to tragic art to clarify an alternative value ideal that might motivate free spirits to revolutionise European culture. In this sense, Nietzsche renews the project he first sketched in *BT*. "*The Birth of Tragedy*" as he declares in the penultimate section of *TI* "was my first revaluation of all values" (*TI* 'Ancients' 5). However, he explicitly rejects the artist's metaphysics that underpinned his first work and returns to Greek tragedy to unpack the psychological basis of strength, health and affirmation. Nietzsche examines tragedy not as a source of metaphysical insight and consolation, but "as a bridge to the psychology of the tragic poet" (*TI* 'Ancients' 5). Rather than holding that tragic affirmation requires transcending the human condition and occupying the transcendent standpoint of an artist-god, as he had in *BT*, Nietzsche now claims that the affirmative stance is one that tragic artists and free spirits can occupy on the basis of their own overflowing strength: "The tragic man says Yes to even the bitterest suffering: he is strong, full, deifying enough to do so" (Raymond 2014: 73). Rather than seeing suffering as an objection to existence, the Dionysian wills and delights in suffering.[13] Rather than responding to pain defensively, through contraction or disavowal, for the Dionysian "it has the effect of a stimulus" (*TI* 'Ancients' 5).

Nietzsche claims that this psychological formulation of Dionysian pessimism simply recovers from his earlier errors the will to tragedy that "has been my perspective from the beginning" (*HAH* 2 P 7). In *GS* 370 Nietzsche reminds his friends of his first great hope in *BT* that nineteenth-century German philosophical pessimism was a sign of a "higher force of thought, of more audacious courage, and of more victorious fullness of life" than eighteenth-century philosophers' superficial sensualism and empiricism. Nietzsche's hope was

---

[13] Following Young (1992: 138–139), Ridley (2007) laments that in his late notion of Dionysian affirmation Nietzsche succumbed to the temptations of his artist's metaphysics.

that Schopenhauer's philosophical pessimism and Wagner's total works of art were signs of a German cultural revolution that would establish the basis for a higher, 'Dionysian' German culture.

Nietzsche acknowledges that he badly misunderstood German philosophical pessimism: he saw it as the expression of Dionysian affirmation rather as a symptom of decline, weariness, and exhaustion (*GS* 370; *BT* ASC 6). Nietzsche recognises, for example, that Schopenhauer failed to conceive Greek tragedy as the expression of the highest affirmation of life, but as teaching renunciation rather than affirmation of life (*BT* ASC 6). Schopenhauer acknowledges that in the tragedy of the ancients the spirit of resignation is rarely seen or expressed: Iphigenia, for example, consents to die, not in resignation that life is worthless, but for the love of her homeland. Greek heroes submit to the will of fate, but they do not, Schopenhauer admits, surrender their will to life. Yet despite this Schopenhauer argues that the "summons to turn away from life remains the true tendency of tragedy". Schopenhauer argues that Greek tragedy solicits the spectator's fear and pity, not to purge or educate these emotions, but as a means to awaken the spirit of resignation (*WWR* 2: 435).[14]

Nietzsche therefore aims to recover Greek tragedy from these moralistic misinterpretations. Against what he calls Schopenhauer's romantic pessimism, Nietzsche claims that "there is a will to the tragic and to pessimism that is as much a sign of strength of intellect (taste, feeling, conscience). With this will in one's heart one has no fear of the fearful and questionable that characterises all existence; one even seeks it out" (*HAH* 2 P 7). It is this that stands behind Nietzsche's title for Book 5: free spirits are "we fearless ones" insofar as they will tragedy, or seek out the terrible, questionable and strange as the very condition for the expenditure of their overflowing energies.

---

[14] Aristotle argues that tragedy is the "imitation of action ... by means of pity and fear accomplishing the *katharsis* of such emotions" (*Poe.* 1449b24–28). Whether Aristotle meant the purging or the education of these emotions remains a matter of controversy (see Nussbaum 1986; Halliwell 1998). Drawing inspiration from Aristotle, Christopher Raymond plausibly argues that Nietzsche fails to see how tragedy stimulates moral reflection (Raymond 2014: 57–79).

Nietzsche's purely artistic doctrine draws on the model of Greek tragedy to identify a 'normative' conception of overflowing, super-abundant health. Nietzsche interprets Greek tragedy as an aesthetic interpretation of the world that expresses an overflowing energy that affirms and embraces the whole of existence. In other words, he identifies the affirmation of eternal recurrence as a symptom of this tragic perspective. It is this tragic perspective that underpins his counter "ideal of the most high-spirited, vital, world-affirming indi-vidual" who "wants what was and what is ... *just as it was and is* through all eternity" (*BGE* 56). Nietzsche takes this Dionysian ideal of overflowing energy that makes it possible to affirm the eternal recurrence as the basis for his concept of a "*the* great health" and as his measure of the value of values. In *GS* Book 5 Nietzsche suggests that the rebirth of a tragic values is the only possible redemption from the modern symptoms of life denial or romantic pessimism. Salvation lies in willing tragedy.

However in *GS* Book 5, Nietzsche's does not focus on the ethics of self-affirmation but on the broader cultural and political implications of his counter-ideal. Where Nietzsche closes Book 4 with the figure of the solitary individual confronting the abysmal thought of his own recurrence, he completes Book 5 evoking a collective of free spirits ('we homeless ones', 'we artists of contempt', 'we who are new, nameless, hard to understand') as opponents of all modern ideals and institutions. Nietzsche conceives this collective as "premature births of an as yet unproved *future*" who seek to discover frontiers beyond modern moral horizons (377/381). In *GS* Book 5, following the lead of *BGE*, Nietzsche expands his conception of the significance of his new ideal well beyond ethical perfectionism to a grand vision of the political transformation of life that is closer to a political perfec-tionism. The last incarnations of Nietzsche's free spirits have a much darker shade than the sceptical, dispassionate inquirer of *HH* intent on dispelling metaphysical clouds or even the intoxicated yea-sayer who appears at the close of *GS* Book 4. From the vantage point of *GS* Book 5 these earlier avatars of the free spirit appear as preludes to a much grander, intoxicating and dangerous 1887 incarnation. Nietzsche no longer writes, as he had in *HH*, under the sign of Voltaire. By 1887 he conceives the ideal of the free spirit as the fulcrum of a radical political and cultural transformation that aims at nothing less than the overthrow the moral foundations of modern European civilisation.

In the context of this shift to his grand politics that we need to address Nietzsche's central positive claims in Book 5. He argues first that that we can discover the highest expression of life affirmation in the will to tragedy. It is a sign of overflowing strength or health to seek out tragedy and to playfully or naively delight in creation and destruction. Tragic insight and action is the luxury of the strong. Second, he argues that free spirits should establish political and cultural institutions on the basis of tragic values because they call forth and cultivate the overflowing energies of the highest human types. Third, he claims paradoxically that his "gaya scienza" is a "secret wisdom": it is an esoteric wisdom that only applies to a few free spirits who have the overflowing energy to want to go beyond contemporary moral horizon for the sake of satisfying their own burning passion to explore a new world of undiscovered ideals (377). Nietzsche conceives this as a secret or esoteric doctrine in a double sense: it can only appeal to those rare free spirits who have the great health that desires tragic rather than moral horizons, and it aims to establish a new order of rank and values that facilitates the enhancement of the highest Dionysian types at the expense of the values that preserve and protect the weak. In short, Nietzsche celebrates Dionysian pessimism as the salvation of modern European culture from the curse of the moral ideal and he argues that this affirmative pessimism necessarily entails an aristocratic politics. In 1887, the year he published *GS* Book 5, Nietzsche enthusiastically endorsed George Brandes' description of his vision as a type of "aristocratic radicalism".[15] Let us briefly consider each of these claims in turn.

---

[15] "The expression 'aristocratic radicalism', which you use, is very good. That is, if I may say so, the shrewdest remark that I have read about myself till now" (Middleton, 1996: 279). Whether or not Nietzsche's philosophy is *necessarily* tied to his aristocratic politics or it in fact lends itself to alternative political ideals, including democratic political views is a matter of controversy. On the one side, some commentators suggest that Nietzsche's philosophy is conducive to formulating an 'agonistic' conception of democracy; see e.g. Hatab (1995), Connolly (2008) and Owen (2008). On the other hand, critics of Nietzsche's politics see him as the arch anti-democrat; see e.g. Detwiler (1990), Appel (1999) and Ure (2013). For a range of recent interpretations of Nietzsche's politics, see Ansell-Pearson ed. (2013b). For an excellent review of some of the contemporary literature on Nietzsche's politics, see

In *GS* 370 Nietzsche elaborates his counter-ideal of Dionysian pessimism. He suggests that overflowing, superabundant life takes delight in the sight of tragedy and in playful creation and destruction. Nietzsche contrast this Dionysian pessimism with what he calls romantic pessimism:

Every art, every philosophy can be considered a cure and aid in the service of growing, struggling life: they always presuppose suffering and sufferers. But there are two types of sufferers: first those who suffer from a *superabundance of life* – they want a Dionysian art as well as a tragic outlook and insight into life; then those who suffer from an *impoverishment of life* and seek quiet, stillness, calm seas, redemption from themselves through art and insight or else intoxication, paroxysm, numbness and madness. (370)

Nietzsche bundles together as 'poor in spirit' Epicureans, Christians and scientific rationalists on the grounds that all seek redemption from suffering. Christians seek salvation from their own suffering from life through a saviour, a 'god for the sick', Epicureans through a hedonistic ethics that aims to eliminate suffering and tragedy, and modern rationalists through the comfort of "the conceptual comprehensibility of existence ... in short, a certain warm, fear repelling narrowness and confinement to optimistic horizons" (370; see also *BT* ASC 1). What they share, he implies, is a desire born of their own weakness to flee from tragic pessimism. By contrast Nietzsche suggests that "he who is richest in fullness of life, the Dionysian god and man can allow himself not only the sight of what is terrible and questionable but also the terrible deed and every luxury of destruction, decomposition and negation; in his case, what is evil, nonsensical and ugly almost seems acceptable because of an overflow in procreating, fertilising forces capable of turning any desert into bountiful farmlands" (370). If romantic pessimists create or destroy out of vengefulness motivated by the fact that they suffer from life, the Dionysian does so from an overflow of procreative, form-giving energy.

Drochon (2010). Elsewhere, Drochon carefully reconstructs Nietzsche's critique of democracy and sees it as issuing a fundamental challenge to modern democratic 'prejudices': "If God is dead, then the question is whether democracy is part of the 'shadows of God' Nietzsche decried ... Can one be democrat if one is no longer a Christian?" (Drochon 2016b: 1067).

In *GS* Book 5 Nietzsche maintains that the rebirth of this Dionysian pessimism requires free spirits to overturn the fundamental ideals and institutions of modern democracy and establish aristocratic political and cultural institutions. We need to take step back to *BGE*, the work immediately preceding *GS* Book 5, to grasp the way Nietzsche connects his ideal of Dionysian pessimism to his aristocratic radicalism. *GS* Book 5, along with *BGE* and *GM*, constitutes Nietzsche first attempt since HH to address the issue of democracy. It is Nietzsche's late, tenebrous version of the free spirit that has caused the most alarm or excitement among his readers. Nietzsche establishes his grand vision on the basis of his conception of the political as fundamentally oriented towards the cultivation of higher human types. In *BGE* Nietzsche assumes politics is the creation of the conditions for the most vigorous growth of "the plant 'man'", (*BGE* 44) or its highest exemplars. In contemporary parlance, we might say Nietzsche endorses an *aristocratic* bio-politics: that is, the cultivation of life for the sake of the maximal enhancement of the best. Conjuring up his free spirits with his signature use of the first-person plural, Nietzsche explains their bio-political project in the following way:

We, who have a different faith – we, to whom the democratic move-ment is not merely a form assumed by a political organization in decay but also a form assumed by man in decay, that is to say in diminish-ment, in the process of becoming mediocre and losing his value: whither must we direct our hopes? – Towards *new philosophers* ... strong and original enough to make a start on antithetical evaluations and revalue and reverse 'eternal values'; ... towards men of the future who in the present knot together the constraint which compels the will of millennia on *new* paths. To teach man the future as his *will* ... and to prepare for great enterprises and collective experiments in discipline and breeding It is the image of such leaders which hover before *our* eyes – may I say that aloud, you free spirits? (*BGE* 203)

Nietzsche endorses a bio-political orientation that he (contro-versially) attributes to modern ideologies: his politics is also about the cultivation of life. Yet his bio-politics is informed by exactly the opposite valuations: the enhancement of the rare, highest types at the expense of the happiness and security of the many, lowest types. Disturbingly, Nietzsche's bio-politics casts aside the Enlightenment conception of individuals as citizens with the inalienable political rights and replaces it with a conception of individuals as members of a species whose value resides in their contribution to "strengthening and enhancement of the human type" (377).[16] Nietzsche conceives politics as the cultivation of life, not the protection and exercise of civic rights. It becomes apparent in *BGE* and *GS* Book 5 that his philosophy is testament to a fateful shift in European political discourse from the politics of rights to the politics of life.[17]

Nietzsche's revaluation of value is motivated by the fear that the whole of Christian-European morality is a fatality that represents the "collective danger that 'man' himself may degenerate" (*BGE* 203). Nietzsche assigns free spirits the "new *task*" of preparing the way for future philosophers who take charge of the development of the species, "the project of cultivation", including the use of political, economic and religious instruments to overturn Christian culture in the name of a new aristocratic order of rank (*BGE* 61 and 62). Nietzsche identifies the political ideal of the free spirit through the distinction between Christian leaders who have until now held "sway over the fate of Europe" with their 'equal before God' and new philosophers who recognising "the abysmally different order of rank, chasm of rank, between man and man" will take responsibility for breeding the highest types (*BGE* 62). These new philosophical legislators will cultivate the unexhausted possibilities of the species and do so first by overthrowing the modern ideals that ensure the "*collective degeneration of man*" (*BGE* 203).

Nietzsche argues that the values and political institutions that systematically favour the enhancement of higher types are such that they necessarily come at the expense of the lowest, and vice versa. In updating his ideal of the free spirit in *BGE* Nietzsche stresses that it is fundamentally antithetical to all contemporary European and American notions of freedom and free thinkers. Nietzsche explicitly identifies his ideal of freedom with the rejection of basic modern

---

[16] Roberto Esposito (2008) plausibly identifies Nietzsche as one of the first to grasp the modern shift to a bio-politics that protect and secures life from all forms of contagion, risk and danger. Nietzsche, he argues, both criticises the nihilistic consequences of this so-called immunitary paradigm and reproduces it, making it more powerful than before (2008: 78).

[17] Hugo Drochon rightly observes that in taking up the language of breeding and cultivation, and with it, I would add, the bio-political framework, Nietzsche is "a prisoner of his own time" (Drochon 2016a: 15).

democratic commitments, which he associates with the slogans of "equality of rights" and "sympathy for all that suffers" (*BGE* 44). In *BGE* Nietzsche pictures his "gay science" as an amulet that wards off the modern morality of pity, which cultivates a morbid sensitivity to suffering and endorses the goal of eliminating suffering (*BGE* 293). Nietzsche interprets these democratic slogans not as expressions of a politics of freedom, but as symptoms of a 'bio-politics' that aims to protect and perfect 'herd animals', uniform, docile creatures content with nothing more than a life free of suffering. "What with all their might they would like to strive after", he declares, "is the universal green pasture of the happiness of the herd, with security, safety, comfort and an easier life for all" (*BGE* 44). For this reason he condemns democracy as the "*collective degeneration of man* ... to the perfect herd animal" (*BGE* 203). It is these values, he argues, that cultivate conditions of existence that preserve the many weak members of the species, partly by eliminating the desire for and the means of cultivating higher types. "When a decadence species of man has risen to the ranks of the highest species of man", as he later explains, "that can happen only at the expense of its antithetical species, the species of the strong and certain of life. When the herd-animal is resplendent in the glow of the highest virtue the exceptional man must be devalued to the wicked man" (*EH* 'Destiny' 5).

Nietzsche claims that the European morality of self-denial effectively serves the many: namely those who suffer from an impoverishment of drives and energies, and who therefore need precisely this morality because it eliminates all the dangers of life. On his view, this morality caters precisely to the needs of the many for a placid, pacified existence (*BGE* 44). European moral values, he argues, are not values in themselves, but particular values brought into existence through two millennia of cultural and psychological invention whose result is the protection of the weakest through the degeneration of the strongest (*EH* 'Destiny' 5). Modern democratic egalitarianism, Nietzsche suggests, is the practical culmination of the Christian morality of self-denial: by abolishing aristocratic orders it ensures that the many have nothing to fear from the strong.

On the other hand, he argues that the conditions that cultivate the highest types are precisely those conditions that undermine the weak. The plant 'man', he insists, grows most vigorously to a height only under the most extreme and dangerous conditions since it transform his drive to adapt and preserve himself to an unconditional will to power and compels him to cultivate everything in him that "is akin to beasts of prey and serpents" (*BGE* 44). Nietzsche also stresses that the elevation of the few requires slavery: "Every elevation of the type man has hitherto been the work of an aristocratic society- and so *it will always be*: a society that believes in an order of rank and differences and worth between man and man and needs slavery in some sense or other" (*BGE* 257, italics added). In his early unpublished essay, 'The Greek State', Nietzsche maintained that slavery is necessary to create a surplus that allows higher types leisure to pursue their goals free from the demands of labour. In *BGE* Nietzsche argues that the distinction between masters and slaves creates what he calls a 'pathos of distance' (*BGE* 257) so that "in looking downwards and outward on slaves their souls are pushed toward the even higher demands and expectations they place on themselves as an internal form of demarcation" (Drochon 2016a: 20).[18] Nietzsche also endorses the view that for the sake of their own flourishing an aristocratic elite must have a good conscience about instrumentalising "the great majority, who exist for service and general utility and who *may* exist only for that purpose" (*BGE* 61). Nietzsche maintains the species' flourishing hinges on the ruling castes' belief that their flourishing justifies enslaving lesser types. "The essential characteristic of a good and healthy aristocracy", he claims, "is that it experiences itself not as a function (whether of the monarchy or the commonwealth) but as their *meaning* and supreme justification – that it therefore accepts with a good conscience the sacrifice of untold human beings, who, for its sake, must be reduced and lowered to incomplete human beings, to slaves, to instruments. Their fundamental faith simply has to be that society must not exist for society's sake but only as the foundation and scaffolding on which a choice type of being is able to

---

[18] Drochon argues that these two reasons are sufficient to explain why Nietzsche insists on the necessity of slavery. Nietzsche therefore does not defend slavery on the grounds that masters need recognition. If "Nietzsche's master is distinguished from Hegel's precisely in the respect that he does not require recognition", as Williams puts it, "this leaves us less than clear why the masters need the slaves at all" (quoted in Drochon 2016a: 20; see also Janaway 2007: 253–254). Yet it is not entirely clear that Nietzsche conceives his higher types as beyond the need for asymmetrical recognition; see e.g. *D* 30.

raise itself to its higher task and to a higher state of being" (*BGE* 258).[19]

In commending the secret wisdom of his '*gaya scienza*' to free spirits Nietzsche identifies them as "we who are homeless" precisely because they are fundamentally opposed to the values of modern democracy: equal rights, individual liberty, humanitarian compassion and progress. In *GS* 377 Nietzsche distils the essence of BGE's aristocratic radicalism. It is worth quoting at length Nietzsche's gloss of all that free spirits must help to break up for the sake of the rebirth of a tragic culture:

> We are not working for progress; we don't need to plug our ears to the marketplace sirens of the future: what they sing – 'equal rights', 'free society', 'no more masters and no servants' – has no allure for us. We hold it absolutely undesirable that a realm of justice and concord should be established on earth (because it would be the realm of the most profound leveling down to mediocrity . . .); we are delighted by all who love, as we do, danger, war, adventure; who refuse to compromise, to be captured, to reconcile, to be castrated; we consider ourselves conquerors; we contemplate the necessity for new orders as well as for a new slavery – for every strengthening and enhancement of the human type also involves a new kind of enslavement – doesn't it? With all this, can we really be at home in an age that loves to claim the distinction of being the most humane, the mildest, and most righteous the world has ever seen? It is bad enough that precisely when we hear these beautiful words, we have the ugliest misgivings. What we find in them is merely an expression – and the masquerade – of a deep weakening, of weariness, of old age, of declining energies. (377)

In *GS* Book 5 Nietzsche exclusively addresses free spirits to clarify this this radical ethical and political project. Unlike his contemporaries Nietzsche does not conceive philosophy an ethically neutral tool to sharpen a disembodied mind; he sees it as a means of cultivating and exhorting a select group of free spirits whose 'task' lies in overcoming in themselves and their culture the moral sickness of humanity. In Nietzsche's grand philosophical vision what is at stake is not the realisation of humanity, but the enhancement of the few.

Nietzsche's style embodies and expresses this fundamentally aristocratic perspective. Following the views he expressed in *BGE* (29–30), he explicitly states that he writes *GS* Book 5 esoterically,

---

[19] Nietzsche glosses Henry Bates (1941); see Ure (2013).

that is to say, only for a select audience of free spirits who have a capacity for independence, which is "a privilege of the strong" (*GS* 381/*BGE* 29). "Books for everybody", he attitudinises, "are always malodorous books" (*BGE* 30). Nietzsche does not express the truth for everyman, only the truth that contributes to the flourishing of the highest types (*BGE* 43). Nietzsche discriminates between the few friends he addresses and the many to whom he wants to be incomprehensible (381). He differentiates the few and the many in terms of health and sickness: "There are books which possess an opposite value for soul and health depending on whether the lower soul, or the higher and more powerful avails itself" (*BGE* 30). "In the end", as he explains, "it must be as it is and has always been: great things for the great, abysses for the profound, shudders and delicacies for the refined and, in sum, all rare things for the rare" (*BGE* 43).

We should note that Nietzsche's rhetoric of exclusion is highly ambivalent. While he stresses that he writes only for rare free spirits and aims to exclude the *profanum vulgus*, by the very same stroke he also seeks to elicit the reader's desire to belong to this elite group. In *GS* 346, for example, he suggests that "we" 'godless', 'unbelievers' and 'immoralists' are "at too advanced a stage ... for *you* to comprehend, my curious gentlemen – how it feels" (346). Nietzsche uses the first (we) and second person (you) plural to split his readers between two different identities and perspectives. On the one hand, he addresses the reader in the second person plural he casts them in the role of "curious gentlemen" who are too naïve, unintelligent or timid to comprehend the epochal break. On the other hand, he uses the first-person plural (we/us/our) to construct for the reader another group of avant-garde free spirits. This rhetorical strategy of exclusions and inclusions splits the reader between opposing groups: between a vulgar, 'outsider' group ('you') that fails to understand or is too weak to endorse the new situation and an elite, 'insider' group (we free spirits) that drives this radical break. Nietzsche's rhetorical strategy compels readers to 'choose' to identify with the weak-minded, antiquated group or the newly emerging strong-minded 'free spirits'. It is a rhetorical strategy that appeals to the pride and contempt of his readers: pride in their own courage in comprehending and confronting the epochal break and contempt for those too weak or cowardly to do so. Nietzsche's use of the royal 'we', as Duncan Large explains, "call on 'us' (readers) to recognise (or not) our affinity with the qualities Nietzsche is describing – to decide for ourselves whether we warrant inclusion in what is always a positively valued category" (Large 2013; see also Westerdale 2013: 136–137).

After declaring in *GS* 381 that he writes esoterically it is not surprising that Nietzsche brings Book 5 to its climax with a lyrical, yet enigmatic evocation of his Dionysian counter-ideal. In section 382 he closes the book's circle. We might recall that in the book's very first section Nietzsche argues that through the moral teachers of the purpose of existence the human animal acquired a metaphysical need to see reason, purpose or meaning in its purposeless natural existence. We cannot thrive without periodic trust in life. Nietzsche sees his gay wisdom, his mocking of European morality, as the opportunity for a new tragic teaching, a new purpose of existence. Gay science is the prelude to a new tragedy. Nietzsche closes *GS* by explaining how his free spirits vanquish European morality with laughter only for the sake of creating a new tragedy, "which gives earth its purpose and man his hope again" (*GM* III. 24).

In *GS* 382 Nietzsche draws yet again on ancient Greek heroic myths of perilous sea journeys to dramatise the adventures of his free-spirited explorers. Just as Odysseus and his precursors the Argonauts required cunning to survive their voyages, Nietzsche suggests that in order to navigate the coasts of the moral ideal his adventurous seafarers must have "a new health that is stronger, craftier, tougher, bolder, and more cheerful than any previous health" (382). Nietzsche stresses that this great health is a "new means" for a "new end" (382). It is a necessary means insofar as this craftiness enables free spirits to navigate the dangerous coasts of modern European ideals and to recover from "shipwreck and damage", but it is not itself the end or goal of their voyage (382). In the terms of Nietzsche mythical framework, his "argonauts of the ideal" set sail to reclaim the golden fleece.

Put another way, Nietzsche recognises that his free spirits require the strength to subject morality to relentless suspicion, but the ultimate end of this is not to sustain suspicion or unbelief. To make suspicion a goal or end, he implies, is to suffer from the "illness of severe suspicion" (*GS* P 4). One must return from such "abysses", he writes, "*newborn* ... more childlike, and at the same time a hundred times subtler than one had ever been before" (*GS* P 4). In *GS* 377 Nietzsche makes the point that his free spirits do not set sail for the sake of unbelief or faith in unbelief, but for a higher end. Just as the Christian believers sacrificed everything for their faith, so too free spirits sacrifice everything:

But for what? For our unbelief? For every kind of unbelief? No, you know better than that, my friends! The hidden Yes in you is stronger than all Nos and Maybes that afflict you and your age like a disease; and you must sail the seas, you emigrants, you too are compelled to this by – a *faith*!" (GS 377)

For Nietzsche then the free spirit's great suspicion is a prelude to and preparation for establishing a new ideal. Nietzsche identifies great health as necessary if they are to "rise climb or fly" to a point "beyond *our* good and evil, a freedom from everything European, by which I mean the sum of commanding value judgement that have become part of our flesh and blood" (380). In what does this great health consist? If sailors must "learn to adjust the sails in a thousand ways", what do Nietzsche's seafarers require (318)? Nietzsche never tires of reminding potential free spirits that strength, cruelty and courage are necessary to pursue their commitment to creating for themselves "eyes to survey millennia" (380). To investigate the truth of morality, the truth of its origins and history, he suggests, requires deploying a whole range of instincts and traits that are morally forbidden: hardness, cunning, ruthlessness (*BGE* 39). Free spirits must be "investigators to the point of cruelty" and this cruelty is directed against their own moral conscience (*BGE* 44). Free-spiritedness requires courage, he suggests, because to subject our moral conscience to examination is to risk being "torn to pieces limb from limb by some cave-minotaur of conscience" (*BGE* 29). Free spirits must wage war against the millennia long script, incarnate in their own moral conscience, in order to have the independence to undertake this trial. Against deeply embedded feelings of devotion, self-sacrifice for one's neighbour, the whole morality of self-denial, the free spirit must deploy a clear-eyed, ruthlessness in order to mercilessly prosecute this morality (*BGE* 39).

If these are the new means free spirits need to undertake their voyage around the old ideals, what is the new end? Put simply, Nietzsche identifies the goal of the free spirit as vanquishing the moral ideal and establishing a new tragic ideal. "If a shrine has to be set up", as Nietzsche puts it, "*a shrine has to be destroyed*" (*GM* II. 24). By means of their great health, Nietzsche's explorers create for themselves eyes to survey the millennia of their previous moral ideals and see these as *beneath* them, but also to see an unmapped "world over-rich in what is beautiful, strange, questionable, terrible and divine" (382). It enables them to both discover the vast, hidden land of past morality for the first time, deciphering "the hieroglyphic script of man's moral past" (*GM* P 7) and as a "reward" to catch a glimpse a whole new vista of unknown, as yet undiscovered moral ideals (382).

Nietzsche identifies the free spirits first reward for setting sail to explore moral ideal as a joyful liberation from moral seriousness. The reward for their courageous and independent exploration of the problems of morality is "one day being allowed to take them cheerfully. That cheerfulness, in fact, or to put it in my parlance, that *gay science* – is a reward: a reward for along, brave, diligent, subterranean seriousness for which, admittedly not everyone is suited" (*GM* P 7). As Nietzsche explains it, 'gay science' is to seriously pursue the problems of morality to the point that one can take them cheerfully. We reach its high tide when we can say with conviction: "Forwards! Even our old morality would make a *comedy*!" (GM P 7). After seeing the old morality from the perspective of "future moralities" (380) free spirits can no longer take seriously "modern man" and "his worthiest goals and hopes" (382):

Another ideal runs before us, a peculiar, seductive, dangerous ideal of a spirit that plays naively, i.e. not deliberately but from overflowing abundance and power with everything that was hitherto called holy, good, untouchable, divine ... the ideal of a human, superhuman well-being and benevolence that will often enough appear inhuman – for example when it places itself next to all earthly seriousness heretofore, all forms of solemnity in gesture, word, tone, look, morality, and tasks as if it were there most incarnate and involuntary parody. (382)

As we have seen, against romantic pessimists who suffer from impoverishment of life and who invent life-denying ideals, Nietzsche pits the Dionysian pessimist who suffers from an over-flowing energy that expresses itself as a total affirmation of life.

Nietzsche identifies this future ideal with the Dionysian pessimist who creates and destroys, not deliberately or reactively, but as an innocent overflow of superabundant energy. His description of the future ideal that runs ahead of his free spirits alludes to Zarathustra's childlike spirit: "Innocence the child is and forgetting, a beginning anew, a play, a self-propelling wheel, a first movement, a sacred Yea-saying" (Z I.i). Nietzsche conceives this childlike innocence, this involuntary parody of all the highest values as the prelude to a new tragedy:

it is perhaps only with [this ideal] that *the great seriousness* really emerges; that the real question mark is posed for the first time; that the destiny of the soul changes; the hands of the clock move forward; the tragedy *begins*. (382)

Nietzsche returns to where he began: he announces himself as a new teacher of purpose who vanquishes old ideals and establishes a new tragedy. Put simply, his future ideal is to delight in tragedy. Nietzsche's *Epilogue* (383) closes with "the real question mark": "Is that what you *want*?"

CHAPTER 8

Nietzsche's Saturnalia: 1886 Preface

On 13 November 1886, Nietzsche completed a Preface to GS, which, along with Book 5, he added to the new 1887 edition (Schaberg 1995: 136). We can consider this his final statement of the ideal of the free spirit's 'gay science'. Nietzsche uses this preface to give his pithiest expression of the meta-philosophical presuppositions that underpin his notion of the philosopher as physician. In many respects the Preface represents the completion and distillation of his much earlier efforts in the unwritten *Philosophenbuch*, which he called '*The Philosopher as Cultural Physician*', to elucidate his own model of philosophy and philosophers.[1] Nietzsche composes his Preface as a memoir that records his experiences of illness, convalescence and recovery. This memoir, he claims, sheds light on the psychology of philosophy, or more particularly on "the relation between health and philosophy" (P 1).

Nietzsche argues we can conceive philosophy as analogous to med-icine insofar as it is a therapeutic exercise. He identifies philosophy as therapeutic in two distinct senses. First, he claims that philosophy has been an *involuntary* mechanism through which philosophers regulate life in response to illness or health, weakness or strength. Nietzsche's meta-philosophy conceives philosophy as an unconscious symptom of life: it is our weaknesses and strengths that philosophise. In this con-text, he also asserts that as a matter of fact most philosophies have been unconscious symptoms of *illness* rather than health. Nietzsche main-tains that past philosophies have not only taken shape through what he

---

[1] Daniel Breazeale recounts the history of Nietzsche's early, never completed project of a 'Philosopher's Book' [*Philosophenbuch*] in his collection of the unpublished notes Nietzsche made for it in the early 1870s; see Breazeale (1979: xiii–xlix).

236

describes as "the *pressure* of illness" (P 2), but they have also misinterpreted these illnesses and as a consequence prescribed 'cures' that deepen our maladies. Nietzsche claims that his convalescence is profoundly important because it represents a recovery from a whole range of cultural sicknesses that modern Europeans have *mistakenly* confused with health. It embodies a recovery from two millennia of European sickness.

Second, Nietzsche suggests that philosophers might become successful physicians capable of properly diagnosing health and sickness. Rather than philosophers remaining victims of their own illnesses and failed cures, he implies, they might become agents of recovery. Nietzsche claims that it is precisely through his own insights into and experiments with the various failed philosophical therapies that he identifies the wrong turns that contribute to degeneration of life and the paths that may lead to healthy, flourishing life. In *GS* P, he illuminates this meta-philosophical framework through a highly compressed, yet compelling philosophical autobiography. Nietzsche takes his personal history of illness as a case study that reveals the various measures philosophers have invented in their attempts to recover from illness. He derives his meta-philosophical insights from the analysis of his own history of illness.

Most importantly of all, perhaps, Nietzsche elaborates the conception of "*the great health*" he identified at the close of Book 5 as the condition of his new, affirmative Dionysian ideal. "'Gay Science'", as he puts it in the 1886 Preface, "signifies the saturnalia of a mind that has patiently resisted terrible, long pressure – patiently, severely coldly, without yielding, but also without hope – and is now all of sudden attacked by hope, by hope for health, by the *intoxication* of recovery" (P 1). Nietzsche defines 'gay science' by analogy to the carnivalesque liberation and reversals that characterised the Roman festival of Saturnalia. According to this analogy, 'gay science' signifies an intoxicating transformation analogous to Roman slaves' liberation from the tyranny of their masters that took place during the Saturnalia festival. During the Saturnalia masters and slaves reversed roles, liberating the latter from tyrannical pressures so that they could yield to their own desires, wishes and hopes without fear.

Nietzsche identifies the free spirit's saturnalia as a liberation from the Platonic-Christian metaphysical imperative to transcend the world of appearances in the name of a higher true world. 'Gay science' is a liberation from the tyranny of the ascetic ideal, the millennial long pressure to devalue life. He argues that his philosophical diagnosis of his own illness illuminates the many philosophical masks of this asceticism. As we shall see, Nietzsche believes that it is this ascetic imperative that also unconsciously motivates the philosophical commitment to truth at any price. The philosopher's saturnalia is both a liberation from the tyranny of the ascetic ideal and the freedom to affirm the world of 'appearances'. Nietzsche claims that it is just this affirmation that defines and differentiates tragic art. Ultimately, then, he identifies free spirits as *artists* of life, or more precisely as tragic artists of life. Nietzsche's saturnalia is the rebirth of tragedy. To arrive at this conclusion, Nietzsche tacks between recalling his own philosophical effort to cure himself and relating its broader significance for the psychology of philosophy and the ideal of the philosophical physician.

In *GS* P 1, as we have noted, Nietzsche identifies the book as an expression of the intoxication of his recovery from a long illness. Once again, he draws on ancient heroic myths of perilous sea journeys to define the book's compass:

This entire book is really nothing but an amusement after long privation and powerlessness, the jubilation of returning strength, of a reawakened faith in tomorrow and a day after tomorrow, of a sudden sense and anticipation of a future, of impending adventures, of reopened seas, of goals that are permitted and believed in again. (P 1)

Nietzsche suggests that his recovery required overcoming romantic pessimism, which he sees as the logical culmination of the ascetic aversion to life that he claims lies at the heart of our philosophical tradition. Nietzsche suggests that he took his first step towards overcoming his own romantic pessimism through what he calls "tyranny of pride" (P 1).

We might recall that in the first two books of the free-spirit trilogy Nietzsche drew on the Hellenistic therapies to cure himself of romantic pessimism. Nietzsche conceived the ancient philosophies as therapies that defend "life against pain" and that strike down "all those inferences that pain, disappointment, ill-humour, solitude, and other swamp-grounds usually cause to flourish like poisonous fungi" (*HH* 2 P 5). Nietzsche suggests that philosophy itself has been a refraction of pain. Pain philosophises. Against pain, he suggests, we can "learn to pit out pride . . . our will power against it" or "withdraw before pain into the Oriental nothingness – called Nirvana – into mute, rigid, deaf self-surrender, self-forgetting, self-extinction" (P 3).[2] Where pain philosophises, Nietzsche suggests, it generates one or another version of the ascetic ideal that only esteems life turned against itself: e.g. metaphysical redemption from life (Plato), withdrawal or retreat from life within life (Hellenism), or radical denial of life itself (Schopenhauer).

In *GS* P 1, Nietzsche observes that in his own recovery from illness he sought to combat his romantic weariness with life through Hellenistic therapies. He deployed Hellenistic styles of "self-defence" against "romanticism" (P 1). Nietzsche describes this Hellenistic self-defence in the following terms:

This stretch of desert, exhaustion, loss of faith, icing up in the midst of youth; this onset of dotage at the wrong time this tyranny of pain surpassed still by the tyranny of pride that refused the *conclusions* of pain. (P 1)

Nietzsche acknowledges that such philosophies of pride formulate principles and practices that make pain endurable. To counteract his own pessimistic weariness with life Nietzsche himself took pride in his capacity to endure misfortune without hope for recovery. He suggests that the desire to oppose pain and suffering imparts a terrible tension to the intellect. "He who suffers", as he explains, "looks *out* at things with a terrible coldness: all those little lying charms with which things are usually surrounded when the eye of the healthy regards them do not exist for him" (*D* 114). Hellenistic and Stoic philosophers conceive old age, thought of as complete self-sufficiency and immunity from the lure of eros, as an ideal goal (see Foucault 2005:

---

[2] Nietzsche's reference to the Buddhist notion of Nirvana is an allusion to the famous closing lines of Schopenhauer's *WWR* I : 411–412. "We must not evade it, as the Indians do, by myths and meaningless words, such as . . . the Nirvana of the Buddhists. On the contrary, we freely acknowledge, that what remains after the complete abolition of the will is, for all who are still full of the will, assuredly nothing. But also, conversely, to those in whom the will has turned and denied itself, this very real world of ours with all its suns and milkways, is – nothing".

109–110). To be old in this sense means to live expecting nothing from life even in the youthful bloom of life. In Seneca's terms, the highest desideratum is to complete our life before our death: "*consummare vitam ante mortem*" (*Ep* .32.4).

However, as we saw in Book 4, Nietzsche argues that in deploying these anti-erotic philosophical therapies he overcame the tyranny of pain only through a petrification of life, or a living death (326). In this way he conceives this strategic retreat into the inner citadel as merely a refraction of a pessimistic denial of life rather than its cure. In *GS* Nietzsche treats Hellenistic therapies as illnesses requiring treatment, refractions of asceticism, rather than as instruments of cure. He aims to develop a therapy to cure the disease these ancient therapies unwittingly reproduce in another form (see Ure 2009; Faustino 2017).

Nietzsche argues that through Platonic metaphysics and Hellenistic physics, especially Stoicism and Cynicism, philosophers exercise tyranny over themselves by eliminating the passions that register their affirmation of the world of appearances. Even Epicurean hedonism, he argues, with its optimistic belief that happiness is attainable through the satisfaction of the simple, natural desires, is a sign of affliction, a flight from and fear of tragedy. "Was Epicurus an optimist", as he asks rhetorically, "precisely because he was *afflicted*?" (*BT* ASC 4). Through these philosophical therapies, he suggests, philosophers sought to extirpate or contract *eros* as a source of tragic suffering. They cultivated the ideal of self-sufficiency to make themselves immune to tragic passions. Nietzsche characterises these classical ideals as symptoms of a fear of tragedy. Ancient tragedies, he implies, fully affirm life as an excess or overflow of forces. Nietzsche argues that the Platonic and Hellenistic resolve *against* tragic pessimism, their various attempts to eliminate the very possibility of tragic experience, is precisely a measure of weakness or affliction. Only those suffering from weariness or impoverishment, he claims, seek to eliminate the tragic character of existence.

Nietzsche repudiates the Platonic and Hellenistic ideal of counteracting tragic pessimism. Against these anti-tragic philosophical ideals, he conceives the tragic passions as an integral part of his new ideal of "superabundant happiness"(326). Against the whole post-Platonic philosophical tradition, as he conceives it, Nietzsche identifies the highest health as a "pessimism of strength" that celebrates the art of tragedy. The affirmation of tragedy, he maintains, is the sign of the highest health:

An intellectual predilection for the hard, gruesome, evil, problematic aspect of existence, prompted by well-being, by overflowing health, by fullness of existence ... The sharp-eyed courage that tempts and attempts, that *craves* the frightful as the enemy, the worthy enemy against whom one can test one's strength. (*BT* ASC 1)

It is on the basis of his analysis of his own recovery that Nietzsche formulates his central meta-philosophical insights. Nietzsche develops his meta-philosophy through his analysis of his experiments with the ancient philosophical 'medicines'. In the first place, he argues that philosophy necessarily translates health and sickness, strength and weakness into "the most spiritual form and distance – this art of transfiguration just *is* philosophy" (P 3). We must, he claims, reconceive philosophy itself as a refraction of physiological and psychological conditions. Our philosophical beliefs and values, he argues, are the unconscious symptoms of our states of health and sickness. Every philosophy, he suggests, is a "cure and aid in the service of growing, struggling life" (370). On this view, philosophies are not true or false representations of the world, but unconscious symptoms of life. What is at stake in these philosophies is not truth, but health or life. As a philosophical physician Nietzsche mockingly repudiates the notion that we should treat metaphysical claims about the value of existence as epistemic claims. Indeed, he later argues that "judgements of value, concerning life, for or against it, can, in the end, never be true: they have value only as symptoms of life ... in themselves they are stupidities" (*TI* 'Socrates' 2). Judgements concerning the value of life, he claims, are not propositions that we can assess as true or false, but symptoms we can diagnose as expressions of the overabundance or impoverishment of life. "For a philosopher to see a problem in the *value* of life", he claims, is "thus an objection to him, a question mark concerning his wisdom, his un-wisdom" (*TI* 'Socrates' 2).

Second, Nietzsche frames this psychology of philosophy in terms of his assertion that we suffer from a superabundance or an impoverishment of life:

For assuming that one is a person, one necessarily also has the philosophy of that person; but here there is considerable difference. In some, it is their weaknesses that philosophize; in others, their riches and strengths. The former *need* their philosophy, be it as a prop, a sedative, medicine, redemption . . . for the latter it is only a beautiful luxury, in the best case the voluptuousness of a triumphant gratitude that eventually has to inscribe itself in cosmic capital letters on the heaven of concepts. (P 2)

As we have seen, Nietzsche suggests that those who suffer from an overabundance of life seek out tragic art and insight (370). In their case, philosophy is a luxury, not a need; they do not create values that alleviate their suffering, rather they forge ideals that express their gratitude to life. Those who suffer from a Dionysian excess of force, as he puts it, inscribe a tragic philosophy "in cosmic capital letters on the heaven of concepts" (P 2). Nietzsche clearly alludes here to the cosmology of eternal recurrence. This cosmological doctrine, he implies, is the symptom of the highest health. Where weakness or illness philosophise they give rise to metaphysical flights 'above' life, the completion of life within life, or even a radical turn against life. By contrast, where our "riches and strengths" philosophise, he suggests, it gives rise to the desire for the complete repetition of life, not the escape from or end of life.

On the other hand, Nietzsche argues that through his analysis of his own struggles to cure his personal pessimism he discovered "where thought is led and misled" when it is subject to the pressure of illness:

Every philosophy that ranks peace above war, every ethics with a negative definition of happiness, every metaphysics and physics that knows some finale, a final state of some sort, every predominantly aesthetic or religious craving for some Apart, Beyond, Outside, Above, permits the question whether it was not illness that inspired the philosopher. (P 2)

Nietzsche casts his net as widely as possible here to catch almost all previous philosophical ideals as unconscious symptoms of illness: Platonic idealism, Epicurean hedonism, Stoic tranquillity, Sceptic *ataraxia*, and Christian consolation all fall within the scope of his description (see also Coker 1997). On the basis of this psychology of philosophy, Nietzsche argues that psychologists must treat all these metaphysics and physics as symptoms of "the body, of its success or failure, its fullness, power, high-handedness, or of its frustrations, fatigues, impoverishments, its premonitions of an end, its will to an end" (P 2). In most cases, as he argues in Book 5, the "philosopher's claim to *wisdom* . . . is a hiding place in which the philosopher saves himself owing to his weariness, age, growing cold, *hardening* – as a wisdom of that instinct which the animals have before death – they go off alone, become silent, choose solitude, crawl into caves, become *wise*" (359). Nietzsche mockingly alludes to Socrates' conception of philosophy as learning how to die and the Stoic ideal of becoming cold and statue-like. That philosophers seek 'wisdom', he implies, is symptomatic of failing, declining, ageing life. In Nietzsche's view the highest classical philosophical ideals have been those that suit the needs of dying animals. "Does wisdom", he provocatively asks, "perhaps appear on earth as a raven which is inspired by the smell of carrion?" (*TI* 'Socrates' 1).

Nietzsche then draws on this psychology of philosophy to ground an ambitious meta-philosophical program. On this basis, he revives the figure of the "philosophical *physician* in the exceptional sense of the term" who risks "the proposition [that] what was at stake in all philosophizing hitherto was not at all 'truth' but rather something else – let us say health, future, growth, power, life" (P 3). Second, he reasserts his ideal of the future philosophical physician who has a "comprehensive responsibility for the collective evolution of mankind" (*BGE* 61). Nietzsche's physician sets himself nothing less than the task of "pursuing the problem of the total health of a people, time, race or of humanity" (P 3).

Nietzsche claims then that the source of his central philosophical insights derives from his own struggles to cure himself of romantic pessimism:

And as for my long sickness, do I not owe it indescribably more than I owe my health? I owe it my *higher* health – one which is made stronger by whatever does not kill it. I also owe my philosophy to it. (*NCW* Epilogue 1)

Nietzsche's psychology of philosophy derives from his analysis of Schopenhauerian resignation, Stoic pride, Epicurean hedonism, Sceptical *ataraxia* as so many missteps in his effort to come to terms with or combat pessimism. By this means he identifies most philosophies as involuntary measures that develop under the pressure of illness; they are defensive strategies analogous to the extreme self-tyranny adopted by Roman slaves to withstand the tyranny of their masters.

Yet Nietzsche argues that philosophers who engage in these experiments with pathologically motivated philosophies find themselves suffering from a *new* illness: viz. a severe suspicion, or an unconditional will to truth or 'truth at any price', that motivates nihilistic doubts about the value of life. "Only great pain is the liberator of the spirit", he explains, "as the teacher of *the great suspicion* . . . Only great pain, that long, slow pain that takes its time and in which we are burned, as it were, over green wood, forces us philosophers into our ultimate depths and puts aside all trust, everything good natured, veiling, mild, average – things in which we formerly may have found our humanity" (P 3). Nietzsche identifies the free spirit's great suspicion as a symptom of pain that promotes a "will to question further, more deeply severely, harshly, evilly" (P 3). Through his experiments with these philosophies, Nietzsche schooled himself in a suspicion that our highest philosophies have been unconscious symptoms of an aversion to life. In doing so, Nietzsche implies, he fuelled a suspicion about the very possibility of affirming life. In other words, he suggests that this suspicion itself is not free of the aversion to life expressed in our philosophical ideals, but is symptomatic of the mistrust that flows from the experience of pain: "The trust in life is gone: life itself has become a problem" (P 3).

Here Nietzsche revisits the dilemma he outlined in the book's very first section. In *GS* 1 we should recall, he suggests that we cannot thrive without periodic trust in life, yet this trust periodically falters (1). Nietzsche acknowledges that this mistrust is not without its rewards. As we have seen, he maintains that philosophical physicians who apply their scientific curiosity to illness can learn a great deal about the relationship between philosophy and health. And exercising mistrust, he adds, yields its own peculiar pleasure. Through this deep mistrust, he claims, we come to know a "new happiness": viz. a delight in all that is problematic "that flares up like bright embers again and again over all the distress of what is problematic, over all the danger of uncertainty, and even over the jealousy of the lover" (P 3).

We should not, however, confuse the goal of Nietzsche's gay science with this delight in suspicion (cf. Reginster 2013). In P 4 Nietzsche immediately adds:

Lest what is most important remain unsaid: from such abysses ... from the illness of severe suspicion, one must return *newborn* having shed one's skin, more ticklish and malicious, with a more delicate taste for joy ... with a more dangerous second innocence, more childlike, and at the same time a hundred times subtler than one had ever been before. (P 4; see also *NCW* Epilogue 2)

Nietzsche stresses that suspicion is a severe illness from which "we convalescents" must recover to enjoy this dangerous second innocence (P 4).

What is this malicious innocence? To answer this question Nietzsche returns to question of the value of the unconditional will to truth, or "'truth at any price'" (344/P 4). To illuminate free spirit's reassessment of the will to truth, he briefly reports three fables, which pivot on the veiling and unveiling of truth. Nietzsche frames these three stories in the context of his suggestion that free spirits have grown sick of their own will to truth at any price.

In the first a young Egyptian, feverish for the truth, sickens and expires after breaking a sacred taboo and unveiling a statue of Isis to reveal the hidden Truth. Truth is fatal. Like the young Egyptian, Nietzsche suggests free spirits are also sickened by their thirst for the truth. On the basis of the youth's dark fate Nietzsche enigmatically observes that perhaps truth does not remain truth when we remove the veils.

Nietzsche then reports a young girl prudishly remarking to her mother that she thinks it is indecent for God to be everywhere and see everything. Nietzsche draws from this a moral lesson for philosophers: they should respect the modesty of nature and not shamelessly expose the immoral truth. Truth, it seems, is indecent. Perhaps Nietzsche then remarks, truth has grounds for not revealing her grounds.

Nietzsche's third literary allusion hints at the meaning of this cryptic remark. Nietzsche personifies truth as the ancient mythical figure of Baubo, an elderly dry nurse who liberates the goddess Demeter from deadening grief by comically lifting her skirt to reveal her vulva. Truth personified is a vulgar character. Beneath the veil she reveals truth as comically profane rather than tragically sacred. Nietzsche has moved from the tragedy of the Egyptian youth dying from the sight of sacred truth, through an Aesopian moral admonition against the shamefulness of truth seekers exposing vulgarity, to the comedy of Demeter cured of tragic grief by profanity.

Is Nietzsche suggesting free spirits desist from profaning the sacred truth; that they return to childlike innocence or naivety; or that they acknowledge that truth is profane rather than sacred? Is truth tragic, indecent or comic? In these vignettes Nietzsche gives a thumbnail sketch of the ebb and flow of tragedy and comedy that frames the entire book. As Nietzsche notes in the Preface, *GS* announces not just the beginning of tragedy ("*incipit tragoedia*"), but also "something utterly wicked . . . : *incipit parodia*" (P 1).[3]

Nietzsche's first story sketches how free spirits are burnt by their own metaphysical flame: i.e. their faith in truth. He recalls the ancient story of the veiled statue of Isis in the Egyptian city of Sais. In Plutarch's report the statue of the goddess has inscribed on it: 'I am everything that is, that was, that will be, and no mortal has yet raised my veil' (Plutarch 1936: 25). Friedrich Schiller's poem, the 'Veiled Image of Sais', embroiders this story. A young Egyptian suffers from "the fierce fever of the wish to know" the whole truth, "Truth one and indivisible". Learning from a hierophant about the divine command proscribing lifting the veil of Isis, he breaks into the temple at midnight and breaks the prohibition. Discovered in the temple the next morning he is speechless and from anguish he goes to an early grave.

Schiller's Egyptian youth is emblematic of the metaphysical desire to uncover a sacred truth beneath the veil of appearances. Nietzsche acknowledges that even free spirits, "we knowers of today, we godless anti-metaphysicians", share this metaphysical faith that truth is divine (344). Even as free spirits scientifically discredit Platonic and Christian metaphysics and morals, unveiling the all-too-human, this-

---

[3] Nietzsche reference to 'incipit tragoedia' directs us back to the close of Book 4 (342), which he will use as the opening of *Z*, as well as to the penultimate section of Book 5 (382). The significance of Nietzsche's suggestion that *GS* announces the beginning not only of tragedy (342, 382) but also of 'parody' is a matter of contention. The controversy concerns what Nietzsche makes the target of parody. Does he imply that Zarathustra's teachings are *self*-parodic? I follow Paul Loeb's view that Nietzsche conceives *GS* as the beginning of the parody of all that Europeans have previously taken 'seriously', which he identifies as the ascetic ideal, in the name of his own tragic counter-ideal (see Loeb 2010: 240–242). For an exhaustive treatment of Nietzsche's concept of parody and its application in *GS* P 1, see Benne (2016).

worldly origins and evolution of the highest ideals, he implies, they are still motivated by this faith. This is the way in which, as puts it, "*we, too, are still pious*" (344). They too burn with the Platonic desire for the divine.

Nietzsche then argues that like all metaphysical faith their commitment to the unconditional value of truth expresses an aversion to life. As we have seen, he argues that the "lie" motivating this will to truth is the ideal of another higher world that stands in contradiction to this world. Nietzsche suggests that the characteristics assigned to the "true" or "real" are "the characteristics of non-being, of *nothingness* – the 'real' world has been constructed out of the contradiction to the actual world" (*TI* 'Reason' 6). Nietzsche argues that this metaphysical ideal is a "moral-optical illusion" that we have invented as expressions of our ascetic aversion to life, a "revenge against life" by means of the phantasmagoria of 'another', 'better' life (*TI* 'Reason' 6/*BGE* 59). As we have seen, he claims that the free spirit's will to truth is motivated by this same ascetic contempt for this world and a desire to take revenge on life. Yet through their own feverish pursuit of truth, Nietzsche claims, they discover that the metaphysical notion of another world is absolutely indemonstrable and that this metaphysical hope expresses an aversion to life. When free spirits in their youthful madness pull off the veils concealing the will to truth, he suggests, they uncover "error, blindness, the lie" (344).

In what sense then have Nietzsche's free spirits been burnt by the fire Plato first lit, the metaphysical ideal of truth as divine, which is the moral ground of the commitment to truth at any price? First, on the altar of this commitment free spirits have sacrificed all metaphysical illusions and errors that once made life endurable. Second, as we saw in the previous chapter, they have also discovered that their commitment to science, the purest expression of the ascetic will to truth, strips the world of value or significance. It is in this sense that we can understand Nietzsche's enigmatic statement that for free spirits "truth does not remain truth": it does not pave the road to the divine, but to an explanation of the natural world that divests it of deeper significance or meaning.

In their feverish devotion to the will to truth at price, it seems, they have unwittingly crossed the threshold to nihilism. As we also saw in the previous chapter, Nietzsche identifies nihilism, the sign of a despairing, mortally weary soul, with "puritanical fanatics of conscience who would rather lie down and die on a sure nothing than an uncertain something" (*BGE* 10). Free spirits, as he explains, must therefore eventually face a terrible Either/Or: 'Either abolish your venerations or *yourselves*!' The latter would be nihilism; but would not the former also be – nihilism? That is *our* question mark" (346). Is it nihilistic to abolish venerations? If so, then Nietzsche's free spirits seem to be nihilists par excellence. Their illness of severe suspicion commits them to nihilism: they prefer to will nothing, a world devoid of sense or meaning, than not will at all.

However, as we observed, Nietzsche conceives *GS* not just as a tragedy, but also as a parody of all earthly seriousness, and the will to truth, he claims, has been the most serious moral commitment. Nietzsche turns then to mock truth on the basis of its obscene or shameful grounds:

Perhaps truth is a woman who has grounds for not showing her grounds? Perhaps her real name is – to speak Greek – *Baubo*? (P 4)

Classical figurines depict Baubo as a lower female torso with a face whose exposed vulva forms the chin. As Pierre Hadot observes, Baubo is a female mythological figure, linked to the mysteries of Eleusis, and therefore to the story of Demeter and Persephone. According to the Orphic poem, Demeter is in mourning after Hades, the god of the underworld, has abducted her daughter Persephone. Baubo alleviates Demeter's grief by lifting her skirt to display her vulva, making Demeter burst into laughter (Hadot 2006: 295). Through her comically obscene act Baubo enables Demeter to overcome the grief that has made her decline her host's offer of wine. Nietzsche's Baubo represents a comic figure who releases Demeter from her mourning so that she can return to the intoxication of life. Baubo's obscene comedy is a therapy of grief and mourning.

How does Nietzsche relate his allusion to the comic Baubo to his concern about free spirits becoming sick from their unconditional will to truth? Nietzsche's allusion mocks the very notion of a metaphysical world behind the apparent world and the free spirit's Platonic inspired contempt for the apparent world. It too is a comic therapy, one that aims to liberate free spirits from their

last vestiges of the 'metaphysical' illness. Nietzsche's Baubo allusion is the comical *reductio ad absurdum* of metaphysics. Baubo
discloses beneath her veil not a deeper truth, not the world as it is
in itself, but simply another superficial, natural appearance.
Nietzsche's parody works through the incongruity between the
free spirit's expectation that truth unveiled will disclose the divine,
and the discovery that there is nothing more than vulgar appearance all the way down. Nietzsche's Baubo allusion also shames
free spirits because it compels them to acknowledge that the
"grounds" of their commitment to truth has been their Platonic
hostility to the world of appearances. Baubo is another version of
Nietzsche's abolition of metaphysics.

Nietzsche, as Williams observes, came to see the idea of the
world in itself as precisely a relic of the kind of metaphysics that
he wanted to overcome (Williams 2001: xxi). As Nietzsche put it
in the famous final section of 'How the "Real World" at Last
Became a Myth': 'The true world is gone: which world is left?
The apparent one, perhaps? . . . But no! *we got rid of the apparent
world along with the true one!*' (*TI* 'Error' 6). That is to say,
Nietzsche suggests that with the end of metaphysics the "antithesis of the apparent world and the true world is reduced to the
antithesis 'world' and 'nothing'". "The apparent world is the only
one", as he explains, "the "true" world is merely added by a lie"
(*TI* 'Reason' 2). Yet, Nietzsche also recognises that even if free
spirits overcome the loss of the metaphysical illusion of depth,
this does not necessarily mean they have overcome the ascetic
contempt for appearances.

Nietzsche implies that the overcoming of the nihilistic devaluation of the world entails moving from comedy to tragedy. Free
spirits might find comic relief in profaning the sacred, but this is
entirely negative: it relieves them of the desire for depth, but it
does not thereby affirm the profane. Nietzsche identifies 'art' as the
overcoming of nihilism. In his final statement on the character of
free spirits he identifies them as "artists" (P 4). As always,
Nietzsche's principal concern is with how we can live well. Art,
he claims, is "the great stimulus to life"; it aims at the "desirability
of life" (*TI* 'Skirmishes' 24). In this regard, he learns from the
ancients:

Oh, those Greeks! They knew how to *live*: what is needed for that is to stop bravely at the surface, the fold, the skin; to worship appearance, to believe in shapes, tones, words – in the whole Olympus of appearance! Those Greeks were superficial – *out of profundity*! (P 4)

Who are these Greeks? Nietzsche clearly means the pre-philosophic Greeks, or more precisely the Greek tragedians. As we have seen, Nietzsche claims that to think in terms of a metaphysical distinction between a true world and an apparent world is a sign of decline of life. Metaphysics is incipient pessimism. "Plato", as he explains, "is a coward before reality, consequently he flees into the ideal" (*TI* 'Ancients' 2). By contrast, the Greek tragedians esteemed appearance higher than reality, but in their case, he claims, 'appearance' is not distinct from or opposed to a true world. Rather, he argues, for the Greeks of the tragic age "'appearance' means reality *once more*, only by way of selection, reinforcement, and correction. The tragic artist is no pessimist: he is precisely the one who says Yes to everything question-able, even to the terrible – he is *Dionysian*" (*TI* 'Reason' 6). On Nietzsche's view, the tragedians do not conceal or veil terrible or questionable appearances; rather, they intensify and accentuate these appearances precisely because they worship these appearances. Unlike Plato, the older Greeks, Nietzsche suggests, had courage in the face of reality (*TI* 'Ancients' 2).

Rather than inventing another true world to slander the apparent world, the tragedians, he argues, artistically transfigure reality. Their profundity lies in worshipping and transfiguring the "surface" rather than in fleeing from the world of appearances into the lie of an ideal, true world. In other words, their profundity and courage consist in acknowledging the world of appearances as the only world. It is a sign of their flourishing or strength that they did not need the metaphysical consolation of another, ideal, eternal world. One must be "sufficiently strong, sufficiently hard, sufficient of an artist", as he puts it, "to get hold of the truth" (*BGE* 59). Nietzsche, then, acknowledges the "truth" of tragic art, which consists in worshipping the 'surface' of things, 'appearances', rather than lyingly inventing another world.

Nietzsche acknowledges in the Preface to *GS* that he is returning to his earliest claims in *BT* that tragedy expressed the highest affirma-tion of life. However, in this Preface he analyses tragic art not through the lens of his earlier Schopenhauerian pessimism, which conceived it as a metaphysical response to the dangers of the pessimistic denial of life. In *BT* Nietzsche understood tragedy as a metaphysical consolation for the Silenian wisdom that for us the best is beyond our reach: "not to be born, not to *be*, to be nothing. But the second best for you is – to die soon" (*BT* 3).

In the final summation of *GS*, by contrast, he conceives tragedy as the ancient Greeks' triumphant affirmation of life: their art glorifies "sublime calamity" precisely because this is what they will as the highest, most praiseworthy condition of life (*TI* 'Skirmishes' 24). Tragedy for the Greeks was the greatest stimulus to life and the affirmation of life. "Before tragedy", he writes, "what is warlike in our soul celebrates its Saturnalia; whoever is used to suffering, whoever seeks out suffering, the heroic man praises his own being through tragedy – to him alone the tragedian presents this drink of sweetest cruelty" (*TI* 'Skirmishes' 24). The tragedian's delight in the fearful and questionable, as puts it, "is a great desideratum" (*TI* 'Skirmishes' 24). Nietzsche conceives tragic art as "truth" in a two-fold sense: it worships surfaces or appearances rather than fleeing into the ideal, and it expresses the most comprehensive affirmation of life.

As we have seen, Nietzsche identifies as the highest peak of this tragic delight in life, the affirmation of eternal recurrence. Greek tragedy identifies the highest flourishing with "Saying yes to life even in its strangest and hardest problems, the will to life rejoicing over its own inexhaustibility even in the sacrifice of its highest types … not in order to be liberated from terror and pity, not in order to purge oneself of a dangerous affect by its vehement discharge … but in order to be *oneself* the eternal joy of becoming, beyond all terror and pity – the joy which included even joy in destroying" (*TI* 'Ancients' 5). In closing *GS* Nietzsche declares that this tragic affirmation of eternal recurrence

is … precisely what we are coming back to, we daredevils of the spirit who have climbed to the highest and most dangerous peaks of thought and looked around from up there, looked *down* from up there… Are we not just in this respect Greeks? Worshippers of shapes, tones, words? And therefore – artists? (P 4)

References

Abbey, R. (1996) 'Beyond Metaphor and Misogyny: Women in Nietzsche's Middle Period', *Journal of the History of Philosophy* 34(2): 244–256.

(2000) *Nietzsche's Middle Period* (London: Oxford University Press).

Allison, D. B. (1985) *The New Nietzsche: Contemporary Styles of Interpretation* (Cambridge, MA: MIT Press).

(1994) '"Have I Been Understood"?', in Nietzsche, Genealogy, Morality, ed. by R. Schacht (Berkeley: University of California Press), 460–468.

Anderson, R. L. (1996) 'Overcoming Charity: The Case of Maudemarie Clark's Nietzsche on Truth and Philosophy', *Nietzsche-Studien* 25: 307–341.

Ansell-Pearson, K. (2013a) 'True to the Earth: Nietzsche's Epicurean Care of Self and World', in *Nietzsche's Therapeutic Teaching*, ed. by H. Hutter and E. Friedland (London: Bloomsbury), 97–116.

(ed.) (2013b) *Nietzsche and Political Thought* (London: Bloomsbury).

Appel, F. (1999) *Nietzsche contra Democracy* (Ithaca, NY: Cornell University Press).

Arendt, H. (1958) *The Human Condition* (Chicago: University of Chicago Press).

Armstrong, A. (2013) 'The Passions, Power and Practical Philosophy: Spinoza and Nietzsche contra the Stoics', *Journal of Nietzsche Studies* 43(1): 6–24.

Ascheim, S. (1992) *The Nietzsche Legacy in Germany* 1890–1990 (Berkeley: University of California Press).

Augustine (1984) *City of God against the Pagans*, trans. by H. Bettenson (Harmondsworth, UK: Penguin).

Bambach, C. (2010) 'Nietzsche's Madman Parable: A Cynical Reading', *American Catholic Philosophical Quarterly* 84(2): 441–456.

Barish, J. (1985) *The Anti-Theatrical Prejudice* (Berkeley: University of California Press).

Barker, E. (1918) *Greek Political Theory: Plato and His Predecessors* (London: Metheun).

Bataille, G. (1985) 'Nietzsche and the Fascists', in *Visions of Excess: Selected Writings, 1927–1939*, ed. and trans. by A. Stoekl (Minneapolis: University of Minnesota Press), 182–196.

Bates, H. W. (1941) 'The Murderer Sipo', in *The Victorians*, ed. by Mary D. Stocks (Manchester: Manchester University Press), 126–128.

Berlin, I. (1969) *Four Essays on Liberty* (Oxford: Oxford University Press).

Berry, J. (2004) 'Nietzsche and Democritus: The Origin of Ethical *Eudaimonism*', in *Nietzsche and Antiquity: His Reaction and Response to the Classical Tradition*, ed. by P. Bishop (Rochester: Camden House), 98–113.

(2005) 'The Pyrrhonian Revival in Montaigne & Nietzsche', *Journal of the History of Ideas* 65(3): 497–514.

(2010) *Nietzsche and the Ancient Skeptical Tradition* (New York: Oxford University Press).

Bett, R. (2000) 'Nietzsche on the Skeptics & Nietzsche as Skeptic', *Archiv für Geschichte der Philosophie* 82: 62–86.

(2005) 'Nietzsche, the Greeks, & Happiness (with Special Reference to Aristotle & Epicurus)', *Philosophical Topics* 33(2): 45–70.

Bittner, R. (2012) 'Nietzsche: Writing from the Late Notebooks', in *Introductions to Nietzsche*, ed. by R. Pippin (Cambridge: Cambridge University Press), 240–263.

Bracht Branham, R. (2004) 'Nietzsche's Cynicism: Upper of Lowercase?', in *Nietzsche and Antiquity*, ed. by P. Bishop (Rochester, NY: Camden House), 170–181.

Breazeale, D. (1979) 'Introduction', in *Philosophy and Truth: Selections from Nietzsche's Notebooks of the Early 1870s*, trans. by D. Breazeale (Atlantic Highlands, NJ: Humanities Press), xiii–xlix.

Brobjer, T. (2008) *Nietzsche's Philosophical Context: An Intellectual Biography* (Urbana: University of Illinois Press).

Calder, W. M. (1983) 'The Wilamowitz-Nietzsche Struggle: New Documents and a Reappraisal', *Nietzsche-Studien* 12: 214–254.

Came, D. (2004) 'Nietzsche's Attempt at Self-Criticism: Art and Morality in The Birth of Tragedy', *Nietzsche Studien* 33(1): 37–67.

Camus, A. (1981) *The Rebel*, trans. by A. Bower (Harmondsworth, UK: Penguin Books).

Caygill, H. (2006) 'Under the Epicurean Skies', *Angelaki* II(3): 107–115.

Cicero (1927) *Tusculan Disputations*, trans. by J. E. King (Cambridge, MA: Harvard University Press).

Clark, M. (1990) *Nietzsche on Truth and Philosophy* (Cambridge: Cambridge University Press).

Clark, M., and Dudrick, D. (2004) 'Nietzsche's Post-Positivism', *European Journal of Philosophy* 12(3): 369–385.

(2007) 'Nietzsche and Moral Objectivity: the Development of Nietzsche's Metaethics', in *Nietzsche and Morality*, ed. by B. Leiter and N. Sinhababu (Oxford: Clarendon Press), 192–226.

(2012) *The Soul of Nietzsche: Beyond Good and Evil* (Cambridge: Cambridge University Press).

Cohen, J. (2014) 'Nietzsche's Second Turning', *PLI* 25: 35–54.

Coker, J. (1997) 'The Therapy of Nietzsche's "Free Spirit"', *International Studies in Philosophy* 29(3): 63–88.

Connolly, W. E. (2008) 'Nietzsche, Democracy Time', in *Nietzsche Power, Politics: Rethinking Nietzsche's Legacy for Political Thought*, ed. by H. Siemens and V. Roodt (Berlin: Walter De Gruyter), 109–143.

Conway, D., and Ward, J. K. (1992) 'Physicians of the Soul: in Sextus Empiricus & Nietzsche', in *Nietzsche und die antike Philosophie*, ed. by Daniel W. Conway and Rudolf Rehn (Trier), 193–223.

Cottingham, J. (2003) *On the Meaning of Life* (London: Routledge).

Crepon, M. (2009) 'The Politics of Music (Nietzsche)', in *Friedrich Nietzsche*, ed. by T. B. Strong (Farnham, UK: Ashgate), chapter 16.

Dahlkvist, T. (2007) *Nietzsche and the Philosophy of Pessimism: A Study of Nietzsche's Relation to the Pessimistic Tradition. Schopenhauer, Hartmann, Leopardi* (Stockholm: Elanders Gotab).

Danto, A. (1988) 'Some Remarks on "The Genealogy of Morals"', in *Reading Nietzsche*, ed. by R. C. Solomon and K. M. Higgins (Oxford: Oxford University Press), 13–28.

Darwin, C. (1856) *Darwin Correspondence Project*, Letter no. 1924, www.darwinproject.ac.uk/DCP-LETT-1924, accessed on 18 June 2018.

Deleuze, G. (1983) *Nietzsche and Philosophy*, trans. by H. Tomlinson (London: Athlone Press).

Della Rocca, M. (2008) *Spinoza* (London: Routledge).

Derrida, J. (1979) *Spurs. Nietzsche's Styles*, trans. by B. Harlow (Chicago: University of Chicago Press).

Desmond, W. (2006) *Cynics* (Stocksfield: Acumen).

Detienne, M., and Vernant, J.-P. (1991) *Cunning Intelligence in Greek Culture and Society*, trans. by J. Lloyd (Chicago: University of Chicago Press).

Detwiler, B. (1990) *Nietzsche and the Politics of Aristocratic Radicalism* (Chicago: University of Chicago Press).

Diethe, C. (1989) 'Nietzsche and the Woman Question', History of European Ideas 11: 865–876.

D'Iorio, P. (1995) 'Cosmologie de l'éternel retour', Nietzsche-Studien 24(1): 62–123.

(2016) *Nietzsche's Journey to Sorrento: Genesis of the Philosophy of the Free Spirit*, trans. by S. M. Gorelick (Chicago: University of Chicago Press).

Drochon, H. (2010) 'Nietzsche and Politics', *Nietzsche-Studien* 39(1): 663–677.

(2016a) *Nietzsche's Great Politics* (Princeton, NJ: Princeton University Press).

(2016b) '"An Old Carriage with New Horses": Nietzsche's Critique of Democracy', *History of European Ideas* 42(8): 1055–1068.

Elgat, G. (2016) '*Amor Fati* as Practice: How to Love Fate', *Southern Journal of Philosophy* 54(2): 174–188.

Empiricus, S. (2000) *Outlines of Scepticism*, trans. and ed. by J. Annas and J. Barnes (Cambridge: Cambridge University Press).

Epictetus (1995) *The Handbook of Epictetus*, trans. by R. Hard (London: J. M. Dent).

Esposito, R. (2008) *Bios: Biopolitics and Philosophy*, trans. by T. Campbell (Minneapolis: University of Minnesota Press).

Faustino, M. (2017) 'Nietzsche's Therapy of Therapy', *Nietzsche-Studien* 46(1): 82–104.

Foucault, M. (1984) *The Foucault Reader*, ed. by P. Rabinow (London: Penguin).

(1985) *The Use of Pleasure: The History of Sexuality*, vol. 2, trans. by R. Hurley (London: Penguin Books).

(2005) *The Hermeneutics of the Subject: Lectures at the Collège de France*, trans. by G. Burchell, ed. by F. Gros (New York: Palgrave).

Franco, P. (2011) *Nietzsche's Enlightenment: The Free-Spirit Trilogy* (Chicago: University of Chicago Press).

Gayon (1999) 'Nietzsche and Darwin', in *Biology and the Foundation of Ethics*, ed. by J. Maienschein and M. Ruse (Cambridge: Cambridge University Press), 154–197.

Gemes, K. (2008) 'Review: *The Affirmation of Life*', *European Journal of Philosophy* 16(3): 459–466.

(2013) 'Nihilism', in *Encyclopedia of Philosophy and the Social Sciences*, vol. 2, ed. by B. Kaldis (Thousand Oaks, CA: Sage), 271–274.

Geuss, R. (1999) 'Art and Theodicy', in *Morality, Culture, and History* (Cambridge: Cambridge University Press): 78–115.

Gillespie, Michael Allen, and Strong, Tracy B. (eds) (1988) *Nietzsche's New Seas: Explorations in Philosophy, Aesthetics and Politics* (Chicago: University of Chicago Press).

Golomb, J. (1997) *Nietzsche and Jewish Culture* (New York: Routledge).

Golomb, J., and Wistrich, R. S. (eds) (2002) *Nietzsche, Godfather of Fascism? On the Uses and Abuses of a Philosophy* (Princeton, NJ: Princeton University Press).

Graver, M. (2007) *Stoicism and the Emotions* (Chicago: University of Chicago Press).

Grimm, S. (2015) 'Wisdom', *Australasian Journal of Philosophy* 93(1): 139–154.

Grundlehner, P. (1986) *The Poetry of Friedrich Nietzsche* (Oxford: Oxford University Press).

Hadot, P. (1995) *Philosophy as a Way of Life: Spiritual Exercises from Socrates to Foucault*, trans. by M. Chase (Hoboken, NJ: Wiley-Blackwell).

(2002) *What Is Ancient Philosophy?* (Cambridge, MA: Harvard University).

(2006) *The Veil of Isis: An Essay on the History of the Idea of Nature*, trans. by M. Chase (Cambridge, MA: Harvard University Press).

(2009) *The Present Alone Is Our Happiness: Conversations with Jeannie Carlier and Arnold I. Davidson*, trans. by M. Djaballah (Stanford, CA: Stanford University Press).

(2010) 'Introduction to Ernest Bertram, Nietzsche Attempt at a Mythology', trans. by P. Bishop, *The Agonist* III(I): 52–84.

Halliwell, S. (1998) *Aristotle's Poetics* (Chicago: University of Chicago Press).

(2008) *Greek Laughter: A Study of Cultural Psychology from Homer to Christianity* (Cambridge: Cambridge University Press).

Hamilton, J. (2004) 'Ecce Philologus: Nietzsche and Pindar's Second Pythian Ode', in *Nietzsche and Antiquity: His Reaction and Response to the Classical Tradition*, ed. by Paul Bishop (Rochester, NY: Camden House), 54–69.

Handfield, T. (2016) 'Genealogical Explanations of Chance and Morals', in *Explanation in Ethics and Mathematics: Debunking and Dispensability*, ed. by U. Leibowitz & N. Sinclair (Oxford: Oxford University Press).

Han-Pile, B. (2011) 'Nietzsche and Amor Fati', *European Journal of Philosophy* 19(2): 224–261.

Hatab, L. (1995) *A Nietzschean Defense of Democracy: An Experiment in Postmodern Politics* (Chicago: Open Court).

(2008) *Nietzsche's Genealogy of Morality: An Introduction* (Cambridge: Cambridge University Press).

Heidegger, M. (1977) 'The Word of Nietzsche: "God Is dead", and "The Age of the World Picture"', in *The Question Concerning Technology and Other Essays*, trans. by W. Lovitt (New York: Harper and Row), 53–114; 115–154.

Heller, E. (1986) 'Introduction' in Human, All Too Human: A Book for Free Spirits, Vol. 1, trans. R. J. Hollingdale (Cambridge: Cambridge University Press,1986), vii–xix.

(1991) *Nietzsche III: The Will to Power as Knowledge and Metaphysics*, ed. by D. F. Krell, trans. J. Stambaugh (New York: HarperCollins).

Higgins, K. M. (2000) *Comic Relief: Nietzsche's Gay Science* (Oxford: Oxford University Press).

Holub, R. C. (2016) *Nietzsche's Jewish Problem: Between Anti-Semitism and Anti-Judaism* (Princeton, NJ: Princeton University Press).

Huddleston, A. (2017) 'Nietzsche on the Health of the Soul', *Inquiry* 60(1–2): 135–164.

Hussain, N. (2004) 'Nietzsche's Positivism', *European Journal of Philosophy* 12(3): 326–368.

Janaway, C. (2002) 'Review: The Gay Science', see https://ndpr.nd.edu/news/23447-the-gay-science-with-a-prelude-in-german-rhymes-and-an-appendix-of-songs/.

(2007) *Beyond Selflessness: Reading Nietzsche's Genealogy* (Oxford: Oxford University Press).

(2013) 'The Gay Science', in *The Oxford Handbook of Nietzsche*, ed. by J. Richardson and K. Gemes (Oxford: Oxford University Press), 252–271.

(2014) 'Beauty Is False, Truth Ugly: Nietzsche on Art and Life', in *Nietzsche on Art and Life*, ed. by D. Came (Oxford: Oxford University Press), 39–56.

Janaway, C., and Robertson, S. (eds) (2012) 'Introduction', in *Nietzsche Naturalism and Normativity* (Oxford: Oxford University Press), 1–19.

Jensen, A. K. (2004) 'Nietzsche's Unpublished Fragments on Ancient Cynicism: The First Night of Diogenes', in *Nietzsche and Antiquity*, ed. by P. Bishop (Rochester, NY: Camden House), 182–191.

Johnson, D. (2010) *Nietzsche's Anti-Darwinism* (Cambridge: Cambridge University Press).

Kafka, F. (1983) Complete Short Stories (Harmondsworth, UK: Penguin Books).

Kain, P. (2007) 'Nietzsche, Eternal Recurrence, and the Horror of Existence', *Journal of Nietzsche Studies* 33: 49–63.

Kaufmann, W. (1974a) Nietzsche: Philosopher, Psychologist, Antichrist (Princeton, NJ: Princeton University Press).

trans. (1974b) The Gay Science: With a Prelude in Rhymes and an Appendix of Songs, by Friedrich Nietzsche (New York: Vintage Books).

Klossowski, P. (2004) 'Nietzsche, Polytheism and Parody', *Bulletin de la Société Américaine de Philosophie de Langue Français* 14(2): 82–119.

Knight, A. H. J. (1933) 'Nietzsche & Epicurean Philosophy', *Philosophy* 8(32): 431–445.

Laertius, D. (1931) *Lives of Eminent Philosophers*, trans. R. D. Hicks (Cambridge, MA: Harvard University Press).

Lampert, L. (1993) *Nietzsche and Modern Times: A Study of Bacon, Descartes and Nietzsche* (New Haven, CT: Yale University Press).

Lange, F. A. (1925) *The History of Materialism* (London: Kegan Paul).

Langer, M. M. (2010) *Nietzsche's Gay Science: Dancing Coherence* (Basingstoke, UK: Palgrave Macmillan).

Large, D. (2013) 'Nietzsche et compagnie: la pluralisation de la première personne', in Nietzsche: un art nouveau du discours (Reims: Éditions et Presses Universitaires de Reims), 103–125.

Leiter, B. (2002) *The Routledge Guidebook to Nietzsche on Morality* (Abingdon, UK: Routledge).

(2015) 'Nietzsche's Moral and Political Philosophy', https://plato.stanford.edu/entries/nietzsche-moral-political/.

Leiter, B., and Sinhababu, N. (eds) (2007) *Nietzsche and Morality* (Oxford: Clarendon Press).

Lemm, V. (2016) 'Is Nietzsche a Naturalist?' *Journal of Nietzsche Studies* 47(1): 61–80.

Loeb, P. S. (1998) 'The Moment of Tragic Death in Nietzsche's Dionysian Doctrine of Eternal Recurrence: An Exegesis of Aphorism 342 in *The Gay Science*', *International Studies in Philosophy* 3: 131–143.

(2010) *The Death of Nietzsche's Zarathustra* (Cambridge: Cambridge University Press).

(2013) 'Eternal Recurrence', in *The Oxford Handbook of Nietzsche*, ed. by K. Gemes and J. Richardson (Oxford: Oxford University Press), 645–671.

(2015) 'Will to Power and Panpsychism', in *Nietzsche on Mind and Nature*, ed. by M. Dries and P. J. E. Kail (Oxford: Oxford University Press).

Long A. A. (2006) *From Epicurus to Epictetus: Studies in Hellenistic and Roman Philosophy* (Oxford: Oxford University Press).

Luchte, J. (2010) 'Preface to the Second Edition', in *The Peacock and the Buffalo: The Poetry of Nietzsche*, trans. by J. Luchte (London: Bloomsbury), 34–44.

Lucretius (1951) *On the Nature of the Universe*, trans. by R. E. Latham (Harmondsworth, UK: Penguin Books).

Mack, B. (2003) *The Christian Myth: Origins, Logic, Legacy* (London: Continuum International).

Magee, B. (2001) *Wagner and Philosophy* (London: Penguin).

Magnus, B. (1978) *Nietzsche's Existential Imperative* (Bloomington: Indiana University Press).

(1988) 'The Deification of the Commonplace', in *Reading Nietzsche*, ed. by R. Solomon and K. Higgins (Oxford: Oxford University Press).

Mann, T. (1959) 'Nietzsche's Philosophy in the Light of Recent History', in *Last Essays*, trans. R. and C. Winston, T. and J. Stern (New York: Alfred A. Knopf).

Meyer, M. (2011) 'Nietzsche's Naturalism and the Falsification Thesis', in *Nietzsches Wissenschaftsphilosophie*, ed. by M. Brusotti, G. Abel, and H. Heit (Berlin: De Gruyter), 59–135.

Middleton, Christopher, ed. and trans. (1996) Selected Letters of Friedrich Nietzsche (Indianapolis, IN: Hackett).

Mitcheson, K. (2017) 'Scepticism and Self-Transformation in Nietzsche: On the Uses and Disadvantages of a Comparison to Pyrrhonian Scepticism', *British Journal for the History of Philosophy* 25(1): 63–83.

Moore, G. (2002a) 'Nietzsche, Spencer and the Ethics of Evolution', *Journal of Nietzsche Studies* 23: 1–20.

(2002b) *Nietzsche, Biology and Metaphor* (Cambridge: Cambridge University Press).

More, N. (2014) *Nietzsche's Last Laugh: Ecce Homo as Satire* (Cambridge: Cambridge University Press).

Mosser, K. (1998) 'Should the Skeptic Live His Skepticism? Nietzsche and Classical Skepticism', *Manuscrito* XXI(1): 47–84.

Nadler, S. (2016) 'Baruch Spinoza', in *Stanford Encyclopedia of Philosophy*, http://plato.stanford.edu/entries/spinoza/.

Navia, L. (1996) *Classical Cynicism: A Critical Study* (Westport, CT: Greenwood).

Nehamas, A. (1985) *Nietzsche: Life as Literature* (Cambridge, MA: Harvard University Press).

(1998) *The Art of Living: Socratic Reflections from Plato to Foucault* (Berkeley: University of California Press).

Nichues-Pröbsting, H. (1996) 'The Modern Reception of Cynicism', in *The Cynics*, ed. by R. Bracht Branham and Marie-Coile Goulet-Gaze (Berkeley: University of California Press), 329–365.

Nussbaum, M. (1986) *The Fragility of Goodness: Luck and Ethics in Greek Tragedy and Philosophy* (Cambridge: Cambridge University Press).

Owen, D. (2008) 'Nietzsche, Ethical Agency and the Problem of Democracy', in *Nietzsche Power, Politics: Rethinking Nietzsche's Legacy for Political Thought*, ed. by H. Siemens and V. Roodt (Berlin: Walter De Gruyter), 143–168.

Parkes, G. (1994) *Composing the Soul: Reaches of Nietzsche's Psychology* (Chicago: University of Chicago Press).

Parush, A. (1976) 'Nietzsche on the Skeptic's Life', *Review of Metaphysics* XXIX: 523–542.

Patton, P. (ed.) (1993) *Nietzsche, Feminism and Political Theory* (Sydney: Allen and Unwin).

Pippin, R. (1999) 'Nietzsche and The Melancholy of Modernity', *Social Research* 66(2): 495–520.

(2008) 'Review: The Affirmation of Life: Nietzsche on Overcoming Nihilism', *Philosophy and Phenomenological Research* 77(1): 281–291.

(2010) *Nietzsche, Psychology, and First Philosophy* (Chicago: University of Chicago Press).

Plato (1959) *Phaedo*, trans. by H. Tredennick (Harmondsworth, UK: Penguin Books).

(1968) *The Republic*, trans. by A. Bloom (New York: Basic Books).

Plutarch (1936) Moralia, trans. by F. C. Babbitt (Cambridge, MA: Harvard University Press).

Porter, J. I. (2000) *Nietzsche and the Philology of the Future* (Stanford, CA: Stanford University Press).

Prinz, J. (2007) *The Emotional Construction of Morals* (Oxford: Oxford University Press).

Raymond, C. C. (2014) 'Nietzsche on Tragedy and Morality', in *Nietzsche on Art and Life*, ed. by D. Came (Oxford: Oxford University Press), 57–79

Rée, P. (2003) *The Origin of Moral Sensations*, in Paul Rée, *The Basic Writings*, trans. and ed. by R. Small (Urbana: University of Illinois Press).

Reginster, B. (2006) *The Affirmation of Life: Nietzsche on Overcoming Nihilism* (Cambridge, MA: Harvard University Press).

(2013) 'Honesty and Curiosity in Nietzsche's Free Spirit', *Journal of the History of Philosophy* 51(3): 441–463.

(2014) 'Art and Affirmation', in *Nietzsche on Art and Life*, ed. by D. Came (Oxford: Oxford University Press), 14–38.

Rethy, R. (1976) 'The Descartes Motto to the First Edition of Nietzsche's 'Menschliches. Allzumenschliches', *Nietzsche-Studien* 5: 289–297.

Richardson, J. (2002) 'Nietzsche Contra Darwin', *Philosophy and Phenomenological Research* 65(3): 537–575.

(2004) *Nietzsche's New Darwinism* (Oxford: Oxford University Press).

Ricoeur, P. (1970) *Freud and Philosophy: An Essay on Interpretation*, trans. by D. Savage (New Haven, CT: Yale University Press).

Ridley, A. (1998) Nietzsche's Conscience (Ithaca, NY: Cornell University Press).

(2007) *Nietzsche on Art* (London: Routledge).

(2014) 'Nietzsche and Music', in *Nietzsche on Art and Life*, ed. by D. Came (Oxford: Oxford University Press), 220–235.

Risse, M. (2007) 'Nietzschean "Animal Psychology" versus Kantian Ethics', in *Nietzsche and Morality*, ed. by B. Leiter and N. Sinhababu (Oxford: Oxford University Press).

Rorty, R. (1989) Contingency, Irony and Solidarity (Cambridge: Cambridge University Press).

Rosen, S. (1995) *The Mask of Enlightenment: Nietzsche's Zarathustra* (Cambridge: Cambridge University Press).

Rougemont, D., de (1983) *Love in the Western World* (Princeton, NJ: Princeton University Press).

Rutherford, D. (2011) 'Freedom as a Philosophical Ideal: Nietzsche and His Antecedents', *Inquiry* 54(5): 512–540.

Safranski, R. (2003) *Nietzsche: A Philosophical Biography* (New York: W. W. Norton).

Scarry, E. (2001) *On Beauty and Being Just* (Princeton, NJ: Princeton University Press).

Schaberg, W. H. (1995) *The Nietzsche Canon: A Publication History and Bibliography* (Chicago: University of Chicago Press).

Schacht, R. (1986) 'Introduction', in *Human, All Too Human: A Book for Free Spirits*, vol. 1, trans. by R. J. Hollingdale (Cambridge: Cambridge University Press), vii–xxix.

(1988) 'Nietzsche's *Gay Science*, or, How to Naturalize Cheerfully', in *Reading Nietzsche*, ed. by R. C. Solomon and K. M. Higgins (Oxford: Oxford University Press), 68–86.

(1995) 'The Spinoza-Nietzsche Problem: Spinoza as Precursor?', in *Making Sense of Nietzsche* (Urbana: University of Illinois Press), 167–186.

Schopenhauer, A. (1965) *On the Basis of Morality*, trans. by E. F. J. Payne (Indianapolis, IN: Bobbs-Merrill).

(1966) *The World as Will and Representation*, 2 vols., trans. by E. F. J. Payne (New York: Dover).

(1974) *Parerga and Paralipomena*, vol. 2, trans. by E. F. J. Payne (Oxford: Clarendon Press).

Scruton, R. (2014) 'Nietzsche on Wagner', in *Nietzsche on Art and Life*, ed. by D. Came (Oxford: Oxford University Press), 236–252.

Sellars, J. (2017) 'What Is Philosophy as a Way of Life', *Parrhesia* 28: 40–56.

Seneca, L. A. (2001) *Epistles*, trans. R. Gummere (Cambridge, MA: Harvard University Press).

Shea, T. (2010) *The Cynic Enlightenment: Diogenes in the Salon* (Baltimore: Johns Hopkins University Press).

Silk, M. S., and Stern, J. P. (1981) *Nietzsche on Tragedy* (Cambridge: Cambridge University Press).

Simmel, G. (1986) *Schopenhauer and Nietzsche* (Amherst: University of Massachusetts Press).

Singer, I. (2009) *The Nature of Love: Courtly and Romantic*, vol. 2 (Cambridge, MA: MIT Press).

Sinhababhu, N. (2014) 'Review: The Oxford Handbook of Nietzsche', *Notre Dame Philosophical Review*, https://ndpr.nd.edu/news/the-oxford-handbook-of-nietzsche/.

Small, R. (1994) 'Nietzsche, Spir, and Time', *Journal of the History of Philosophy* 32(1): 85–102.

(2005) *Nietzsche and Rée: A Star Friendship* (Oxford: Oxford University Press).

(2017) 'Review: Michael Allen Gillespie, *Nietzsche's Final Teaching*', *Notre Dame Philosophical Review*, https://ndpr.nd.edu/news/nietzsches-final-teaching/.

Smith, P. (2015) *M Train* (London: Bloomsbury).

Soll, I. (1973) 'Reflections on Recurrence: A Re-examination of Nietzsche's Doctrine, *die ewige Wiederkehr des Gleichen*', in *Nietzsche: A Collection of Critical Essays*, ed. by R. Solomon (Garden City, NY: Doubleday).

(1998) 'Schopenhauer, Nietzsche, and the Redemption of Life through Art', in *Willing and Nothingness: Schopenhauer as Nietzsche's Educator*, ed. by C. Janaway (Oxford: Clarendon Press), 79–115.

Sommer, A. U. (2012) 'Nietzsche's Readings on Spinoza', *Journal of Nietzsche Studies* 43(2): 156–184.

Sorabji, R. (1997) 'Is Stoic Philosophy Helpful as Psychotherapy?', *Bulletin of the Institute of Classical Studies* 68(suppl.): 197–209.

Spinoza, B. (1994) *The Ethics*, in *A Spinoza Reader*, ed. and trans. E. Curley (Princeton, NJ: Princeton University Press).

Stambaugh, J. (1994) 'Amor dei and Amor fati: Spinoza and Nietzsche', in *The Other Nietzsche* (Albany, NY: SUNY), 75–94.

Stegmaier, W. (2016) 'Nietzsche's Orientation towards the Future', *Journal of Nietzsche Studies* 47(3): 384–401.

Strawson, P. F. (2008) *Scepticism and Naturalism: Some Varieties* (Abingdon, UK: Routledge).

Strong, T. B. (1988) *Friedrich Nietzsche and the Politics of Transfiguration* (Berkeley: University of California Press).

Swanton, C. (2015) *The Virtue Ethics of Hume and Nietzsche* (Chichester, UK: Wiley Blackwell).

Tanner, M. (1993) 'Introduction', in *The Birth of Tragedy*, trans. by S. Whiteside (London: Penguin Books), vii–xxx.

Taylor, C. (1991) The Ethics of Authenticity (Cambridge, MA: Harvard University Press).

Ure, M. (2008) *Nietzsche's Therapy: Self-Cultivation in the Middle Works* (Lanham, MD: Lexington Press).

(2013) 'Nietzsche's Free-Spirit Trilogy and Stoic Therapy', *Journal of Nietzsche Studies* 38: 60–84.

(2013) 'Nietzsche's Political Therapy', in *Nietzsche and Political Thought*, ed. by K. Ansell-Pearson (London: Bloomsbury), 161–178.

Ure, M., and Ryan, T. (2014) 'Nietzsche's Post-Classical Therapy', *PLI: Warwick Journal of Philosophy* 26: 91–110.

Ure, M., and Ryan, T. (2019) 'Eternal Recurrence: Epicurean Oblivion, Stoic Consolation, Nietzschean Cultivation', *in* Epicurus and Nietzsche, ed. by V. Acharaya and R. Johnson (London: Bloomsbury). 26: 91–110.

Vattimo, G. (2006) *Dialogue with Nietzsche*, trans. by W. McCuaig (New York: Columbia University Press).

Westerdale, J. (2013) *Nietzsche's Aphoristic Challenge* (Berlin: De Gruyter).

Wienand, I (2015) 'Writing from a First-Person Perspective: Nietzsche's Use of the Cartesian Model', in *Nietzsche and the Problem of Subjectivity*, ed. by J. Constancio, B. Mayer, B. Maria, and B. Ryan (Berlin: De Gruyter), 49–64.

Williams, B. (1994) 'Do Not Disturb: Review of Martha Nussbaum, Therapy of Desire', *London Review of Books* 16(20): 25–26.

(1997) 'Stoic Philosophy and the Emotions: A Reply to Richard Sorabji', *Bulletin of the Institute of Classical Studies* 68(suppl.): 211–213.

(2001) 'Introduction', in *The Gay Science*, trans. by J. Nauckhoff (Cambridge: Cambridge University Press), vii–xxii.

(2004) Truth and Truthfulness: An Essay in Genealogy (Princeton, NJ: Princeton University Press).

(2006) *The Sense of the Past: Essays in the History of Philosophy* (Princeton, NJ: Princeton University Press).

Williams, W. D. (1952) *Nietzsche and the French* (Oxford: Basil Blackwell).

Wollenberg, D. (2013) 'Nietzsche, Spinoza and the Moral Affects', *Journal of the History of Philosophy* 51(4): 617–649.

Young, J. (1992) *Nietzsche's Philosophy of Art* (New York: Cambridge University Press).

(2006) *Nietzsche's Philosophy of Religion* (Cambridge: Cambridge University Press).

(2010) *Nietzsche: A Philosophical Biography* (Cambridge: Cambridge University Press).

Yovel, Y. (1989) 'Spinoza and Nietzsche: Amor Fati and Amor Dei', in *Spinoza and Other Heretics: The Adventures of Immanence* (Princeton, NJ: Princeton University Press), 104–135.

Index

265